UNIVERSITY OF NORTH CAROLINA
STUDIES IN THE ROMANCE LANGUAGES AND LITERATURES
Number 79

ARTHUR DE GOBINEAU
AND THE SHORT STORY

ARTHUR DE GOBINEAU AND THE SHORT STORY

BY

REBECCA M. VALETTE

CHAPEL HILL

THE UNIVERSITY OF NORTH CAROLINA PRESS

depósito legal: v. 1.127-1969

artes gráficas soler, s. a. - jávea, 30 - valencia (8) - 1969

To my parents

ACKNOWLEDGMENTS

I should like to thank Richard Chadbourne for his initial encouragement and inspiration in this study and express my appreciation to Normand Cartier for his careful reading of the manuscript.

WORKS BY ARTHUR DE GOBINEAU

Table of Abbreviations

A: *Mademoiselle Irnois suivi de Adélaide,* eds. A. B. Duff and F. R. Bastide. Paris: Gallimard, 1961.

CA: "La Cour d'Amour," ed. R. Béziau. *Mercure de France,* CCCXI (1963), 260-299.

CB: And Mère Bénédicte de Gobineau. *Correspondance 1872-1882,* ed. A. B. Duff. Paris: *Mercure de France,* 1958.

CP: *Correspondance entre le comte de Gobineau et le comte de Prokesch-Osten,* ed. Clément Serpeille de Gobineau. Paris: Plon, 1933.

CR: *Les Conseils de Rabelais,* ed. A. B. Duff. Paris: *Mercure de France,* 1962.

CT: *Correspondance d'Alexis de Tocqueville et d'Arthur de Gobineau,* ed. M. Degros. Paris: Gallimard, 1959.

DD: *Les Dépêches diplomatiques du Comte de Gobineau en Perse,* ed. A. Hytier. Geneva: Droz, 1959.

E: *Essai sur l'inégalité des races humaines.* 5ᵉ ed. Paris: Firmin-Didot, n.d.

EC: *Etudes critiques (1844-1848).* Paris: Kra, 1927.

EP: *Ecrit de Perse, treize lettres à sa soeur,* ed. A. B. Duff. Paris: *Mercure de France,* 1957.

LDA: *Lettres à deux Athéniennes,* ed. N. Méla. Athens: Kauffmann, 1936.

MP: "Le Mariage d'un Prince," ed. René Guise. *NRF,* XIV (1966), 357-384.

MR: *Le Mouchoir rouge et autres nouvelles,* ed. J. Gaulmier. Paris: Garnier, 1968.

N: *Nouvelles.* Paris: Pauvert, 1956.

NA: *Nouvelles asiatiques,* ed. J. Gaulmier. Paris: Garnier, 1965.

OJ: *Histoire d'Ottar Jarl, pirate norvégien.* Paris: Didier, 1879.

P: *Les Pléiades,* ed. J. Mistler. Monaco: Editions du Rocher, 1946.

S: *Stendhal par Gobineau,* ed. C. Simon. Paris: Champion, 1926.

SV: *Souvenirs de voyage,* ed J. Mistler. Monaco: Editions du Rocher, 1948.

TA: *Trois Ans en Asie.* Paris: Hachette, 1859.

VTN: *Voyage à Terre-Neuve.* Paris: Hachette, 1861.

TABLE OF CONTENTS

			Page
Table of Abbreviations		...	11
Chapter	I.	Introduction ...	15
—	II.	The Picaresque Narrative ...	29
—	III.	The Dynamic Heroine ...	49
—	IV.	The Power of Love ...	102
—	V.	The Confrontation of Cultures ...	131
—	VI.	A Persian "Candide" ...	164
—	VII.	Conclusion ...	180
A Selected Bibliography		...	185

Chapter I

INTRODUCTION

The French brief narrative, whether termed *conte* or *nouvelle*, has generally been considered a secondary genre by both critics and authors. In the nineteenth century, Daudet and Maupassant sought literary fame through their novels. Earlier Mérimée had focussed much of his energy on historical and philological studies. Arthur de Gobineau, a diplomat like Mérimée, hoped to enter the Académie Française on the merit of his philosophical and archeological works and based his claim to literary renown upon his epic poetry. It is for his short stories, however, that he is now most often praised. In this genre Gobineau developed an original narrative technique which enabled him to incorporate both his personal ideas and the experiences of his travels into a single literary work.

Born in 1816 of royalist parents, Gobineau was educated in a German Swiss school where, his sister Caroline would have us believe, the emphasis lay not only on Greek and Latin but also on Oriental studies. Although he probably did not translate Persian poetry, he did immerse himself in the *Arabian Nights* which was to become his lifelong bedside book.[1]

---

[1] Until recently most biographers accepted the myth of Gobineau's early introduction to the languages of the Near East. Jean Gaulmier, however, has actually investigated the linguistic capabilities of the faculty at the Collège de Bienne in the early part of the last century and failed to uncover a single teacher with fluency in Persian or Arabic; *Spectre de Gobineau* (Paris: Pauvert, 1965), p. 33.

Having finished his formal schooling in 1835, Gobineau went to Paris where he hoped to establish a career. After several years marked by pecuniary difficulties, he was able to supplement the modest income of his uninspiring governmental job with the sale of several critical articles; he soon turned to the more remunerative *roman feuilleton*. "Le Mariage d'un Prince," his first work of fiction, appeared in *La France* in 1840. "Scaramouche" was published in *Unité* in 1843. Gobineau did not give up his literary endeavors upon becoming Tocqueville's secretary. Since he soon had a family to support, he wrote and published six more serials. During the second year of his marriage with Clémence Monnerot, a marriage which was to end in separation thirty years later, a daughter, Diane, was born; Christine was born nine years later, in 1857.

When Tocqueville was named minister of foreign affairs in 1849, he chose his protégé as *chef de cabinet*. Although the former remained in office for only a few months, Gobineau did not leave the diplomatic corps until his retirement in 1877. After being named secretary of the embassy in Berne, he was subsequently sent to Germany, first to Hanover in 1851, and then to Frankfurt in 1854. The following year Gobineau was assigned to a special mission to Tehran and was finally able to visit the Orient which had so delighted his imagination. Upon returning to Paris in 1857, he was sent first to Newfoundland to resolve a fishing dispute and then to Savoy. Finally in late 1861, he was again transferred for two years to Tehran, this time as minister. From 1864 to 1868 he was a member of the French delegation in Athens. During these various diplomatic assignments he wrote his *Essai sur l'inégalité des races humaines* (1853 and 1855), *Traité des écritures cunéiformes* (1864), *Les Religions et les philosophies dans l'Asie centrale* (1865), and *Histoire des Perses* (1869). He also published two accounts of his voyages: *Trois Ans en Asie* (1859), which related his first visit to Tehran, and *Voyage à Terre-Neuve* (1861). Tancrède de Visan gives a succinct characterization of the cosmopolitan author: "Gobineau fut diplomate par occasion, mais écrivain de métier et l'homme le plus éloigné qui soit de tout pédantisme, bref, le plus français.

Dès l'âge de vingt ans il entre dans la carrière des lettres et ne quitte la plume que le jour de sa mort." [2]

It was during his last two foreign missions at the relatively unimportant embassies in Rio de Janeiro and in Stockholm that Gobineau returned to the writing of fiction, composing his *Souvenirs de voyage* and *Nouvelles asiatiques* in addition to *Les Pléiades* and *La Renaissance*. Upon retirement he made several voyages, spending much of his time in Italy. Even the platonic love of the Countess Mathilde de la Tour and the friendship of Richard Wagner were not able to dispell the misery of his financial worries nor dissipate the painful realization that literary renown was not forthcoming He died a disappointed man, in 1882.

Wagner's admiration stands as an early indication that Germany would be the first country to cultivate Gobineau's memory. The Gobineau-Verein, under Ludwig Schemann's dynamic leadership, established its seat in Strasbourg and not only undertook the translation of the late count's works, but also collected manuscripts, letters, sculpture, and personal effects. The association followed Gobineau's lead in emphasizing the importance of the *Essai sur l'inégalité de races humaines*. In the preface to the second edition which he prepared just before his death, Gobineau wrote that during the three decades which had elapsed since the *Essai*, his fundamental ideas had not changed. "Mes convictions d'autrefois sont celles d'aujourd'hui," [3] he insists. Moreover, the *Essai* may be considered the foundation of his other works: "... ce livre est la base de tout ce que j'ai pu faire et ferai par la suite" (E: I, xix). The error of the Verein lay in its misinterpretation of the text, in transforming the concept of the Aryan race into the basis of subsequent affirmations of German superiority and of the rationale for violent anti-Semitism.

Gobineau himself, while asserting the superiority of the Aryan branch of the Caucasian race and postulating the decline of a civilization to be proportionate to the racial impurity of its peoples,

---

[2] "Introduction" to Gobineau, *Nouvelles asiatiques* (Paris: Perrin, 1913), p. vi. Further references to this introduction will be prefaced with "Visan".

[3] E: I, xvi. Henceforth all references to Gobineau's writings will be noted in the text. See the table of abbreviations on pp. i-ii.

in no way extolled the qualities of the German nation. "La famille ariane, et, à plus forte raison, le reste de la famille blanche, avait cessé d'être absolument pure à l'époque où naquit le Christ" (E: II, 562). By the nineteenth century, he felt, the country with the highest degree of racial purity was England, which by reason of its isolation had resisted contamination more successfully than the Aryan peoples on the continent. He saw no hope for rejuvenation in either Britain or Germany and concludes his *Essai* with the following remark: "On serait donc tenté d'assigner à la domination de l'homme sur la terre une durée totale de douze à quatorze mille ans, divisée en deux périodes: l'une, qui est passée, aura vu, aura possédé la jeunesse, la vigueur intellectuelle de l'espèce; l'autre, qui est commencée, en connaîtra la marche défaillante vers la décrépitude." (E: II, 563)

Already in 1853, Tocqueville foresaw the dangers inherent in the *Essai* and wrote to his protégé: "Ne voyez-vous pas que de votre doctrine sortent naturellement tous les maux que l'inégalité permanente enfante, l'orgueil, la violence, le mépris du semblable, la tyrannie et l'abjection sous toutes ses formes?" (CT: p. 203) Gobineau, however was preoccupied with what he felt to be the truth of his ideas and considered their possible misapplication to be of lesser concern. When the second part of his treatise was published he wrote to Tocqueville: "Suis-je vraiment l'homme à flatter une opinion qui me semblerait fausse et ne serais-je pas plutôt un peu trop enclin à accuser celle qui ne me semblerait pas suffisamment vraie? Qu'est-ce que mon *Essai sur les Races* sinon une preuve que je ne crains ni n'accepte les idées les plus reçues et les plus chères à ce siècle-ci?" (CT: p. 271)

It was not until the early part of the twentieth century that the French began to express interest in their compatriot and, specifically, began to study Gobineau as a philosopher and moralist. Unwilling to accept the German interpretation of the philosophy contained in the *Essai* and the insistence that Gobineau was truly a German by taste and temperament while a Frenchman merely by birth, certain French scholars sought to define the "real" Gobineau. Consequently they studied not only his philosophical and historical writings, but also his literary works in their attempt to establish a definitive moral and philosophical biography. Typical of this attitude is the following sentence in Ernest Seillière's book on Gobineau: "Prenons à regret congé de ces *Souvenirs de voyage* qui nous ont fourni de si précieuses données sur l'état moral de leur auteur." [4] Thus the short stories are analyzed only for their philosophical and moral content.

Seillière discovers three tendencies which are already apparent in the young Gobineau and which seem to dominate his adult life and works. The first is a legitimist, Catholic orientation which stems from the family traditions. The second element is his early contact with the German language and his travels in that country. The third is his enthusiasm for the Orient, its languages and its culture; in part, this preference for Oriental philosophies arose from a reaction against Latin culture and more precisely from an extreme dislike for one of his Latin teachers. [5]

Gobineau's intellectual development is made to fall into a theoretical, an Asian, and an ascetic period, which Seillière conveniently uses as a basis for dividing his study into three parts. The theoretical period includes the preparation and composition of the *Essai sur l'inégalité des races* and dates approximately from Gobineau's arrival in Paris in 1835 until 1855; the Asian part of his philosophical evolution begins with the first visit to Persia in 1854, and contains writings such as the *Histoire des Perses* (1869) and the *Nouvelles asiatiques* (1876); the ascetic period already has its beginnings in 1861 with the publication of the *Voyage à Terre-Neuve* and embraces all the non-Oriental works written by Gobineau until his death in 1882. Seillière's divisions appear to be quite arbitrary and chronologically overlapping; although they do facilitate a presentation of Gobineau's theory of Aryanism, they manifest little validity for a study of his literary works. Seillière's conclusion, however, reveals a certain perspicacity: "D'un ensemble d'impressions divergentes, on ne saurait tirer une sentence motivée et définitive. Tout au plus pourrait-on dire que le gobinisme est un état d'esprit foncièrement aristocratique et impérialiste vers le dehors, mais qui, une fois

---

[4] *Le Comte de Gobineau et l'aryanisme historique* (Paris: Plon, 1903), p. 324.

[5] Seillière, pp. 3-5.

son adepte renfermé dans le groupe élu où il se complaît, revêt toutes les allures d'un utopisme égalitaire." [6]

Gobineau's dominating belief in aristocracy links him to a major nineteenth-century trend. However, it is in his publicized attempt to base this superiority on racial differences that Gobineau parts company with the majority of his contemporaries.

Robert Dreyfus, in the series of lectures he gave at the Ecole des Hautes Etudes Sociales during the academic year 1904-1905, centered his remarks on this very notion of aristocracy. Dreyfus felt that Gobineau had devoted his life to reaching one key goal: "constituer scientifiquement et philosophiquement la morale de l'élite." [7] However, the attainment of such an aim presupposes the definition of this elite, whose foundation Gobineau first sought to discover in the "race," then in the "individual," and finally in the "family."

While engaged in scholarship in the confines of his office and the Parisian libraries, Gobineau became obsessed with the formula of the "race," just as Taine had been with the idea of *milieu*. [8] Then Gobineau had the opportunity to travel, thanks to his career in the foreign service, and slowly revised his theory by placing more emphasis on the individual; Dreyfus adds, "...même s'il reste vrai que l'action de la *race* n'est pas un facteur négligeable, il faut accorder aussi quelque influence aux moeurs, au climat, aux croyances et beaucoup, et infiniment, à l'instinct individuel." [9]

Gobineau found the historical study of different civilizations to be an indispensable tool for establishing and presenting a racial hierarchy (white, yellow, black). But he turned to creative literature in his attempt to delineate an individual hierarchy. While the *Essai* and the *Histoire des Perses* reveal Gobineau's preoccupation with "race," the literary works, and specifically *Souvenirs de voyage*, *Nouvelles asiatiques*, *Les Pléiades*, and *La Renaissance*, show his efforts to establish an aristocracy of

---

[6] Seillière, p. 444.
[7] *La Vie et les prophéties du comte de Gobineau* (Paris: Cahiers de la Quinzaine, 1905), p. 15.
[8] Dreyfus, p. 19.
[9] Dreyfus, p. 20.

individuals, of the "fils de Roi" (P: p. 21). Our study of the short stories will confirm this view. And yet, Gobineau's form of aristocracy is only a "poussière d'aristocratie." [10] He postulates no links between individuals, except those of friendship and understanding; consequently, for this aristocracy there is no possibility of permanence.

Near the end of his life, Gobineau tried to combine the idea of race and the idea of the individual within the concept of the family. In his *Essai* the yonug Gobineau had insisted that any mixture of blood led inevitably to the degeneration of the race; twenty years later, however, he modified that theory by adding that certain strong characteristics could be transferred from father to son. Conceivably these traits could remain latent for several generations and then suddenly appear in one of the offspring, in the individual. In *L'Histoire d'Ottar Jarl*, Gobineau poetically traces his own genealogy back to the Viking pirates who established themselves in Normandy; here the author's ingenious imagination helps fill any gaps which history had left open. Dreyfus underlines the importance of *Ottar Jarl* for a study of Gobineau's philosophy: "C'est là que nous recontrerons l'expression la plus hardie et la plus complète de sa morale, qui est la morale de l'honneur." [11]

While Seillière read the short stories of Gobineau in order to portray their author as a philosopher, Dreyfus used the literary works as source material to define Gobineau the moralist.

Maurice Lange manifest little concern with the political or moral philosophy of Gobineau and still less with his literary art; Lange's aim is to compile an accurate biographical study. [12] By a careful reading of the correspondence and by a study of accounts by persons who knew Gobineau, Lange refutes conclusions about Gobineau's character drawn by those who had read only the author's published works. Lange points out that, although there is a certain pessimism in Gobineau's works concerning the moral and political state of the world and more specifically of France,

---

[10] Dreyfus, p. 31.
[11] Dreyfus, p. 33.
[12] *Le Comte Arthur de Gobineau, étude biographique et critique* (Strasbourg: Istra, 1924).

Gobineau was quite optimistic about his personal abilities and those of his friends.[13] His extremely independent thought, not only in politics but also in religion, is evident in his letters to Tocqueville and later in those to his sister Caroline who took the veil under the name Mère Bénédicte. In literature Gobineau preferred depicting periods of history in which individual independence could be glorified, periods such as the twelfth century, the Renaissance, and the Napoleonic Empire. Furthermore, even though the older Gobineau toyed with the idea of asceticism, a critical reading of his personal writings shows that he never endeavored to put that philosophy into practice.[14] Lange concludes that the keystone to Gobineau's thought was a belief in the existence of an elite, based on individual intelligence and energy.

Forty years after Lange had finished his biographical study, Jean Gaulmier delved into the Gobineau archives at the University of Strasbourg and reread Gobineau's published works with the hope of clarifying some of the myths surrounding this enigmatic writer. *Spectre de Gobineau,* which appeared in 1965, points up several inaccuracies of fact and presents a fresh interpretation of Gobineau the man. For Gaulmier, the key to an understanding of Gobineau is contained in the "grande trilogie romantique": *Essai sur l'inégalité des races humaines, Histoire des Perses,* and *Histoire d'Ottar Jarl.* He goes on to explain: "Ces trois ouvrages n'appartiennent en fait ni à la philosophie, ni à l'histoire, mais traduisent une vision poétique de l'aventure humaine. Ils éclairent Gobineau et permettent de le replacer, ce que l'on omet toujours de faire, dans la génération du désespoir, entre ses contemporains Flaubert et Fromentin, Baudelaire et Leconte de Lisle."[15] A combination of circumstances, an unhappy childhood and marriage, a relatively unsuccessful diplomatic career, and the failure to find acceptance as a scholar and writer, all reinforce Gobineau's pessimistic view of humanity and increase his scorn for those who neglected to appreciate him. "Poète maudit, par l'ironie hautaine, la morgue, l'humour noir, Gobineau se console

---

[13] Lange, pp. 32-33.
[14] Lange, pp. 173-174.
[15] Gaulmier, p. 45.

de sa misère en la portant aux dimensions d'une tragédie où l'espèce humaine toute entière deviendra, au même titre que lui-même, une victime de la Fatalité." [16] However, Gobineau possessed the determination to continue in spite of adversities and even to plunge into new and challenging areas of endeavor, as is exemplified in his later years by his work in sculpture: a victim, yes, but vanquished, never.

These four critics seem to agree that the basic concept evident in Gobineau's published works and personal correspondence is that of aristocracy, although Gaulmier would emphasize the tortured aspect of "le Titan indigné." [17] Gobineau, when he was twenty-four, had encouraged his friends to form an elite club, the *Scelti* (chosen ones); the name of the group speaks for itself. In a letter to his sister, Gobineau explained: "Trois choses sont communes aux membres de la Sérénissime Société: l'ambition, l'indépendance d'esprit, les idées aristocratiques." [18] These characteristics followed Gobineau throughout his life, playing a dominant role in the formation of his philosophical and moral ideas and providing much of the substructure of his short stories.

Already in 1844, at the age of twenty-eight, Gobineau had expressed a liking for the short story as a genre. He considered it to be a most demanding art form. In an essay on Alfred de Musset's prose works, he compared the short story with the novel: "Ce genre de composition est beaucoup plus près que le roman de la poésie et, nous oserions presque dire, de l'art" (EC: p. 66). Thus Gobineau, while still in his twenties, extols the challenge of the short story and its artistic possibilities. Further in the same article on Musset he describes his theory in more detail:

> Dans le roman, certaines qualités qui n'ont rien d'artistique, peuvent assurer le succès. Ainsi Richardson, le plus sec des puritains, a composé un livre immortel du récit des affections et des pruderies d'une miss anglaise, le tout à force d'observations fines, mais sans mélange d'un seul grain de poésie... Mais toute la finesse d'observation

---

[16] Gaulmier, p. 87.
[17] Gaulmier, p. 190.
[18] Quoted in Lange, p. 35.

> possible, toute la philosophie, toute la raison du monde ne sauraient suffire à produire une bonne nouvelle. Prenez plutôt un sujet absurde, comme a fait Boccace et que le développement soit savamment combiné, que la forme arrête à chaque instant l'esprit amusé et séduit: que pas un tour de phrase, pas un mot ne s'échappe de la plume de l'écrivain sans être aussitôt assujetti et comme enchâssé à la place qui lui convient; dans une nouvelle, traitez la prose comme vous feriez pour des vers; car rien n'est trop bon, ni trop soigné pour ce petit cadre où tout doit se voir de si près (EC: pp. 66-67)

Gobineau concludes his comments by expressing his admiration for Mérimée: "Il existe aujourd'hui un grand maître en fait de nouvelles; difficilement on ferait mieux que *Colomba* et que la *Double Méprise;* leur auteur unit aux qualités que nous avons énumérées, celle plus indispensable encore d'une grande originalité de style." (EC: p. 67)

After the 1847-1848 series of *romans feuilletons* which included "Mademoiselle Irnois," Gobineau left the domain of imaginative writing for twenty years to direct his attention to the composition of non-fictional studies dealing with philosophy, archeology, religion, history and travel. It was in the period between 1869 and 1874 that Gobineau wrote the outstanding brief narratives of his literary career. While his early *feuilletons* were inspired by a knowledge of history, the later short stories find their origin in the diplomat's actual experiences. In 1872, Gobineau wrote to his friend Prokesch-Osten saying that he considered the *Nouvelles asiatiques* to represent a new type of artistic transcription, "une manière de peindre ce que j'ai vu" (CP: p. 358).

Near the end of his life, Gobineau was again engaged in the composition of a new collection of short stories, but this time he returned to the historical setting which interested him as a young man. Upon his death in 1882, he left two unfinished short stories, "Le bourgeois de Jérusalem" and "La Cour d'Amour," which were intended to be part of the newly conceived *Nouvelles féodales*. Apparently the short story is the fiction form which most attracted Gobineau's attention, from his youth until the end of his life.

Admiration for Gobineau's literary works has grown in recent years. In December, 1952, the *Figaro Littéraire* sponsored a poll to select the twelve best novels of the nineteenth century; Gobineau's *Les Pléiades* was one of the works chosen.[19] Similarly his short stories have acquired increasing popularity, one indication being their numerous reeditions. The recent television adaptation of "Adélaïde" by Jean-Louis Curtis was first performed over the "première chaîne" of the O.R.T.F. on May 3, 1966.

Already at the turn of the century the lengthy studies by Seillière and Dreyfus encouraged the literary to read or reread Gobineau's novels and stories, the original publication of which had aroused little critical comment. *Nouvelles asiatiques*, for example, received only one review, and that by Robert Lytton in Britain (*Nation*, December 7, 1876). Most articles published in the last fifty years discuss limited aspects of Gobineau's works or try to compress the man and his work into a single formula.

The short stories have been given scanty attention. Eugen Kretzer devoted about one hundred pages to an analysis of Gobineau's works, but in only two of these pages did he treat the short stories, generously terming them "Kleine Meisterwerke."[20] Seillière studied the short stories for their philosophical content, and this overly-serious reading occasionally led him to mistake Gobineau's humor and irony for biting criticism. Dreyfus, in his series of Parisian lectures on Gobineau, allowed himself a brief digression concerning the short stories and the short story itself which he considered an inferior literary genre: "C'est une notation. Comme telle, elle convient à ceux qui sont assez doués pour être capables d'animer un coin d'humanité ou de nature, mais qui pourtant ne portent pas en eux un monde d'accents et de personnages. M. de Gobineau était de ceux-là, en littérature: il avait moins d'invention que de sensibilité et d'intelligence dans le domaine de l'art."[21]

---

[19] Quoted in Michael Riffaterre, *Le Style des Pléiades de Gobineau* (New York: Columbia University Press, 1957), p. 5.

[20] *Joseph Arthur Graf von Gobineau, sein Leben und sein Werk* (Leipzig: Seemann, 1902), p. 194.

[21] Dreyfus, pp. 267-268.

Paul Souday is the first critic to treat Gobineau's literary works with a degree of finesse and perception, but just ten pages in the brief essay are devoted to the short stories. [22] Concerning the *Nouvelles asiatiques* and the *Souvenirs de voyage* Souday writes: "Ces deux volumes de nouvelles... contiennent ce que M. de Gobineau a écrit de plus achevé. Il y montre une grâce charmante et un esprit souvent éblouissant." [23]

Another French critic who came to appreciate Gobineau's literary achievements was Tancrède de Visan. Author of many articles treating various aspects of Gobineau's ideas and art, he was responsible for the reprinting of the *Nouvelles asiatiques* (1913), *Mademoiselle Irnois* (1914), and *Ternove* (1921), for which he wrote prefaces. [24] He grew especially enthusiastic about the first of these which he termed a "chef d'oeuvre littéraire": [25] "En mettant entre les mains du grand public les *Nouvelles asiatiques* on a conscience de dévoiler un des côtés les plus riants de l'oeuvre de Gobineau, et quand même les plus représentatifs. Cet ouvrage plaira aussi bien aux savants qu'aux amateurs, aux érudits comme aux simples lettrés, à ceux qu'on appelait les honnêtes gens." [26]

Arnold Rowbotham, the first critic to consecrate an entire book to Gobineau's literary production, confines his study primarily to the presentation of lengthy résumés of all Gobineau's major and minor works; only a few pages are devoted to the short stories. [27] Here Rowbotham imposes a rigid criterion without demonstrating its validity; he insists that in the successful short story an equilibrium must be maintained between three elements: character, action, and atmosphere or background. [28] He infers that Gobineau's narratives, consequently, with the exception of "Akrivie Phrangopoulo," lack harmony. In support of his conclusion he gives a summary of "La danseuse de Shamakha," ridiculing Gobi-

---

[22] "Gobineau," reprinted in *Le Livre du Temps*, 2ᵉ série, nouvelle édition (Paris: Editions Emile-Paul, 1929).
[23] Souday, p. 19.
[24] For a list of essays by Tancrède de Visan, see "Gobineau et le mouvement gobiniste," *NRF*, XLII (1934), pp. 289-310.
[25] Visan, p. xii.
[26] Visan, p. viii.
[27] *The Literary Works of Count de Gobineau* (Paris: Champion, 1929).
[28] Rowbotham, p. 79.

neau's clumsy characterization; here, however, Rowbotham only calls attention to his own blatant misreading of the story for he confuses Assanoff and Grégoire Ivanitch, reducing them to a single character. [29]

In 1934, recognition of Gobineau as a literary figure became more widespread in France as the *Nouvelle Revue Française* devoted the entire February issue to a series of articles in his memory. Jean Cocteau in discussing *Les Pléiades* expresses his admiration for "Adélaïde." [30] In another article Abel Bonnard categorically states, "Gobineau n'est pas un grand romancier, mais c'est un admirable conteur," [31] adding that among the short stories "La Guerre des Turcomans" must be considered a masterpiece. Alain emphasizes the sobriety and simplicity of Gobineau's style, basing his remarks primarily on "Mademoiselle Irnois" and "Adélaïde," which he terms "le drame le plus court et le plus émouvant que Gobineau ait écrit." [32]

In his *Spectre de Gobineau*, Gaulmier refers only incidentally to the short stories. Although he feels that Gobineau's fiction may have been praised excessively, he does make the following concession: "Certes, plusieurs de ses nouvelles ne manquent pas d'un charme original. Il a su trouver un ton qui lui est propre de désinvolture et d'ironie, parfois très supérieur à la glaciale perfection de son ami Mérimée. *Adélaïde* —qu'il n'a pas publiée sans doute parce qu'elle raconte une histoire vraie où le héros aurait pu se reconnaître— est un authentique chef-d'oeuvre de pénétration." [33] Gaulmier has also brought out annotated editions of Gobineau's narratives in which the problems of genesis and sources are carefully set forth. [34]

The only full-length literary study to appear in recent years is Michael Riffaterre's doctoral dissertation, *Le Style des Pléiades de Gobineau*. Underlining the author's constant preoccupation with form, Riffaterre presents the salient characteristics of Gobi-

---

[29] Rowbotham, p. 80.
[30] "Eloge des Pléiades," *NRF*, XLII (1934), p. 196.
[31] "Gobineau," *NRF*, XLII (1934), p. 183.
[32] "Gobineau romanesque," *NRF*, XLII (1934), p. 204.
[33] Gaulmier, p. 43.
[34] Both volumes are in the "Classiques Garnier" series: *Nouvelles asiatiques*, 1965, and *Le Mouchoir rouge et autres nouvelles*, 1968.

neau's fictional style as manifested in *Les Pléiades*. A chronological history of Gobineau's earlier works has recently been published by René Guise.[35]

The short stories themselves, though often admired, have never been the object of detailed analysis. In this book the content and structure of each individual narrative will be studied, with special emphasis on character, plot, theme and point of view. "Character" denotes the study of the protagonists, their personalities, and the manner in which they are presented. "Plot" refers to sequence of events and structure. The predominant themes will be isolated and the imagery employed to express such themes will be analyzed. The "point of view" generally assumes one of three forms: omniscient (in which the narrator enters the minds of his characters at will), third person (in which the narrator implicitly or explicitly presents the story as seen by one of the characters) and first person (in which the protagonist relates the story). The point of view may be "non-interpretive," if the reader can accept the narrator's version of the happenings without reservation, or "interpretive," if the reader must temper the actual narration with personal observation in order to discover the real meaning of the events or the true personality of the protagonist. In conclusion, the results of the separate analyses will be synthesized to define the originality of Gobineau's short stories and his contribution to French literature.

---

[35] "Le Poète malchanceux ou les débuts littéraires d'Arthur de Gobineau," *Etudes gobiniennes 1966*, pp. 159-215.

Chapter II

THE PICARESQUE NARRATIVE

In "Scaramouche," which he published in 1843, Gobineau experimented with the picaresque genre. He returned to that form thirty years later with "L'Histoire de Gambèr-Aly." In the literature of roguery emphasis is placed on actuality rather than ideals, on the low life rather than the heroic, on manners rather than emotion and conscience. The rogue engages in occasional or even habitual theft but is distinguishable from the villain in that he avoids physical violence. Frank Wadleigh Chandler, in his study *The Literature of Roguery*, defines the "classical" picaresque novel as "the comic biography (or more often the autobiography) of an anti-hero who makes his way in the world through the service of masters, satirizing their personal faults, as well as their trades and professions. It possesses, therefore, two poles of interest, — one, the rogue and his tricks; the other, the manners he pillories." [1] In France this form was perfected in Lesage's *Gil Blas*. During the eighteenth and nineteenth centuries European writers experimented with variations of this model, often stressing one aspect at the expense of others. This very freedom attracted French authors such as Marivaux, Hugo and Gautier.

Gobineau's primary consideration in the composition of "Scaramouche" was a financial one: the *roman feuilleton* demanded action-packed stories which would hold the reader's interest. Gobineau tempered the typical *roman d'aventures* with the introduc-

---

[1] (New York: Burt Franklin, 1958), I, 5.

tion of a picaresque element which becomes most noticeable in the final chapter. In the composition of the narrative he found the opportunity to experiment with certain ideas which later would form the core of his work. Moreover he could unleash his humor and irony, poking fun at existing literary practices, throwing barbs at social hypocrisy, while amusing himself and his readers.

Matteo Cigoli, chased from his village home, sets out for Bologna and meets an itinerant *commedia dell'arte* troop in need of a new actor. In Venice, Scaramouche (Matteo assumed the name of the personage he was to portray) falls in love with the beautiful but unknown Rosetta; the young coquette rewards his attentions with a practical joke by having him tossed into a canal. Scaramouche gains revenge and has Rosetta convicted of treason and sent to a convent. In the second chapter, the troop, having incurred the wrath of the Duchess of Florence, sets out for Naples. In a small village Scaramouche discovers Rosetta's former fiancé courting Doña Paula, the gypsy heiress of wealthy Don Geronimo. He determines to prevent the marriage; however, it is Doña Paula herself who decides to obtain her liberty not through marriage but by fleeing with her tutor, Corybante. In the final chapter Scaramouche, who has been "identified" as the long-lost Don César, son of the Marquise Bianconero, returns to Venice as a wealthy playboy and offers to assist in the escape of two young nuns from a convent. The veiled Rosetta, for it is she, declares her intention of entering a stricter convent in Germany; when the two arrive in Trieste, Scaramouche learns that Polichinelle has been acknowledged the "true" Don César. Matteo, again penniless, resumes the directorship of the *commedia dell'arte* troop and marries the lovely, faithful Columbine.

The scene is laid in Italy, primarily in the cities of Florence, Venice, and Naples. The time span covers about six or seven years. The events of the first two and a half chapters are chronologically compact; the years during which Matteo travels as Don César are omitted and the last chapter ends with the second Rosetta episode at Venice and Trieste. The narrator gives no precise dates but mentions that the actors' financial difficulty in Naples was due to Goldoni's recent successes (N: I, 342); this would place the narrative toward the middle of the eighteenth century.

Matteo Cigoli, a cheerful fellow, "était, de l'aveu général, le meilleur garçon, le plus gai, le plus actif et le plus spirituel qu'eût produit son village" (N: I, 271). When through talent and application he had perfected his acting technique so that he became the star of the company, he spent his free time, at Rosetta's suggestion, studying grammar, elocution, singing and fencing in his effort to acquire social grace. Young Scaramouche on first coming to Venice possesses an open personality free of hypocrisy or dissimulation. His confidence in the generosity of others shattered by Rosetta, he learns how to surmount his feelings. In the first chapter he plans his cheerful vengeance against Rosetta; in the second chapter his unique aim is to prevent the impoverished Don Foscari from acquiring Don Geronimo's property. He is also devoid of sympathy for the mistreated Abbé Corybante, who had been Rosetta's tutor.

Material things have little attraction for young Scaramouche. The narrator comments, "Ce qui distingue tout homme habitué aux brusques revirements de la fortune et, partant, tout homme vraiment digne de ce titre si estimé des anciens Grecs, c'est la facilité avec laquelle il accepte les coups les plus funestes." (N: I, 308).

As the actors leave Florence and the duke's favor pursued by their debtors, they manage to escape with very few possessions. "Les temps étaient changés, la garde-robe de la troupe n'était ni de velours, ni de soie, ni garnie de dentelles comme par le passé; mais sous la serge et la bure bariolées on avait conservé tout entiers cette verve et cet esprit qui avaient enthousiasmé deux grandes capitales" (N: I, 312-313).

Gil Blas had been impervious to changes in fortune until he became so accustomed to the power and luxury of his position as minister that his outlook on life became warped: during his imprisonment Lesage's hero rediscovers the true values of life. In the final chapter Matteo, on learning that he is no longer Don César, reacts first with anger, then with tears. Although promised a handsome income, he is disturbed by the loss of social position, until he finds happiness with Columbine.

The two characters who are more clearly defined, even though they play a smaller role in the narrative, are women: Rosetta and especially Doña Paula. In the first chapter the narrator presents Rosetta as a rich Venetian heiress "dans toute sa jeune beauté, fraîche comme les roses" (N: I, 287). This cliché description mirrors Rosetta's lack of individuality. Bored by her fiancé, Don Foscari, she looks for light amusement elsewhere. Secretly flattered by the knowledge that Scaramouche's acquired elegance is due to her encouragement, Rosetta nevertheless suffers no remorse after having him thrown into the canal. As a result of this escapade, Scaramouche suffering from laryngitis was humiliated at the opera and forced to leave Venice. Convinced of her influence over the actor, Rosetta wagers with a friend that Scaramouche would again return to Venice to see her. As she sees him from her gondola, "Rosetta échangea un brillant regard avec son amie; ce regard voulait dire bien des choses! Le triomphe, l'orgueil, la moquerie s'en disputaient l'éclat; mais aussi le dépit de se voir si bien et si mal à propos entourée" (N: I, 303). Light-headed Rosetta, totally taken aback by the judge's decision sending her to a convent, suffers most deeply upon noticing the satisfied expression on Scaramouche's face (N: I, 304).

When Rosetta reappears in the third chapter, she distinguishes herself through her bearing, for "l'on pouvait préjuger, d'après sa demarche naturelle et ferme, une certaine fierté de caractère" (N: I, 360). This very pride motivated the change in Rosetta's personality. As a sense of contrition and shame for her actions permeated her consciousness, she began to experience a true religious vocation. However, her taste for the "romanesque" coupled with a desire for stricter discipline inspired her to look for retreat in a German convent; in Italy the monastic vows of poverty, chastity and obedience were scarcely observed. The transformation in her character is most evident when she is with Scaramouche. He proposes, "mais Rosita [sic], bien qu'avec une douceur infinie, ne voulut lui laisser aucune espèce d'espérance" (N: I, 364). She manifests this kindness and gentleness again in the Trieste hotel scene, when, having learned of Scaramouche's sudden lack of fortune, she offers him a permanent income which he politely refuses. It is she who arranges the marriage between Scaramouche and Columbine. Generosity has overcome all desire for self-gratification.

The characterizations of Scaramouche and Rosetta depend on brief descriptions and sketches. In the third chapter the narrator comments, "...si les caractères de nos personnages sont tracés dans votre esprit, je puis dire, grâce à Dieu! que ce n'est avec l'aide d'aucune analyse psychologique" (N: I, 342). He states that his primary concern has been to amuse the reader with a series of episodes. There is very little resemblance between the Rosetta of the first chapter and the generous nun of the last chapter; the change in character is affirmed and not discussed.

Doña Paula is the one original character who distinctly stands out from the remainder of the narrative. Don Geronimo, loath to bequeath his property to the Bianconeros, finally discovered Doña Paula, the natural daughter of his deceased brother Giulio and an errant Gypsy. The fourteen-year-old girl, however, is guided by only one desire: freedom. "Quand sa mère, pour une modique somme, l'avait livrée à don Geronimo Torrevermiglia, la jeune bohémienne n'avait ressenti de douleur que pour la perte de sa liberté" (N: I, 338-339).

In the hope of being sent back to her tribe, the energetic young Gypsy makes herself unbearable by breaking dishes, letting the horses out of the stable at night, firing the servants in her uncle's absence and generally wreaking havoc. The only thing she would learn from her tutor Corybante was pistol shooting, for she was determined to kill her uncle if that should prove to be the only means of escape.

The elderly count originally thought he could tame her spirit, but after several years of struggle he realized that his niece was the stronger: "son plus beau rêve était de s'en voir débarrassé et il soupirait après le jour où le jeune fille, prenant le chemin de l'autel, le laisserait libre de prendre celui de Rome où il comptait aller passer des jours pleins de repos" (N: I, 329). Rumors concerning Doña Paula's character had spread over the entire district and discouraged suitors who might otherwise have been attracted by her dowry. Don Geronimo was as delighted with Don Foscari's assiduous courtship as he was dismayed with his niece's categorical refusal of the match. Once Doña Paula learns that Foscari is an impostor she consents to the marriage because she feels that Foscari will readily give her both money and freedom.

Determined to elope with Foscari she suddenly changes her plans when she notices that Corybante possesses unsuspected resources. After locking Foscari in a closet, she forces the tutor to accompany her to a nearby city. Her unique desire had been to escape the restrictions of civilization; but once free she realizes that the life of luxury and the absence of menial labor has spoiled her. After spending Corybante's fortune, she becomes a courtesan, rather than rejoin her primitive kinsmen, and dies several years later.

In the presentation of Doña Paula, Gobineau goes beyond the simple technique of defining a character with several descriptive adjectives. Doña Paula's identity is surrounded with an aura of mystery. First the comedians meet Don Geronimo on the highway under unusual circumstances. Doña Paula's name is mentioned by the local priest who tells Scaramouche: "vous raconterez à don Geronimo tout ce que vous m'avez dit [about Foscari] et vous aurez eu le double mérite de démasquer un fripon et d'arracher une jeune fille, d'ailleurs peu intéressante, à un hymen qu'elle déteste" (N: I, 319). When Scaramouche finally sees this "uninteresting" girl, she is quietly sitting next to her uncle and concentrating on a piece of embroidery. On learning of Foscari's true character, she abruptly changes her attitude toward the suitor: "Je vous aime, et je vous épouserai" (N: I, 324). The reader's reaction is reflected in Scaramouche's exclamation: "Quel démon de femme!" (N: I, 324). After letting the village priest explain Doña Paula's background, the narrator confidentially reveals the motivating forces of her personality. "En définitive, que voulait-elle, me demanderez-vous, ami lecteur? Elle voulait que Don Geronimo Torrevermiglia la mît à la porte et que sa famille campée dans les Apennins lui rouvrît ses bras et lui rendît sa liberté. Pour cela, jamais elle ne put l'obtenir, comme on va le voir" (N: I, 330). This final comment is calculated to increase the reader's desire to continue with the narrative.

After this preparation, Doña Paula is directly presented in her apartment with Foscari and Scaramouche, and then in the highway scene where Scaramouche and the actors stop her carriage. The subsequent years of Paula's dissolute life in the city and her death are succinctly recounted in one paragraph:

Bientôt les ressources de Corybante furent dévorées; dans la compagnie assez délurée où Paula se lança bientôt, elle trouva des adorateurs; sans goût et sans plaisir, sans amour de l'argent, elle céda, pour éloigner le terme qu'elle avait fixé à sa réunion avec sa famille. Enfin arrivée à trente ans, la vieillesse précoce, ordinaire à sa race, flétrit sa beauté; elle sentit que l'insolence et la rudesse de ses manières allaient manquer de ce qui faisait adorer; elle se résolut, ruinée d'ailleurs qu'elle était, à recommencer la vie de son enfance, qui, après tout et de loin, lui paraissait pleine de charme; et, ayant donné une grande fête qui devait être ses adieux à la vie élégante, elle gagna une fluxion de poitrine et en mourut (N: I, 339).

The emotionless style of this account contrasts strongly with the humorous, ironic tone of the narrative as a whole.

The other characters in the story are presented as personality types. Don Foscari, who appears first as Rosetta's fiancé and then as Doña Paula's suitor, represents the impoverished young noble who must marry a rich heiress in order to repay his debts. This financial motivation precludes all other tastes or desires, since all he seeks in a wife is her dowry. The *commedia dell'arte* actors, who compose a colorful background, are presented not as individuals, but rather as caricatures whose offstage personalities closely resemble their theatrical roles.

The plot development is uneven. In fact, each chapter could almost be considered a short story in itself. The first part of the narrative portrays the beginnings of Scaramouche's dramatic career. The action moves from Bologna to Venice and then shuttless between Venice and Florence. Accepted into the company of actors, Scaramouche perfects his technique and develops his social graces in an effort to please Rosetta. His unfortunate bath in the canal the night of his serenade results in the termination of his Venetian career and cures him of his infatuation with the beautiful Rosetta. The method of his revenge is a mere device, which sets the scene for the third chapter.

Doña Paula's psychological make-up is analyzed more closely, and correspondingly the second chapter is constructed with greater care. The opening scenes in Florence dramatize the vicissitudes of fortune and explain the company's trip to Naples. The comedians meet the unidentified Don Geronimo as they enter a small village; and beginning with this touch of mystery, the narrator develops the elopement interlude. The fortuitous arrival of Tartaglia at the end of the chapter finishes the Florence episode and allows the troop to travel quickly to Naples.

The final chapter is constructed around an extremely weak plot line. Scaramouche's sudden rise to fortune, his meeting with Rosetta, his return to the theater group and marriage with Columbine represent the chain of chronological events which pulls together all the loose threads of the two previous chapters. This simplified construction allows the narrator to satirize contempory French society and literature under the guise of eighteenth-century Italy.

The fluid story line is characteristic of the picaresque novel which by nature is a series of adventures experienced by a rogue of lowly origins. "Scaramouche" however lacks unity of purpose and therefore remains a literary experiment rather than a work of art.

In "Scaramouche," Gobineau experiments with the themes of energy, of race and heredity, of feminine will power, and of society's unhealthy influences. These are hinted at, however, rather than consciously developed.

Energy is the attribute which distinguishes the positive characters. Scaramouche's determination and application transform him from a country peasant into an accomplished actor and an accomplished member of society. His strong desire for revenge dictates his attitude toward Rosetta in chapter one and his opposition to Foscari in the second chapter. Rosetta finds strength of purpose in the convent and determines to escape alone in order to find refuge in Germany. Doña Paula is the dynamic heroine, the prototype of the Caucasian Omm-Djéhâne ("La Danseuse de Shamakha").

Race and heredity have determined Doña Paula's character. Gobineau was familiar with Mérimée's "Carmen" and the young Spanish gypsy might well have served as the model for his strong-willed Doña Paula. Rosetta's transformation in the last chapter is not due to the convent, where moral laxity would rather have tended to produce the opposite effect; it is traced to inherited qualities which had been suppressed up to that time: "La solitude, l'éloignement des mauvais conseils avaient réchauffé le bon sang qui coulait dans ses veines" (N: I, 362).

Civilization did stifle Doña Paula's ambitions. She had rebelled against Don Geronimo because he represented a civilization whose limitations she wished to flee, but the presence of material comforts corrupted her intentions and perverted her purpose. Although her death is not directly caused by her years of dissipation, the narrator suggests an indirect relationship between the two.

Neapolitan society is to some extent a projection of Parisian society, which, in the eyes of Gobineau possessed no positive virtues, but demanded novelty and distraction: "...c'est bien simple: dans le monde on aime à voir changer souvent la décoration" (N: I, 351). The system of values is based on fashion; for example, concerning the convent raid, the narrator informs the readers: "Ne jetez pas les hauts cris... et soumettez-vous à ce sacrilège, en commentant cette phrase magique: 'C'était la mode!'" (N: I, 358). Fashion and etiquette supersede honesty and generosity in importance. It is this society that Gobineau ridicules and lightly condemns, for as long as Scaramouche masquerades as Don César, he is lost to Columbine's generous love.

The narrator of "Scaramouche" is the omniscient author of the *feuilleton*. Conscious of his role as creator, he destroys any atmosphere of verisimilitude by frequently interrupting the narrative. Not only does he discuss his art, as do many authors of the period, but he jokes about literary techniques. The opening paragraph of the narrative begins in this manner:

> Ami lecteur, t'attendrais-tu par hasard à me voir commencer cette historiette par: "La lune pâle se levait sur un ténébreux horizon..." ou par "Trois jeunes hommes, l'un blond, l'autre brun et le troisième rouge, gravissaient péniblement..." ou par... Ma foi, non! tous ces débuts, étant vulgaires, sont ennuyeux et, puisque je n'ai pas assez d'imagination pour te jeter sur la scène de mon récit d'une manière un peu neuve, j'aime mieux ne pas commencer du tout et t'avertir tout bonnement que Matteo Cigoli... (N: I, 271).

At the end of the last chapter the narrator tells of the marriage between Scaramouche and Columbine and then hastens to explain that since Lesage and Hugo both ended their works in this manner, the technique must be an acceptable one.

The narrator often apologizes for his lack of analysis and lack of precision (N: I, 280, 299, 365, et passim). In the final chapter he parodies the traditional recognition scene. The unveiling of Scaramouche as the Marquise de Bianconero's lost son is prefaced by a scene in which the Marquis interviews Polichinelle in order to determine the hero's identifying marks. The actual meeting between Scaramouche and the Marquise acquires additional humor through its very brevity:

> Mme de Bianconcero était une femme d'un certain âge, qui avait pu être fort belle, mais qui ne l'était plus. Elle était pourtant tirée à quatre épingles et avait un air très avenant. Quand Matteo Cigoli entra, elle courut plutôt qu'elle n'alla à sa rencontre, le considéra quelques instants d'un air passionné, et se précipitant enfin dans ses bras:
> —Mon fils, mon cher fils, je te retrouve donc enfin! s'écria-t-elle.
> Et elle s'évanouit (N: I, 345).

In utilizing a scene of false recognition, where each of the persons involved pretends to believe the travesty, Gobineau pokes fun at a traditional *deus ex machina* device.

As the narrative progresses, the dramatic element varies in prominence. The proportion between straight narration and actual scenes is about two to one in the first chapter. In the second chapter this proportion is six to five, and in the last chapter four to three. Since the second chapter is the most tightly constructed, it is not surprising to note the importance of the dramatic element.

"L'Histoire de Gambèr-Aly," one of Gobineau's last short stories, was written in August 1872 and published four years later in the collection *Nouvelles asiatiques*. The narrative closely follows the typical picaresque model in that it describes the rise to wealth and power of a young man of lowly origins. The hero is one of the Persian "mirzas," a group which Gobineau had described in *Trois Ans en Asie*:

> La plupart des mirzas aspirent à des fonctions civiles, mais on en trouve aussi parmi les militaires. Lorsqu'ils

sont partis d'une position très-humble, il est évident que la route ascendante de ces personnages ne saurait être la même que lorsque la fortune favorise leurs premiers pas. Alors, on les voit étendeurs de tapis ou porteurs de kalyans jusqu'à ce qu'une circonstance favorable les conduise plus haut. Rien ne s'oppose à ce qu'ils arrivent aux emplois les plus éminents.... Le genre d'existence que mènent ces personnages n'est pas très-favorable au maintien d'une grande moralité. Ils ont les vertus et les vices des solliciteurs de tous les pays. Beaucoup de patience, de la souplesse, infiniment d'amabilité, de la disposition à prendre le temps comme il vient, un grand scepticisme pratique, de la gaieté, de la finesse, de l'esprit d'à-propos; ce sont des Gil Blas (TA: pp. 390-391).

The handsome young Persian, Gambèr-Aly, is in a Shyraz cafe with a pishkhedmèt, or servant of the Prince. A brawl takes place and it is his good fortune to have protected his companion. Subsequently introduced into the royal service, Gambèr-Aly manages to acquire a certain prestige and affluence. In Tehran, where he has gone following the Prince's disgrace, Gambèr-Aly accidentally kills his companion Kérym and is forced to flee the reprisals of the latter's family since his superiors, whose disfavor he has incurred, refuse to come to his assistance. After first requesting refuge in the Shah's stables, he seeks asylum in the mosque of Shah-Abdoulazym. Fear of treachery induces him to refuse the Shah's pardon. Délices du Pouvoir, a rich widow attracted by his beauty and pitiful physical condition, pays his debts and has him carried to her home. Gambèr recovers to find himself in an ornate apartment and graced with the position of intendant of the widow's fortune. Eventually he solidifies his social status by marrying his protectress.

In "Gambèr-Aly," social satire is of greater importance than characterization. Therefore, Gobineau simplifies the psychology of the characters, for he wishes to present not particular Persians, but individuals representative of specific aspects of the Persian mentality and makeup.

Gambèr-Aly, the only child of Mirza-Hassan-Khan, an impoverished artist, and Bibi-Djânèm, his energetic wife, leads a carefree existence, visiting the bazaars and shoplifting confections until he is old enough to go to school. "Il faut bien que tout le monde passe par là; Gambèr-Aly le savait et se résigna" (NA: p. 133). His mother sees to it that he studies under a teacher who shuns physical coercion and who gives glowing reports of her son's progress. At sixteen, having finished his education, he spends his days in idleness parading as a dandy; "il fréquentait les taverniers arméniens; ... en un mot, il voyait fort mauvaise compagnie; ce qui, pour beaucoup de gens d'humeur joviale, équivaut à s'amuser parfaitement" (NA: pp. 134-136). Devoid of the least concept of duty or responsibility, Gambèr is motivated only by vanity and a desire for leisure.

Gambèr-Aly is endowed with a vivid imagination, which colors the accounts he gives of his adventures. Returning home the evening of the brawl, he tells his parents: "Je viens de sauver la vie au lieutenant du prince-gouverneur. Il était attaqué dans la campagne par vingt hommes de guerre, des tigres en fait d'audace et de férocité...." (NA: pp. 143-144). After his first day in the palace as a simple servant he reports to his parents: "Je suis accablé de fatigue.... Le Prince a tenu absolument à me faire dîner avec lui" (NA: p. 152). Gambèr is not merely trying to impress his parents; his imagination is so powerful that he himself confuses fantasy with reality. "Il croyait plus d'à moitié ce qu'il venait d'inventer à la minute même, et cela provenait des lois particulières qui régissent l'optique des esprits orientaux. Un pishkedmèt du prince, qui voulait du bien au pauvre et intéressant Gambèr-Aly, était nécessairement un homme du plus rare mérite, et, dès lors, comment n'eût-il pas été le favori de son maître? Puisqu'il était le favori de son maître, il était son véritable lieutenant...." (NA: pp. 144-145). It is this same imagination which almost leads to his ruin; having found refuge in the mosque he refuses imperial pardon because of an unreasonable fear of betrayal. The narrator comments: "Les gens d'imagination forte n'ont jamais qu'une seule sensation à la fois" (NA: p. 164).

Although many of Gambèr's words are tempered with harmless exaggeration, he often avoids the truth entirely. Gobineau feels that among certain Orientals a prime motive for action is self-interest. It is not uncommon to swear one thing and then do the contrary. Gambèr promises the pishkedmèt not to mention the tavern fight to anyone: "Il jura sur la tête de cet ami, sur celle de sa mère, de son père et de ses grands-pères paternel et maternel, et consentit à être appelé fils de chien et de damné, s'il ouvrait jamais la bouche sur leur commune aventure" (NA: p. 142). That Gambèr's subsequent account to his parents departs from the actual facts is due to his enthusiasm and not at all to an intentional mental reservation. These tendencies explain his rise to fortune in Shyraz and his downfall in Tehran. When sent to collect money from debtors, he pockets a part of what he obtains before giving an account of his dealings. Pleading poverty, however, in contrast to the growing manifestation of his affluence, he fails to pay his superiors the sum agreed upon at the outset of his employment. Consequently after the Kérym episode he finds himself without protectors.

Gambèr is alert, but he lacks foresight. Although he outwits his competitors and clients, he falls victim to the sin of presumption. In describing Gambèr, the narrator writes: "Il éprouvait une envie folle de courir les aventures et de s'amuser à tout prix, sauf au prix de sa peau, car il était extrêmement poltron" (NA: p. 134). This cowardice is the key to his success: his protection of the pishkhedmèt was motivated by fear. In the mosque, Gambèr's emaciated condition, which attracts favorable attention, is the result of his fear of poison.

The narrator characterizes Gambèr-Aly in a straightforward fashion, citing his natural air of bravado and his fear of physical violence. In the subsequent scenes Gambèr vacillates between carefree exhibitionism and trembling cowardice. The reader laughs at Gambèr's predicaments and finds himself accepting the hero's advancements. The narrator occasionally includes an ironic touch; for example, in describing Gambèr's first day in the Shyraz court he writes: "Bref, il parut à chacun ce qu'il était en réalité, un fort joli garçon au physique et au moral" (NA: p. 152). Toward the end of the story, wen Gambèr is installed in the rich widow's home and proud of his popularity in the bazaars, the narrator continues: "Il avait raison de l'être, ce qui prouve bien, soit dit en passant, pour faire plaisir aux gens qui veulent un sens moral à chaque histoire, que le vrai mérite finit toujours par obtenir sa récompense" (NA: p. 177).

Gambèr's mother, Bibi-Djânèm, surpasses both her husband and her son in strength of character. An energetic woman, she typifies the lower middle class Persian mother and housewife, for it is she who runs the household. If her husband contradicts her, or if she has heard rumors about his fidelity, she castigates him physically with the pointed heel of her slippers. Bibi-Djânèm is similarly direct in protecting her son, and woe to the shopowner who chastises Gambèr-Aly for shoplifting.

> [Bibi-Djânèm] ajustait son voile et se précipitait hors de sa porte, comme une trombe, secouant les bras en l'air et poussant ce cri:
> —Musulmanes! on égorge nos enfants!
> A cet appel, cinq à six commères qui, mues par un esprit belliqueux, étaient accoutumées à lui servir d'auxiliaires dans les expéditions de cette sorte, accouraient du fond de leurs demeures et la suivaient en hurlant et en gesticulant comme elle; en route, on se recrutait, on arrivait en force devant la boutique du coupable. Le scélérat voulait s'expliquer, on ne l'écoutait pas, on faisait main basse sur tout. Les désoeuvrés du bazar s'empressaient de se mêler à l'action, les gens de la police se jetaient dans la bagarre et cherchaient vainement à rétablir l'ordre à coups de pieds et de gaules. Ce qui pouvait arriver de plus heureux au marchand, c'était de ne pas être mis en prison; car, une amende, il finissait toujours par la payer, s'étant permis de troubler la paix publique (NA: p. 132).

Bibi-Djânèm devoutly believes in astrology. At her son's birth she consults an astrologist who, upon reception of a generous gift, assures her that Gambèr-Aly is destined to become prime minister. Ostensibly a practicing Moslem, Bibi-Djânèm chooses a house in Tehran near the mosque where she goes every day with the double intention of impressing her neighbors and of collecting gossip. At the loss of her husband, she goes into deep mourning: "Le désespoir de Bibi-Djânèm éclata et renversa toutes les bornes; elle se déchira le visage avec un tel emportement et poussa sur la tombe du défunt des cris si aigus, que, de l'aveu de ses amis, on n'avait jamais connu dans le monde une femme aussi fidèle et aussi attachée à ses devoirs" (NA. p. 178).

Bibi-Djânèm is a strong, self-confident woman, preoccupied only with herself. Her husband's position is that of companion during the days of felicity and scapegoat in times of displeasure. She dotes on her son because she sees in him the object of her creation. On hearing of Gambèr's exploits with the pishkedmèt, she exclaims: "Voilà, cependant, le fils que j'ai mis au monde, moi seule!... Embrasse-moi, mon âme! embrasse ta mère, ma vie!" (NA: p. 144).

Were Bibi-Djânèm to undergo a strict psychological analysis, she would appear as an unpleasant egoist. However, Gobineau avoids description and analysis and portrays her as a colorful active figure, a person to be enjoyed simply for what she is. The narrator's presence is only evident in the humor and light irony of the narration.

Gobineau sketches many of the characters to resemble actual acquaintances. Bibi-Djânèm recalls the prowess of a slipper-wielding young girl of thirteen (TA: p. 447). Moussa-Riza or Monsieur Brichard, the European convert to Islam who takes political asylum in the Shah-Abdoulazym mosque, was created in the likeness of a certain Monsieur Richard whom Gobineau knew in Tehran.[2] Many of Gambèr's exploits are based on those of two youths, Redjêb and Kambèr, the latter of whom inspired both his name and his personality traits. Kambèr "était jeune, bien découplé, de jolie figure, toujours élégant, très-poli, extrêmement poltron, et portant toutes sortes d'armes à la ceinture" (TA: p. 434). He accidentally kills a comrade named Aly, the model for Kérym, and seeks refuge in the Shah-Abdoulazym mosque. He refuses the king's offer of protection, but is saved by "une veuve de haute considération" (TA: p. 436). Gobineau ends the brief account in *Trois Ans en Asie* with the following comment: "La morale de ceci est qu'en Perse tout le monde est disposé à se mêler de ce qui ne le regarde pas, et par conséquent qu'une affaire n'est jamais désespérée" (TA: p. 436). Redjêb, having also committed murder, finds refuge under his master's horse: "C'est un asile sacré, et qu'on ne peut violer en aucun cas" (TA: p. 430). In composing the short story Gobineau developed these several

---

[2] This question has been carefully studied by A. B. Duff in his "En Marge d'une 'Nouvelle asiatique,'" *Mercure de France*, CCCVII, (1959), 684-702.

anecdotes at greater length, combining them into a tightly constructed narrative.

The interest of the reader centers on the action; he wonders what will happen to Gambèr rather than what Gambèr himself will do. Gambèr is a coward, however, Gobineau's aim is not to analyze the emotion of fear, but only to add humor to the narrative.

The presentation is chronological. The story opens with a description of Gambèr's parents and their situation in society. Then the narrator follows Gambèr from his birth to his marriage with Délices du Pouvoir. Unity of construction is found in the person of the astrologist, from his initial prediction to the final paragraph; the narrator writes: "L'histoire finit ici: elle a souvent été racontée avec des variantes par l'admirable et profond astrologue dont il a été question au commencement. Il la citait comme une preuve sans réplique de la solidité de son art. N'avait-il pas prédit, au jour de la naissance de Gambèr-Aly, que ce nourrisson serait premier ministre? Il ne l'est pas encore, sans doute; mais pourquoi ne le deviendrait-il pas?" (NA: p. 179). In spite of this explicit avowal of sources, the narrator consistently presents Gambèr's point of view and not the astrologist's. Gobineau simultaneously maintains two levels of narration: first, the sequence of events as experienced by the protagonist and, secondly, the humorous account rendered by the narrator.

The primary objective of the story is to present a picture of contemporary Persia and implicitly to contrast Oriental civilization with European society; thus, the locale furnishes the basis of the narrative. Many of Gambèr's traits, his imagination, his dislike for work, Sare those which Gobineau had considered typically Persian. More especially, Gambèr resembles his fellow townspeople of Shyraz. In *Trois Ans en Asie* Gobineau had written: "Les Schyrazys ont en Perse la réputation d'être les plus grands coquins de l'empire. Tout me porte à croire qu'ils méritent ce renom. Ils ont du gamin de Paris l'insolence et l'amour de mal faire. On leur reconnaît aussi de l'esprit, mais c'est un esprit de jeu de mots et d'impertinence... C'est le seul point de l'Iran où je n'aie pas la moindre envie de retourner" (TA: p. 164). Time had eradicated the bitterness from Gobineau's memory, but Gambèr none the less incarnates the Shyraz insolence, rascality and the spirit of the Parisian "gamin."

The fluidity of Persian society, which had greatly impressed Gobineau, becomes an underlying theme illustrated in Gambèr's rise in fortune. At the end of the narrative his former masters become his servants. "Les affaires de l'ancien gouverneur de Shyraz ayant mal tourné, le Ferrash-Bachi et Assad-Oullah-Bey se trouvèrent sans emploi. Ce ne fut pas pour longtemps; Gambèr-Aly, devenu Gambèr-Aly-Khan, les prit à son service et il se déclara très satisfait de leur zèle" (NA: p. 178). In the account of his first visit to Persia, Gobineau writes: "On l'a observé de tout temps dans l'Asie musulmane, où les élévations et les chutes de fortune sont si subites, si rapides et si extraordinaires... il n'y est pas aussi commun que les serviteurs de la veille y deviennent les maîtres du lendemain" (TA: p. 205).

This extreme social mobility, while allowing for rapid rises in fortune, conversely leads to rapid disgrace. The repercussion of this awareness in the private lives of the citizens is their tendency to live in the present without concern for the future. Money is to be spent; and when times are bad, debts are incurred and possessions put in hock (Cf. TA: p. 399). Gobineau humorously describes the unfortunate financial condition of Gambèr's family:

> On se résignait donc. On empruntait, à ses amis, aux marchands, aux Juifs, et, comme c'était une opération toujours difficile, attendu que le Khan jouissait d'un faible crédit, on livrait des habits, des tapis, des coffres, ce qu'on avait. Lorsque le bonheur venait à sourire et laissait tomber quelque pièce de monnaie dans les mains du ménage, on appliquait un système financier très sage: on s'amusait avec un tiers de l'argent; avec l'autre on spéculait; avec le troisième, on dégageait quelque objet regretté ou bien on amortissait la dette publique. Cette dernière combinaison était rare (NA: p. 129).

In the same spirit the Persians avoid paying taxes; the tax-collectors keep what money they can, giving only a portion of what they received to their superiors. The economic and political system is based on bribery rather than any objective criterion of values. The fact that Gambèr gives inaccurate reports of the money he collects from his masters is no less remarkable than the fact that he never actually receives his salary. As the pishkedmèt explained to him:

> Vos gages... sont de huit sahabgrans (à peu pres dix francs par mois), mais l'intendant de Son Altesse n'en paie généralement que six. Vous lui en laissez deux pour sa peine; il vous en reste donc quatre. Vous ne voudriez pas témoigner de l'ingratitude à votre digne chef en ne lui en offrant pas, au moins, la moitié? Je vous connais, vous en êtes incapable; ce serait le procédé le plus inconvenant! Nous disions donc qu'il vous reste deux sahabgrans. Que pouvez-vous en faire, si ce n'est d'en régaler le naybèferrash, le chef de votre escouade, pour vous faire un ami sûr et dévoué, car, ne vous y trompez-pas! sous des formes un peu abruptes, c'est un coeur d'or! (NA: pp. 146-147).

In this concept of finances Gobineau sees the Oriental attitude towards truth. Exaggeration and even small lies are not considered as evil as long as one is not apprehended.

Gobineau had found that the Persian housewife definitely dominated the household: "Les femmes n'étant, comme je viens de le dire, responsables de rien, sont extrêmement colères et violentes" (TA: p. 446). These traits are not only characteristic of Bibi-Djânèm and Délices du Pouvoir, but also of the groups of women in the bazaars, at the mosque, and along the highway.

The feature which distinguishes the story from the fragments of Gobineau's travelogue is the style. *Trois Ans en Asie* was a series of impressions and experiences recorded by a European for other Europenas. In "L'Histoire de Gambèr-Aly" the narrator appears to be telling the story for a mixed audience of Persians and Europeans. In describing the Shyraz palace the narrator mentions a large hall, "qu'un Européen aurait prise pour la scène d'un théâtre" (NA: p. 185). In *Trois Ans en Asie,* concerning the same scene, Gobineau had written: "La perspective était terminée par une sorte de grand théâtre ouvert...." (TA: p. 165). The Oriental terms are not always defined, but the narrator discreetly arranges the context so that the meaning of Persian words becomes clear. For example, the pishkedmèt tells Gambèr: "J'ai parlé de vous au ferrash-bachi, chef des étendeurs de tapis de son Altesse" (NA: p. 146).

The narrative is told with the humor of a person who knows and loves the Persian people, and who can laugh with them about their shortcomings. Towards the beginning of the narration Gobineau describes the poor financial position of Gambèr's artisan father: "C'était pourtant dommage; tant d'illustres protecteurs de l'art croyaient faire assez pour leur grand homme en acceptant ses oeuvres, et oubliaient toujours de le payer, et il était assez simple pour ne pas le leur rappeler" (NA: pp. 130-131). With more realism the narrative could be transformed into a petty bourgeois tragedy, with more bitterness into a diatribe against the profiteering upper classes.

Lightness of tone pervades the narrator's comments as well as his descriptions and narrations. In describing Gambèr's tendency to deny reality, he writes: "C'est une chose admirable que la vérité! Elle se glisse partout, au travers du mensonge, sans que les hommes puissent savoir comment" (NA: p. 153). The politics of Tehran are briefly characterized as the narrator explains the attempt of the Prince of Shyraz to retain his post:

> De part et d'autre, beaucoup de ruses furent déployées, on menaça, on fit des promesses sans nombre, on chercha des moyens termes. Tantôt la question avançait, tantôt elle reculait. Le grand-vizir était porté à la sévérité; la mère du Roi inclinait à l'indulgence, ayant reçu une belle turquoise, bien montée et entourée de brillants d'un prix convenable. La soeur du Roi montrait de la malveillance; mais le chef des valets de chambre était un ami dévoué; il était contredit, il est vrai, par le trésorier particulier du palais, soit! mais, quant au porteur de pipe ordinaire, on ne pouvait douter de son désir de voir tout finir pour le mieux. Gambèr-Aly se souciait peu de ces grands intérêts (NA: p. 161).

The narrator's conversational style is especially obvious in the interpolation of interjections like "soit". The prevailing tone of understatement and light irony is typical of Gobineau's most successful short stories and distinguishes him from his contemporaries.

"Scaramouche," Gobineau's second venture into narrative fiction, must be considered as an unsuccessful experiment with the picaresque form. The narrative itself was written for financial rather than literary reasons; an example of the author's apparent lack of interest in his creation is the third chapter where Gobineau inadvertently changes the heroine's name to "Rosita." The narrative's major shortcoming lies in Gobineau's failure to unify the diverse elements which entered into its composition.

"Scaramouche," however, in contrast to the bland "Mariage d'un Prince" published three years earlier, presents a fertile ground of research for the scholar, since many of Gobineau's future works are here present in embryonic form. The picaresque form becomes the basis of "Gambèr-Aly." Doña Paula is the prototype of the dynamic Gobinian heroine. The theme of generosity in love, as incarnated in Columbine and in the later Rosetta, is again picked up in "Mademoiselle Irnois," and later in "Les Amants de Kandahar" and "L'Illustre Magicien." The criticism of contemporary society recurs in the introduction of the *Essai sur l'inégalité des races* and in many of the short stories. The themes of race and heredity form the cornerstone of Gobineau's philosophical system. The plot structure of the Doña Paula episode is refined in "Mademoiselle Irnois" and in "Adélaïde." In "Scaramouche" Gobineau fluctuates between a humorous and a dramatic narrative style. In his later works he separates these two techniques and consciously maintains a consistent style.

"L'Histoire de Gambèr-Aly," one of Gobineau's most successful short stories, was composed in a manner quite the opposite of that of "Scaramouche." In the latter story Gobineau began with a central character and then branched out in several directions as he wrote the chapters; even Scaramouche's personality differs somewhat in each installment. "Gambèr-Aly" is based on a variety of sources and experiences, yet from this diversity Gobineau successfully creates artistic unity. Gambèr becomes a convincing individual even though he is the composite of several Persians. Gobineau creates a single plot —Gambèr's rise to wealth— and treats it in a light conversational tone. The point of view is consistently that of Gambèr; thus Gobineau indirectly employs the autobiographical style typical of the picaresque novel. In "Scaramouche" the picaresque form was used as an expedient; in "Gambèr-Aly" the form becomes the foundation of the story.

CHAPTER III

THE DYNAMIC HEROINE

The fusion of two themes, woman and energy, pervades several of Gobineau's short stories written during different periods of his literary career. "Mademoiselle Irnois," "Adélaïde," "Le Mouchoir rouge," and "La Danseuse de Shamakha" all focus on the presentation of a forceful heroine. His first published short story, "Le Mariage d'un Prince," presents the negative counterpart of this theme: the weak hero.

While still in his twenties, Gobineau had expressed his concern with the role of the female protagonist in narrative fiction. In 1844, in an article on Musset, Gobineau mentions his appreciation of Richardson's *Pamela* and Mérimée's *Colomba* (EC: p. 67). Several months later he explicitly comments on the artistic importance of a strong heroine: "*La Chartreuse de Parme* est un roman conduit par une femme: nous dirons volontiers que les meilleurs sont ainsi, parce que les développements y gagnent toujours en finesse" (S: p. 11). In the same Stendhal article Gobineau lauds the concept of energy, insisting that the "esprits vigoureux" are not intimidated by violence or excess (S: p. 10). About forty years later, in *Ottar Jarl*, he writes: "Quand on est résolu, on plaît aux gens violents; on les enthousiasme, on les attire" (OJ: p. 78). In this last prose work published before his death, Gobineau, in tracing his genealogy back to the Viking pirate, insists that the character of the father determines the character of the offspring: "... il faut induire que le principe mâle est plus important dans le mélange que l'apport féminin" (OJ: p. 291). Gobineau here appears to relegate woman to the secondary position of childbearer, a position which would forestall any further inquiry into her character or her personality; but such a conclusion would fail to take into account his other works. Probably Gobineau felt constrained to emphasize only the male side of his presumed family tree in order to simplify the gargantuan task of linking his own intelligence, his sensitivity and his energy to that supposed representative of the pure Aryan race, Ottar Jarl.

An individual analysis of the four stories, "Mademoiselle Irnois," "Adélaïde," "Le Mouchoir rouge," and "La Danseuse de Shamakha," will indicate the variations which Gobineau introduced into the two basic themes: woman and energy. But first we shall consider "Le Mariage d'un Prince."

"Le Mariage d'un Prince," which appeared in four installments in *La France* in 1840, lay forgotten until its discovery by René Guise and subsequent publication in the *Nouvelle Revue Française* in 1966. The story itself is quite weak, a fact which would support Guise's supposition that the *feuilleton* was written for pecuniary reasons (MP: p. 359).

Young Monsieur de Chalais was called to the French court by Cardinal Richelieu and given the position of "maître de la garde-robe" to Louis XIII. He betrays his protector by participating in an unsuccessful plot to prevent the marriage between Monsieur and Mademoiselle de Montpensier. Chalais admits his guilt and is condemned to death for treason.

Through the narrator, Gobineau gives expression to his anti-democratic sentiments. In reference to Chalais' opponents, he says: "Par bonheur, il avait à faire à des gentilshommes: c'était un avantage des révolutions d'alors; les torrents étaient dévastateurs comme toujours, mais ils n'étaient pas de fange" (MP: p. 370). The conclusion reflects the royalist sentiments of the author and more particularly of the newspaper in which the story first appeared. In a last letter to his mother, Chalais writes: "Mais oui! oui! j'ai trahi le Roi qui, pour moi, avait été un si bon maître, trahi le cardinal qui m'avait aimé et protégé comme son fils; trahi mon Dieu en faussant mes devoirs" (MP: p. 383). Herein lies the didactic nature of this *roman feuilleton* which preaches loyalty to king, country and God.

The characters have been hastily delineated. Chalais is a two-dimensional protagonist lacking in psychological complexity. Although René Guise feels that Chalais possesses "toute la sympathie de l'auteur" and ranks the young hero among the "fils de roi" (MP: p. 361), such an interpretation appears exaggerated. Admittedly the young man is handsome and gifted. "M. de Chalais était beau, séduisant, aimable au-delà de toute expression. Sa blonde chevelure tombait en anneaux parfaits et nombreux sur son cou gracieux et noble; ses minces moustaches se liaient à ravir au contour souriant de sa bouche et à ses yeux bleus pleins à la fois de douceur et de force. Nul mieux que lui ne savait réciter un sonnet de Desportes .... Il faisait des armes à merveilles, montait à cheval comme le Roi" (MP: p. 364). He courageously rallies the participants in the plot to block Monsieur's marriage, but his oratorical gifts outweigh his intelligence. The narrator characterizes the Chalais project as "un plan absurde" (MP: p. 370) and subsequently comments: "L'enthousiasme fébrile de l'ambition ne remplace pas la force et la vigueur native du génie" (MP: p. 371). Chalais was ambitious to the point of envisioning himself a successor to Richelieu, but he lacked the ability to discern his own weaknesses. When Chalais finally is imprisoned, the narrator comments: "Voilà donc où l'avait conduit l'ambition, le désir d'employer ces riches facultés dont il se croyait doué!" (MP: p. 383). At this point, to the great surprise of the reader, the experience of the dungeon transforms Chalais into a saint (MP: p. 384)!

Guise states that Gobineau accepted the anti-Richelieu stance taken by the editors of *La France,* but one of the two dynamic characters in the story is definitely the Cardinal. In the first installment of the *feuilleton,* Gobineau introduces Richelieu and mentions "l'ordinaire énergie de sa volonté" (MP: p. 363). Richelieu, however, does not at first recognize Chalais as a traitor: "...il avait le coeur aussi haut que l'esprit, et croyait tard à une perfidie" (MP: p. 372).

As the story progresses, Gobineau seems to change his opinion about his characters. Ambition makes Chalais haughty, but he remains inwardly uncertain and somewhat fearful about the decision he has made to betray the Cardinal. Richelieu becomes suspicious upon noticing a change in Chalais who has grown less impertinent and more reserved. The narrator cannot resist inserting a little moral at this point: "C'est ainsi que trop de précaution sont souvent une plus grande imprudence que l'imprudence même" (MP: p. 376). In part three of the *feuilleton,* Chalais' weaknesses become more apparent: "Et en voyant les dangers qui les [Chalais and the conspirators] entouraient, ceux qu'il fallait vaincre, ceux auquels il fallait échapper avant de toucher le but, il se sentit pris d'un tel découragement que son ennemi mortel, s'il en eût un, aurait dans ce moment conçu pour lui une pitié profonde" (MP: p. 378). The narrator continues: "... pris d'une étrange faiblesse, il fut obligé de se baisser très bas sur l'arçon de sa selle pour dérober à son page la vue de son visage couvert de larmes" (MP: p. 378).

In the opinion of Don Petro Alcuna, the other energetic character in the story, the conspirators have one remaining chance for success: the murder of Monsieur d'Aspion. Chalais considers such a plan repugnant. Later, when accused of treason, he freely confesses rather than seeking a means to confound his accusers. His final "religious" experience, which seems to stem from weakness rather than strength, hardly constitutes a credible conclusion.

"Le Mariage d'un Prince," an ineffective story which Gobineau himself quickly wrote and forgot —there is not a single mention of the *feuilleton* in his notebooks or correspondence—, does interest the critic on three minor accounts. Chalais is the first example of a weak, vacillating hero. Jérôme Lanza (in "Le Mouchoir rouge") resembles Don Petro Alcuna in his perception and lack of scruples. Finally, the terse remark about Monsieur after his marriage ("... il se hâta de prendre le nom [Duc d'Orléans] qu'il méritait à tant d'égards," MP: p. 384) is an early indication of Gobineau's lifelong attraction to the ironic aside.

Although "Mademoiselle Irnois," Gobineau's third venture into the brief narrative, was published in installments as a *roman feuilleton,* it is more carefully structured than the "Scaramouche" and "Le Mariage d'un Prince" and possesses both unity of character and unity of effect.

Monsieur Irnois, a speculator who has amassed considerable wealth and power during the years following the Revolution, centers his vapid existence on young Emmelina, a child crippled both mentally and physically. When the story opens, a certain Count Cabarot, attracted by Emmelina's position as sole heiress to the Irnois fortune, obtains the Emperor's promise to "suggest" the marriage to the girl's father. Thinking the proposed fiancé to be a young carpenter whom she has spent her days of solitude observing from her window, Emmelina acquiesces to the idea of leaving her parents. The young girl collapses after the marriage ceremony and dies a week later, due in part to the final realization that from the window of her new room she sees only the Cabarot gardens and not the workshop of the carpenter who had given meaning to her existence.

Certain vestiges of the serialized form in which the story was written tend to interrupt the flow of the narrative. The division into chapters reveals Gobineau's attempt to arouse an artificial curiosity in his readers, in order to retain their attention until the appearance of the following installment. Thus Chapter I ends with:

> On s'attend sans doute à entendre un récit merveilleux de perfections inouïes, à contempler une jeune fille douée par les fées de tous les charmes de la beauté et de l'esprit... Nous allons voir! (A: p. 42).

And Chapter II begins:

> Emmelina, cet ange, cette divinité, cet objet de tant de voeux, était, à dix-sept ans, une pauvre créature de la taille d'une fille de dix ans, et qu'un sang mauvais avait privée tout à la fois de croissance, de conformation régulière, de force et de santé (A: p. 43).

Similarly Chapter III ends with Madame Irnois asking her daughter's advice in regard to Cabarot's proposal of marriage; Chapter IV begins by depicting the general consternation resulting from Emmelina's simple assertion of willingness to leave the family.

In addition to this somewhat strained effort to end the chapter on an "up-beat," the narrator occasionally interrupts the story to address comments to the reader. In describing Emmelina he inserts his own opinions: "... Ce n'est plus même un corps, si l'on veut bien me permettre de poursuivre aussi loin que possible l'image de ce qu'elle me produit à moi, l'auteur, à moi qui la vois" (A: p. 95). Further on, the narrator avows that Emmelina's simple life makes boring reading: "Ces menus détails ne sont rien pour le lecteur, et pas davantage pour l'auteur de ce récit, on peut le croire; mais ils faisaient toute la vie d'Emmelina" (A: p. 102).

The above remark reveals Gobineau's concept of the *roman feuilleton*. In an article on Balzac written in 1844, Gobineau described the educative value of the serialized novel. "Pourquoi l'éducation d'un peuple ne serait-elle pas soumise aux mêmes nécessités fâcheuses que celle d'un individu... Le roman-feuilleton joue donc, en quelque sorte, à ce moment de notre existence sociale, le rôle d'un abécédaire perfectionné et orné d'images en taille douce" (EC: p. 16). Thus the narrator, in his role as teacher, gently tries to increase the sensitivity of the bourgeois reader and to introduce him to the complexities of human nature. This effort to enlighten the masses, this surge of liberalism, in part traceable to Gobineau's friendship with Tocqueville and the latter's influence on the young protégé, contains a degree of superficiality (cf. CT: p. 17); in spite of Gobineau's generous intentions, his belief in aristocracy and in the strength of the race forms the foundation of "Mademoiselle Irnois." Acting under the immediate inspiration of Vigny's widely publicized attack on Napoleon's practice of arranging marriages (Discours de réception à l'Académie Française, le 29 janvier 1846), Gobineau paints the intrigues of the Premier Empire, the unscrupulous social-climber, the facades behind which men plot petty schemes for acquiring wealth.[1] This episode between the adroit Cabarot and clumsy Irnois would be ironic or even funny if it were not for the defenseless victim. In this sense Gobineau foreshadows the naturalist novel and the stories of Maupassant. The tender, delicate soul is unable to acquire happiness. Emmelina's fault lies in her heredity, a prison from which even her love offers no lasting escape, and yet she gradually achieves dramatic stature.

Seventeen-year-old Emmelina Irnois is a congenital cripple. "Sans être précisément bossue, elle avait la taille déjetée, et, en

---

[1] Guido Saba, "Gobineau, 'Mademoiselle Irnois' e Vigny," *Studi Francesi*, VIII (1964), pp. 229-238.

plus, sa jambe droite était moins longue que sa jambe gauche. Sa poitrine était comme enfoncée, et sa tête, penchée de côté par le vice de sa taille, s'inclinait aussi en avant" (A: p. 43). Nor was her face pretty; only her eyes and hair could be considered beautiful. Her intellectual development had not gone beyond the reading of fairy tales and her days were often spent sitting dumbly on her mother's knees; "son tempérament était apathique; jamais elle ne voulait ni ne désirait rien; elle ne paraissait pas s'ennuyer, mais elle ne s'amusait pas non plus" (A: p. 45). The only positive feature of her personality, in fact the only feature, was her tendency to daydream, her "disposition rêveuse" (A: p. 49).

Gradually as these flights of imagination become focussed on a single point, the window across the court, love enters Emmelina's life. What at first was dreaming attains the level of meditation and contemplation, reaches a state reminiscent of religious ecstasy; "elle ressemble à ces chérubins dont parlent les écrivains mystiques de l'Eglise, qui sont tout amour, toute passion et que, pour cette cause, on ne représente qu'avec une tête entourée d'ailes de flamme" (A: 95). The simple, mentally retarded child becomes "une sorte d'extatique" (A: p. 106). Her sole joyful experience is the visit of the young carpenter one afternoon when he is called in to repair a kitchen chair. She gives him her gold coins, representing all the money she thought she possessed, and thus, symbolically, gives herself to the object of her love. Once the young man has left she cries, but without bitterness: "son coeur était comme fatigué par l'excès du bonheur" (A: p. 120).

As love brings serenity and deep contemplation, it also brings a certain beauty to this misshapen creature. Her cheeks acquire a rosy glow: her body gains in physical strength: "elle vivait pour la première fois" (A: p. 100). The most important result for Gobineau, however, is the acquisition of a will. Emmelina suddenly refuses her mother's caresses. She demands that her door be closed and that anyone desiring to enter knock first; this artifice allows her time to draw the curtains. She naively desires marriage for she imagines the proposed fiancé to be the young carpenter. The narrator explains: "l'amour ne pouvait pas se vanter de lui donner de l'esprit. Il ne lui apprit ni la ruse ni la réflexion; mais il lui découvrit, comme nous l'avons vu, le secret d'avoir une volonté .... Il lui donna une âme" (A: pp. 104-105). This, then, is the key to Emmelina's transfiguration. Her personality has been nourished on the contemplation of the cheerful workman; once the object is removed, once she is married and installed in Cabarot's luxurious apartments, the soul withers and Emmelina dies. Her former simple life is no longer possible; she has tasted love and known ecstasy, and she realizes that the view from her new windows would never change.

Gradually Emmelina assumes tragic proportion. Were this merely the story of a retarded cripple who dies owing to extreme physical strain and emotional shock the reader would experience pity for the victim. However, Emmelina realizes that her fiancé is not the carpenter, but rather a Count Cabarot who often called on her and thus prevented her from passing the afternoon at her window. Aware of the import of the vows exchanged at the altar, she declines to answer yes, but her silence is mistaken for acquiescence. Since her hysterical scene upon meeting Cabarot, she remains calm; this new serenity is not the product of ignorance but springs from Emmelina's conscious control of her emotions. After describing the wedding reception, the narrator says: "Le moment de la séparation fut assez pénible. Comme je l'ai dit, Emmelina comprenait ce qui avait lieu, et en ressentait profondément l'ébranlement; mais elle ne dit rien" (A: p. 135). Later we read:

> La comtesse traîna encore huit jours. Tous les matins, elle faisait ouvrir sa fenêtre pour voir si elle apercevrait la mansarde; puis, trompée, elle soupirait.
>
> Elle ne fit pas une plainte et ne prononça pas un seul mot qui pût donner à conaître ce qui se passait en elle.
>
> Le huitième jour, elle mourut (A: pp. 136-137).

Seemingly conscious of his aim to educate his readers and of the difficulties to be faced in presenting such an untypical heroine, the narrator employs a variety of artistic devices. First Emmelina is presented indirectly by the description of her effect on others; she is the joy and delight of the Irnois household and the only person capable of calming her father's bad humor. But the dull, lifeless Irnois household is governed by standards entirely different from those of society. Therefore, in the eyes of Cabarot, she is an unavoidable burden. On seeing his fiancée for the first time, ironically at the moment when Emmelina herself is expecting to see the carpenter, he exclaims to himself: "Vrai Dieu, . . . elle est horrible cette malheureuse éclopée, et furieusement vive!" (A: p. 86).

The reader's understanding of Emmelina is dependent on the narrator's explanations and interpretations. Her direct conversations are few and limited to simple expressions of her desires, such as "Porte-moi," "Oui" and "Non." Even in the scene with the carpenter she manages to tell the maid only: "Donne-lui cela." After arousing the reader's curiosity about Emmelina during four chapters, the narrator finally explains his heroine and the change in her personality wrought by the carpenter's presence.

The other characters in the story are two-dimensional figures whose actions and reactions remain predictable. Monsieur Irnois is presented as physical repulsive: "Mal bâti, grand, maigre, sec, jaune, pourvu d'une énorme bouche mal meublée, et dont la mâchoire massive aurait été une arme terrible dans une main comme celle de l'Hercule hébreu, il n'avait dans sa personne rien qui, par la séduction, fût de nature à faire oublier les défectuosités de son caractère et celles de son intelligence" (A: p. 28). Moreover, he never thinks about things, or people, or even himself. When he felt the need to marry, he chose a wife similar to himself, "sotte et ennemie du faste et des plaisirs" (A: p. 36); he ruled his family despotically because neither his wife nor his two sisters-in-law, the Demoiselles Maigrelut, dared contradict him.

As a young man he acquired the beginnings of his fortune through his cowardice. Finding himself in what he thought to be an ambush, he became so frightened that he said and did nothing to avert certain catastrophe. Then he came to the realization that the men facing him thought he was the representative of their competitor and intended only to offer payment for timber rights; he was bright enough to take the money and leave. Later, Monsieur Irnois shows uneasiness at receiving an Imperial Summons: "le mot *gouvernement* le faisait frissonner" (A: p. 61). His general ineptitude and inability to make positive decisions become even more noticeable when he learns of the proposed match between his daughter and Count Cabarot: on returning home he is victim of "un sentiment profond de frayeur" (A: p. 71). Monsieur Irnois accepts the loss of his daughter and the reduction of his fortune without even attempting to prevent the marriage with the means afforded by his wealth and influence. Indicative of his uncertain position and chronic disability to think or act is an increase of vituperations.

Monsieur Irnois is less elaborately characterized than Emmelina. The narrator describes his background and the manner in which he stumbled into his fortune; then, during the remainder of the narrative, M. Irnois is objectively shown in scenes and conversation. Once the narrator has given a brief description of his two-dimensional or "flat" personality, no more explanations are necessary. Monsieur Irnois' actions are always in accordance with his character.

Count Cabarot, an intelligent though impoverished lawyer, possesses an acute political acumen. "Horriblement laid" (A: p. 125) Cabarot is motivated by his desire for social advancement and more especially by his extreme need for money. Once he feels certain of his marriage with the Irnois heiress, his happiness is so evident that a friend remarks: "Faites-moi le plaisir de me dire ce qui charme si fort Cabarot ce soir?" (A: p. 59). Cabarot is representative of the same society described by Balzac's Gobseck: "L'or est le spiritualisme de vos sociétés actuelles." "L'or représente toutes les forces humaines." [2] Cabarot quickly vanquishes any repugnance he might feel for Emmelina; in fact he assiduously spends two hours daily visiting his fiancée. With an ironic touch the narrator adds: "Il faut ici connaître le comte Cabarot tout entier. Pour six cent mille livres de rente et même pour beaucoup moins, il aurait donné sans hésiter sa main à Carabosse avec tous les travers de taille et les monstruosités d'humeur de cette fée célèbre. Le comte Cabarot était un homme positif" (A: p. 60). The description of Don Foscari's motivations in *Scaramouche* is quite similar. Foscari lacks Cabarot's intelligence, but his need for money has led him to similar conclusions

---

[2] *Oeuvres complètes*, ed. M. Bouteron and H. Longnon, vol. V (Paris: Conard, 1948), 398, 389.

regarding the choice of a spouse. "Quand le comte Foscari s'aperçut de tout cela [Doña Paula's extravaganzas and impossible disposition], on peut croire qu'il en prît quelque inquiétude; pas le moins du monde. Il en fut ravi. Toute autre femme me gênerait, se dit-il; pour celle-ci, en la claquemurant dans un cloître, je lui rendrai justice et tout le monde, loin de m'accuser, me plaindra" (N: 329).

Cabarot, too, is a "flat" character; all his actions, the half hour spent at his dying wife's bedside, and the subsequent lavish funeral remain within the purview of the accepted social etiquette. His own thoughts are presented through several interior monologues.

In this narrative, Gobineau was experimenting with a variety of characterization techniques. The reader's attention is focussed on the changes and subtleties of Emmelina's personality. The narrator assumes the position of a psychoanalyst endeavoring to explain the various aspects of his case to the uninitiated layman. Emmelina reacts to the background stimuli which are shown two-dimensionally and only presented in their relationship to her; consequently the young carpenter remains nameless. Her fate is determined by Cabarot's opportunism which her timid, inept father is unable to vanquish.

Gobineau maintains a consistent imagery. Emmelina's love is consciously elevated to the level of a religious experience. The first time the narrator mentions the young girl's existence, he employs imagery reminiscent of the Twenty-third Psalm: "Mais ainsi que dans ces vallées étroites, stériles, affreuses, que la nuit couvre d'ombres épaisses, et où le voyageur marche d'un pas chancelant et effrayé, il finit toujours par apparaître quelque clarté lointaine qui vous rend la joie, ainsi, dans l'antre de M. Irnois, il y avait une clarté; clarté faible et douteuse, il est vrai, mais charmante cependant pour les yeux qu'elle éclairait et qui n'avait pas besoin d'un grand jour" (A: p. 38). Emmelina's hair and eyes are the positive features of an otherwise misshapen body. The day she expects the carpenter to be her proposed fiancé, her eyes, "pleins d'une ivresse angélique" (A: p. 86), reflect her emotions. Throughout the narrative her eyes are made the expression of her soul; thus when she does meet the carpenter: "Soudain on vit aussi s'animer ses grands yeux, et je ne crains pas de dire qu' avec toutes les imperfections de sa personne, elle eut à ce moment une exquise beauté" (A: p. 115).

Emmelina inherited her parents' lack of intelligence, of wit, of feeling. She experiences an ethereal love, "un amour angélique" (A: p. 137), because she is a cripple; yet at the same time this very inability to react and to act normally indirectly causes her death. The author, unwilling to create a fictitious plot or to insert an unexpected climax, consciously maintains an atmosphere of reality: "Le mélodrame n'est pas vrai; la vérité seule est triste" (A: p. 134). Emmelina docilely submits to her fate, just as she has always accepted her limitations. A similar preoccupation with reality is expressed by the narrator of "Adélaïde"; traditional morality would demand the punishment of a girl who seduces her stepfather, but the baron states: "Si je vous détaillais un roman, je ferais tranquillement ici mourir l'un et l'autre d'épuisement, de confusion et de douleur. Il y aurait de quoi. Mais pas du tout. Les choses n'ont guère de ces conclusions dans la vie réelle" (A: p. 181).

The wit and irony evident in "Scaramouche" and "L'Histoire de Gambèr-Aly" are found to a lesser degree in "Mademoiselle Irnois." A certain lightness of tone appears in the first paragraph in which Monsieur Irnois is compared to the conquerors of antiquity: "enfin, il n'imita pas Annibal: il sut vaincre d'abord, puis conserver sa victoire; sa race, si elle eût duré, eût pu le comparer à Auguste" (A: p. 27). The preposterousness of likening this weakling to Hannibal or Augustus brings a smile to the reader's lips. In the same chapter Gobineau ridicules the abstract discussion of the eighteenth-century *philosophes*. Young Irnois, having just escaped deportation, seeks refuge in a Parisian salon.

> Le récit du vagabond déguenillé servit de texte heureux à différentes considérations trop justes, hélas! sur l'ordre social. M. Rousseau de Genève embrassa publiquement Irnois en l'appelant son frère; M. Diderot l'appela aussi son frère, mais il ne l'embrassa pas; quant à M. Grimm, qui était baron, il se contenta de lui faire de la main un geste sympathique en l'assurant qu'il voyait en lui l'homme, ce chef-d'oeuvre de la nature. L'expression de cette grande vérité, reconnue par toute

> la compagnie, ne suffisait pas au pauvre diable. Par le plus étonnant des hasards, en le renvoyant, on pensa à lui faire donner une soupe et un lit (A: p. 30).

This incident, though scarcely related to the story, helps set an initial tone of humor and light sarcasm.

Towards the end of this chapter, the narrator describes the father's affection for his daughter, an affection which only manifests itself negatively. Monsieur Irnois is never abrupt with Emmelina; he is in bad humor during the day if he learns that she has not slept well the previous night. "Bref, il l'aimait passionnément" (A: p. 40), comments the narrator, half-seriously in that for Irnois this affinity was the only feeling he had ever experienced, and half-ironically, for such affection would never commonly be termed love. The final paragraph of the narrative is structurally similar to the above statement. There heroine is summed up in one last sentence: "Emmelina n'avait que le pouvoir d'aimer, et elle aima bien!" (A: p. 138). This phrase has always been interpreted literally, and considered an essential expression of Gobineau's early philosophy of love. And yet, perhaps the same ironic undertone is present. Given Emmelina's nature, her only force was her love, a love which developed her soul and her will; furthermore, this love was a total, all-absorbing passion. For a healthy individual, however, this love would be incomplete. The reader laughs at Monsieur Irnois's "passion," and hesitates before accepting Gobineau's concluding statement. Yet the real irony is rather that few can understand such an angelic or platonic love felt by a girl mutilated in body but not in soul.

"Adélaïde" was composed in Rio de Janeiro over twenty years after "Mademoiselle Irnois"; the two narratives are now often published together. Apparently Gobineau, gifted conversationalist that he was, had related this anecdote to a group of friends who subsequently encouraged him to write it down. The manuscript bears the date December 15, 1869, a fact which gave rise to the belief that the story had been composed in a single day; certain stylistic flaws do indicate that the manuscript was not reworked in a leisurely fashion. The story contains over twelve thousand words, which would represent a good stint of continuous writing.

Gobineau mailed a copy of the unpolished manuscript to his wife adding: "Je crois qu'elle te plaira. J'en suis plus sûr que de l'Akrivie Phrangopoulo. Il y a de la passion et du racontage et pas l'ombre de sentiment où je suis toujours moins sûr de mon fait." [3] Despite Gobineau's enthusiastic appraisal of the story, "Adélaïde" remained unpublished until André de Hévésy printed it in the *Nouvelle Revue Française* in 1913.

The story is told as a court anecdote, the scene being set in the brief prologue and epilogue. The baron reveals the details of a scandal dating back several years: Elisabeth de Hermannsburg, after the death of her husband, succeeds in winning her former lover, Frédéric Rothbanner, away from her daughter Adélaïde and marrying him. A battle of cunning develops between the two women, with the weak irresolute Frédéric turning first to his wife from a sense of duty and then to Adélaïde out of love. Over the years the two women, growing to recognize each other's strength and realizing Frédéric to be an unworthy target of such energies, unite in tormenting their defenseless victim.

In its rough outlines, the plot is similar to that of "Mademoiselle Irnois"; in the latter Emmelina is the pawn in the struggle between Cabarot and Irnois (perhaps "struggle" is too strong a term since Irnois simply acquiesces without trying to prevent the match). The focus of attention, consequently, is not on the conflicting interests of Cabarot and Irnois, but rather on the emotional development of the "pawn." Frédéric becomes the pawn in the struggle between mother and daughter, but the narrator centers his presentation on the development of the conflict.

Elisabeth, who dominates the narrative, is introduced at the age of thirty-five as she bestows her favors upon young Frédéric Rothbanner. Not only is she astonishingly beautiful, but also intelligent and vivacious. "La comtesse, de sa nature esprit fort, ne s'était jamais becaucoup préoccupée des questions au-dessous d'elle. Son rang dans le monde, son sang-froid et, pour tout dire, son audace avaient toujours commandé et obtenu le respect, et il était convenu qu'on lui pouvait et devait passer becaucoup de

---

[3] Quoted in Gerald Spring, *The Vitalism of Count de Gobineau* (New York: Publications of the Institute of French Studies, Inc., 1932), p. 257.

choses" (A: p. 146). The narrator describes her personality, "cette âme toute domination, toute puissance, tout orgueil" (A: p. 171). Of her background we know nothing. Elisabeth is a striking woman, adored and admired by the society of the small German court; she realizes, however, that as she grows older her beauties will fade, and her present position will be usurped by some younger, more attractive rival. "Pour savoir ce qu'une femme adorée devient d'ordinaire, elle n'avait eu besoin que de jeter les yeux autour d'elle, et les jardins d'Armide où elle régnait lui avaient montré en foule leurs gazons verdoyants peuplés de vieilles cigales dont les voix prophétiques n'étaient comprises de personne hormis d'elle-même" (A: p. 143). In order to avoid such a fate, Elisabeth decides to single out a young man whom she can dominate and who would owe his social advancement entirely to her good graces: she chooses Rothbanner. In the midst of all this reasoning, the essential for Elisabeth is not the love and devotion of her admirer, but rather society's opinion of the situation. Five years later Elisabeth's felicity is interrupted by her husband's death. While observing the customary mourning, she realizes that the only means of retaining domination over Frédéric would be to marry him. At this point Elisabeth becomes doubly motivated: not only is she concerned with society's image, but she discovers that in her drive for Frédéric's devotion and fidelity she is in competition with her daughter.

Elisabeth's forces and energies are subsequently directed towards two goals, conserving a flattering image in the eyes of society and maintaining her dominion over Frédéric. When offered the choice between professional and social ruination or marriage, Frédéric obviously chooses the latter. Elisabeth is not restrained by any scruples and regularly searches her husband's apartment. Even when she is thwarted in her purposes, even when she knows that for the moment Frédéric has chosen Adélaïde's affection rather than her own, she carefully camouflages her true sentiments. "Mme de Rothbanner fut sublime dans son genre; elle céda, ne pouvant mieux faire, et ne se découragea jamais" (A: p. 180). As the years went by, as Frédéric gradually outgrew his infatuation for Adélaïde, Elisabeth could well congratulate herself on having attained both her goals.

In characterizing Elisabeth, Gobineau relied on a direct presentation. The baron describes her beauty, her preeminent role in society; then it is Elisabeth herself whom the reader meets. In an interior monologue near the beginning of the narrative, she explains the considerations governing her choice of Rothbanner.

> Elle se dit: "Je ferai un heureux. J'aurai un esclave qui me devra tout, et le premier succès et le premier bonheur et la première gloire et la première expérience. Il m'adorera, et si je l'adore, je ne le lui dirai pas comme je le sens et je régnerai sur lui; je l'entraînerai où il me plaira qu'il aille et je le connaîtrai à fond, tête et coeur, bien et mal, vices et vertus: des premiers, je flatterai ceux qui me serviront; des secondes, j'étoufferai celles qui pourraient se dresser contre moi. Je l'aurai tout à moi, d'abord parce qu'il sera très jeune et qu'il se donnera sans réserve, et je profiterai de ce moment pour le pétrir et le repétrir de telle sorte que, s'il songe jamais à se révolter, il n'aura plus ni nerfs ni muscles pour servir son intention; de cette façon-là, je réaliserai une des plus belles fictions des romans, j'aurai créé un de ces amours hypothétiques qui durent toujours et, jusqu'à mon dernier soupir, si cela me plaît, je serai servie, je serai aimée; du moins le monde, et c'est l'essentiel, me croira telle. Enfin, en admettant que ce soit là une chaîne propre à devenir lourde, moi et non pas lui, ma volonté et non la sienne, décidera de la rupture" (A: pp. 143-144).

Her reasoning is vigorous; the style she employs when thinking to herself is succinct and to the point. Here Elisabeth is portrayed as an intelligent reasoning woman, absolutely blunt and candid.

After this introduction, the narrator presents Elisabeth in action: her conversations with Rothbanner, her brief scenes with her daughter, her comments to other members of the court. It is the reader who interprets, but this task is simplified since Elisabeth is basically treated as a "flat" character. Gobineau emphasizes her energy, her will, and is unconcerned with personality changes. The final comment about Elisabeth is made, not by the baron, but by one of the gentlemen hearing the story. "Ce satané baron est bien la plus mauvaise langue que je connaisse! Toutes ces balivernes n'empêchent pas Mme de Rothbanner d'être une personne charmante et elle joue au whist comme jamais femme n'y a joué!" (A: p. 183). Not only has Elisabeth attained her goal of charming society, but society has seen in her mastery of whist the mark of a woman possessing acute analytic and deductive powers.

Adélaïde, having inherited her mother's beauty as well as her force and intelligence, struggles to win Frédéric's total affection and devotion. Even though she does not dominate the action, she furnishes the title of the narrative; she is the more "rounded" character, she is the one whose personality gradually changes. Just as Elisabeth is accusing Frédéric of delaying the marriage because of his liaison with her daughter, the latter enters the scene. "Adélaïde venait d'atteindre ses dix-huit ans. Elle était blonde extrêmement, blanche à éblouir, une taille de reine, des bras admirables, rien d'une jeune fille, beaucoup d'une impératrice, au grand moins l'esprit de sa mère, et son audace et sa hauteur implacable et, en plus, ce qui n'était pas à dédaigner, le sentiment parfaitement défini qu'elle tenait le pas comme femme aimée vis-à-vis de celle qui ne l'était plus et comme beauté dans sa fleur vis-à-vis de la rose d'à demi effeuillée" (A: pp. 150-151). Adélaïde, too, is strongly motivated, but in a different sense from her mother: "... L'amour de la lutte dominait de bien loin tous les autres penchants d'Adélaïde; et pendant la vie entière de cette héroïne, ces penchants étant, grâce à Dieu, devenus des passions, avec le temps l'amour de la bataille a chez elle prédominé sur tous les autres genres d'amour" (A: pp. 161-162). As a child she had been spoiled by her father and ignored by her mother. At the age of sixteen she decides that the most beautiful thing in the world would be to foil her mother's goals; to this end she seduces Frédéric and then fights to maintain her advantage.

When sent to visit an aunt at the time of her mother's marriage, she adroitly handles public opinion and professes such love for her mother that Elisabeth is forced to bring her back to the household. Frédéric, however, directed by a sense of duty towards his wife, remains cold towards his daughter-in-law until Adélaïde arouses his jealousy by letting society assume that she is soon to be engaged to Christian Grunewald. At Frédéric's request she publicly breaks with Christian at a court function and returns home with her father-in-law. The two in no way hide their renewed liaison from Elisabeth; society rumors that young Adélaïde had finally grown to accept the father-in-law for whom she had publicly avowed such dislike. "On félicita l'heureuse Mme de Rothbanner qui, fière comme le cacique indien attaché par l'ennemi au poteau de torture, accueillait ces compliments avec le plus doux sourire" (A: p. 173).

As Frédéric's fervor gradually diminishes and feelings of guilt about his irregular position increase, he returns to Elisabeth. Adélaïde goes through a series of broken engagements followed by periods of renewed felicity with Frédéric. Frédéric is handsome, but Adélaïde recognizes the fluctuations of his intentions and the weakness of his will. She had already realized his failings when she first conceived of this liaison as a means of antagonizing her mother. Over the years Adélaïde grows to despise Frédéric and even marries a court official. But within the year she is back with her mother, for the two women have gradually grown to respect their mutual energy and join (as we have seen) in devoting their energies toward the moral torture of Frédéric.

Adélaïde may be considered the counterpart of Mademoiselle Irnois. Emmelina, dull, crippled, ugly, was motivated by one desire, the opportunity to watch the young carpenter; this "love" resulted in the development of her soul, of her will. Young Adélaïde, intelligent, energetic and beautiful, channels all her potential toward one goal, the foiling of her mother's desires. All else in her life is sacrificed so that after some years she becomes unable to develop a life of her own independent of her mother. Emmelina's growth in personality, even though that growth is limited, may be contrasted to the narrowing of Adélaïde's horizons.

Just as Gobineau relied on indirect presentation, on a narrator's explanation, in order to portray the expansion of Emmelina's personality, so does he resort to indirect presentation in the description of Adélaïde. Adélaïde is portrayed confronting her mother before the latter's marriage with Frédéric, she is presented manipulating public opinion in an effort to leave her aunt's house, and her first reconciliation with Frédéric is recorded in detail. Then the baron intervenes to temper his listeners' image of Adélaïde by explaining her upbringing and by describing her gradually changing attitude towards Frédéric and towards her mother.

Frédéric figures in the story only in relation to the two women. Of him the reader is informed that by the age of forty, he had increased in girth, had invented "sa fameuse culasse à mortier" (A: p. 181) and was trying to obtain a military decoration. In the same tone in which the reader is assured that Cabarot is "un homme positif," the narrator affirms that Rothbanner "est assurément ce qu'on appelle un homme distingué" (A: p. 165); not only is Frédéric well considered by his military colleagues for his achievements, but he is also a fine administrator and an amiable member of society.

Frédéric is evidently not totally lacking in intelligence, but he is no match for Elisabeth and Adélaïde. The narrator vividly paints Frédéric's position after he has been cowed into accepting Elisabeth's marriage proposal: "Frédéric eut bien l'idée de le contester; mais il perdit du temps à réfléchir à la meilleure manière d'essayer son opposition et il se trouva, au bout d'un quart d'heure, si bien enguirlandé, paqueté, emballé, cloué dans sa caisse, que... ce n'est pas qu'il n'eût par moments des spasmes et des soubresauts; mais rien de plus inutile!" (A: p. 156). Frédéric is merely a colorful insect in the hands of an experienced collector.

Both Elisabeth and Adélaïde know that the only passion which will rouse Frédéric is jealousy. With age, however, this unique expression of will gradually loses its force. Speaking of Frédéric's jealousy, the narrator comments: "Il est curieux que les passions de ce dernier ordre-là ont d'autant plus d'énergie et de cruauté que ceux qui les éprouvent sont plus faibles" (A: p. 175). Perhaps Gobineau feels that the strong individual develops his will to such an extent that he can master his feelings, whereas the weak person, who subconsciously considers himself inferior to the one he adores, is unable to dominate his jealousy.

Frédéric is primarily characterized by a series of unflattering comparisons. At the outset of the story, he is a mere name mentioned by the narrator; subsequently he assumes stature as Elisabeth's conquest. At this point he is compared to a bug pinned in a collector's box. Even though Rothbanner is respected by society, the baron admits: "... il me fait exactement l'effet d'un chapeau de Paris. C'est ravissant, bien chiffonné, d'un air exquis, ça coûte très cher, et quand on analyse le fait, ça ne vaut pas quatre sous de bon argent" (A: pp. 165-166). The baron continues: "Les gens comme Rothbanner sont comme les vélocipèdes; ils ne roulent que sur les trottoirs; hors des trottoirs, ça tombe. Moi, j'aime mieux les gens qui son gênés sur les trottoirs, mais qui peuvent très bien marcher dans les bois" (A: p. 166). Because of his incapacity to understand Adélaïde's seductive powers Frédéric is referred to as a "machine à vapeur mal construite" (A: p. 173). Towards the end of the story we are told: "Il devint comme une espèce de spectre" (A: p. 180). Frédéric is not only weak, but empty; society in admiring men like Frédéric shows itself, from Gobineau's point of view, to be similarly devoid of force and life.

The Adélaïde-Elisabeth anecdote is told as a "story within a story." At the primary level, that is, in the prologue and epilogue, Gobineau presents four additional characters: the baron who narrates the story, Monsieur and Madame Hautcastel, and Georges de Hamann. The last three are of interest in that they contribute to Gobineau's ironic criticism of society and his caricature of social stereotypes. The gracious Madame de Hautcastel reflects society's demands on women: she is poised, highly conscious of her bearing, and appears to be scandalized at certain parts of the narration. Georges de Hamann exemplifies society's values; he in no way comments on the baron's story, but looking at the clock remembers another engagement and discreetly leaves. Society requires punctuality. Monsieur de Hautcastel considers Elisabeth incapable of such scheming because he finds her a charming person and an excellent whist player: his reasoning demonstrates the point that society only judges by outward appearances.

The baron seems to be a transposition of Gobineau himself whom we know to have been an excellent conversationalist. Conscious of his listeners, he at one point stops the narrative in order to explain Adélaïde's background: "Mais je m'aperçois que me laissant trop entraîner par le courant des faits je ne vous ai pas arrêtés assez longtemps sur la personne même d'Adélaïde" (A: p. 160). He avoids passing any moral judgment; yet by not assessing Elisabeth's and Adélaïde's actions according to the standards of conventional morality and by humorously contrasting

Frédéric's lack of conviction with society's high opinion of his qualities, the baron reveals his personal sympathies.

"Adélaïde" is structurally simple. The plot relates the struggle between Elisabeth and her daughter over Frédéric's loyalty and affection and the development of their mutual relationships. The conflict between the two women is presented chronologically, the reader being introduced first to Elisabeth and Frédéric and then to Adélaïde. The action of the initial pages occurs when Elisabeth is thirty-five years old and Frédéric twenty-two. The bulk of the narration takes place six years later after her husband's death. The first fluctuations of Frédéric's will are carefully described and then the reader is allowed to imagine the passage of time, the succession of broken engagements, reconciliations, and betrayals.

The reader realizes that in this conflict there can be no clearly defined victor. The development of the strange relationship between mother and daughter is the strand which unifies the narrative. As the story opens the narrator remarks: "Quant à une notion quelconque des rapports de fille à mère, pas l'ombre" (A: p. 151). However, as time progresses the two women realize that they have grown dependent on one another. "Ces femmes avaient une telle habitude de se détester et d'employer l'esprit que le ciel leur a donné à aiguiser des mots sanglants l'une contre l'autre et à torturer Rothbanner d'un commun accord, dernière et unique marque d'attention qu'elles ne lui ont pas retirée, qu'on les voit décidément inséparables, et telles gens qui disent s'aimer ne se tiennent pas de cette force" (A: pp. 181-182).

The point of view is carefully developed and skillfully camouflaged. The baron is purportedly telling his audience the story he just learned from Frédéric Rothbanner. The actual tale, however, mirrors Elisabeth's view of events. Her motivations are made clear to the audience in the monologue, and nothing in the final part of the story would indicate that she has revealed these inner reasons to her husband. The manner in which Monsieur de Hermannsburg's death is reported also reflects Elisabeth's point of view: "Mme de Hermannsburg avait alors quarante années échues et les choses [her liaison with Frédéric Rothbanner] allaient à merveille, quand, aussi sottement et mal à propos que tout ce qu'il avait fait dans sa vie, son mari s'avisa de mourir" (A: p. 145). The epithets used to characterize Adélaïde, "ange des ténèbres" and "ce petit Satan" (A: p: 164), indicate the young girl is being seen through the eyes of her mother. There are only two scenes where Adélaïde and Frédéric are alone together; however, Elisabeth could easily have obtained a verbatim report of those conversations from Frédéric during one of his docile and repentant moments. Moreover throughout the whole affair, Frédéric is shown in an unfavorable light, so much so that the baron occasionally feels prompted to give a generous explanation of the young man's actions. It is highly improbable that Frédéric would have revealed such past events to the baron. One would assume that during the dinner at which the baron supposedly learned of the story, Rothbanner, since he was asking for assistance in obtaining "la croix de Louis le Pieux," would be discussing his merits rather than his failings. The baron himself, because of his own character, his wit and irony, his intelligence, and his criticism of society, is on the other hand a person in whom Elisabeth might easily have confided.

The two themes which predominate are energy and will. At the outset Elisabeth is determined to dominate Frédéric; Adélaïde has decided to foil her mother's plans. Both protagonists adhere to their resolutions, while tempering their actions to retain a favorable image in the public eye. The force which gradually pulls mother and daughter together is the mutual recognition of their energy: "... à force de lutter ensemble et de se trouver également inépuisables en ressources, en haine, en courage, elles prirent l'une pour l'autre cette estime secrète que l'énergie inspire aux gens énergiques mêmes les plus ennemis" (A: p. 180); the force which cements this unity is the intensity of their scorn for the unworthy Frédéric. Frédéric appears a little less ridiculous when, at the ball, his jealously forces him to make a positive decision; for the first time he exerts his will.

The strategy of the two protagonists is presented in terms of a game of whist. Elisabeth, having succeeded in arranging her marriage with Frédéric and in sending Adélaïde away for several months, finds herself forced to bring her daughter back home through a combination of social pressure and suspected infidelity on the part of Frédéric. The narrator concludes: "Il n'en est pas moins vrai qu'ayant gagné la première manche, elle venait de perdre la seconde et elle avait trop de sens pour chercher à se le dissimuler" (A: p. 160). However, when Adélaïde finally does arrive home, Frédéric, again under the domination of Elisabeth, returns her letters and expresses his desire to break their liaison. "Il parla très bien, oh! très bien! et quand il eut fini, il se leva et voyant qu'Adélaïde regardait fixement devant elle et ne répondait pas un mot, il sortit. Elle avait perdu la troisième manche" (A: pp. 167-168). Figuratively, Elisabeth has won the rubber. It is no surprise that Monsieur de Hautcastel considers Madame de Rothbanner an excellent whist player.

The role of the locale is limited. The characters do recognize the power which public opinion exercises in the small German court, but the nobility maintains a solid front to the bourgeoisie. After mentioning the succession of engagements and reconciliations which follow the Grunewald episode, the narrator states: "La maison était un enfer, bien que les apparences furent gardées toujours. On se douta bien au-dehors de quelque chose et je n'aurais pas conseillé à des bourgeois de mener cette petite vie; mais comme il n'y eut pas d'éclat bien clair, la bonne compagnie protégea les siens" (A: p. 179). As have already remarked, Gobineau employs gentle irony to condemn society and its values; he sketches unflattering caricatures of the Hautcastels and of Georges de Hamann. The baron as narrator ridicules the accepted system of values by pointing out the dichotomy between Frédéric's charcter and the image he created for himself in the Court.

"Adélaïde" is a tightly constructed narrative. The witty social criticism is carried from the prologue into the baron's narration. The theme of strategy and whist is developed by the baron and then echoed in the epilogue. The energy which the reader admires in the protagonists is reflected in the character of the baron himself and in the manner of his presentation. The goals which Elisabeth sets for herself at age thirty-five are achieved in the time span of the narration; this success is reflected in the final comments of Monsieur de Hautcastel. In spite of occasional stylistic flaws, stemming from Gobineau's failure to revise the manuscript, "Adélaïde" may be ranked as a masterpiece of the French brief narrative.

"Le Mouchoir rouge," published in *Souvenirs de voyage* (1872), depicts a similar matching of wills between parent and child; in this instance, however, the latter is victorious. The action takes place in Argostoli, on the island of Cephalonia, in 1835. In August, 1865, Gobineau, then with the French Embassy in Athens, accompanied the King of Greece to Corfu and returned by British steamer via Cephalonia, Zante and Patras. In an official dispatch he wrote: "Les nobles Zantiotes avaient conservé, jusqu'à une époque très récente, l'habitude vénitienne de se débarrasser de leurs rivaux de toute nature en les faisant tuer par quelques personnes du peuple." [4] The neighboring island of Cephalonia possessed the same Venetian heritage. "Le Mouchoir rouge" is dated Athens, May 25, 1868, but Jean Mistler believes that date to be an indication of the conception of the story or, at most, of a rough sketch. The final version was apparently written in Brazil. [5]

Wealthy, powerful Jérôme Lanza, intimate friend of the Palazzi family, and godfather (secretly the natural father) of beautiful Sophie Palazzi, tries to prevent her marriage to Gérasime Delfini. The young suitor is the son of Catherine Delfini and César Tsalla, who just before his mysterious disappearance ten years earlier had been an intimate friend of Madame Palazzi. Gérasime, having been forbidden by Madame Palazzi to see Sophie, unwittingly accepts Lanza as confidant. Sophie manages to send the young man a dagger wrapped in a red handkerchief thereby indicating her desire for blood, and after Mass that Sunday she surreptitiously designates the victim. Several weeks later Lanza falls into an ambush and is mortally wounded. Upon his death bed he leaves his fortune to Sophie but has the young girl and her mother promise that Gérasime, whom he had recognized, be assassinated in a similar manner with the same dagger. A month after the funeral, Sophie softly reminds her mother of Lanza's probable role in Tsalla's death and receives parental consent to her marriage with Gérasime who was just returning from Naples.

---

[4] Quoted in Jean Mistler, "Avec Gobineau, en Grèce," *Les Nouvelles Littéraires*, 31 août 1961, p. 6.

[5] "Introduction" to Gobineau, *Nouvelles* (Paris: Hachette, 1961), p. 16. Hereafter referred to as "Mistler."

After a brief description of Argostoli the narrator presents the genealogy of the Lanza family. Jérôme Lanza is a man of energy and, like Elisabeth Hermannsburg, strives to maintain his high position in Cephalonian society. A proud individual, he demands Madame Palazzi's fidelity and Sophie's devotion. "Le comte Jérôme Lanza avait au fond du coeur des passions fortes, et s'il était, en réalité, assez indifférent aux affaires des autres, il ne l'était nullement, tant s'en faut, à ses intérêts, ses plaisirs et ses affections" (SV: pp. 14-15). Upon returning to Argostoli as a young man many years earlier, immediately following his graduation from the University of Padua, he fell in love with Madame Palazzi. Lanza became an intimate friend of the young bride's husband, and as the years went by twice paid the latter's debts and often encouraged his infidelities. As Stendhal pointed out in *La Chartreuse de Parme,* this role of "sigisbé" was generally accepted in Italian society.[6] Around 1825, Lanza discovered that Count César Tsalla was becoming an ardent admirer of Madame Palazzi, and noticed the latter often blushing in his presence. The young man mysteriously disappeared, but Lanza was able to forestall the investigation of the British commissioner.

As Sophie matured, Lanza's mania for possession focussed on his attractive godchild. One afternoon he observed Sophie's emotional reaction to Gérasime's singing: "On peut se demander s'il avait éprouvé une douleur plus poignante le jour où la fidélité de la mère lui parut douteuse" (SV: p. 24). Impulsive in his decisions and ready to resort to physical violence, Lanza none the less possesses a shrewd mind. He has easily been able to retain political influence under the three successive foreign powers which ruled Cephalonia; it is a simple matter for him to gain Gérasime's confidence once the latter has been refused admittance to the Palazzi residence.

On his death bed Lanza's last considerations are consistent both with the public image he has created of himself and with his true personality. Publicly he avows that he had not recognized his assailants and subsequent judicial inquiry exhumes no clues. But privately he elicits the promise of Madame Palazzi

---

[6] (Paris: Garnier, 1960), p. 3.

and Sophie to have Gérasime assassinated. Throughout his life Lanza thinks only of himself, his political advancement, his passions; interference with these values leads to the certain disgrace or disappearance of the guilty party. Confronted with death, he is motivated neither by repentance nor by compassion, but by vengeance. During his lifetime he has been obeyed through fear rather than love; yet he never suspects that his last wish will not be respected.

Given Lanza's consistent personality traits, Gobineau is able to characterize him much in the same way he portrayed Elisabeth in "Adélaïde." Lanza is briefly described in the first few paragraphs. His ancestry is traced to Michel Lanza, a Venetian nobleman who settled in Argostoli towards the end of the seventeenth century. "[Michel] donna naissance à une lignée d'avocats et de médecins redoublés, qui s'appelèrent à tout jamais les comtes Lanza, firent fortune, se signalèrent par une avarice sordide, prêtèrent leur argent à gros intérêts aux bourgeois, aux ouvriers, aux paysans frappés de respect, et prirent rang, de l'aveu général, parmi les cinq ou six maisons citées comme les plus respectables et les plus illustres des îles vénitiennes" (SV: p. 13). The Lanza avarice was so great that the counts were reputed never to have given away even a glass of water. When the last doge abdicated, the citizens of the Ionian islands placed their confiance in Jérôme Lanza. Lanza's political astuteness and diplomacy are indirectly descibed in terms of his accomplishments: "Le front grave, la bouche serrée, il lui arriva de hocher la tête d'un air composé qui donna beaucoup à réfléchir. Il fut dévoué aux Français, très dévoué aux Russes, extrêmement dévoué aux Anglais, et professa toujours hautement l'opinion que la domination qui précédait celle sous laquelle il parlait avait été désastreuse et bien heureusement remplacée" (SV: p. 14).

Knowing Lanza's energy and passion, the reader can easily interpret the discreet allusions to Lanza's paternal attitude towards Sophie and to his role in the disappearance of Tsalla. Lanza, during the time between his discovery of Sophie's love for Gérasime and his death, is always presented directly through physical description or conversation; the narrator leaves the interpretation to the reader. Lanza, the courtier who so successfully conceals his true thoughts and easily maintains an elevated position in society, cannot restrain his jealousy; his churning emotions betray themselves in his speech. The conversation in which Lanza asks Madame Palazzi no longer to receive Gérasime begins in a very reserved tone: "Par quelle singulière idée, ma chère, admettez-vous dans votre salon ce Gérasime Delfini?" (SV: p. 24). Several moments later, however, Lanza's anger overflows and his efforts at self-control are singularly unsuccessful: "Et vous ne voyez pas que cette petite sotte de Sophie... mais non! je ne veux pas le croire! je ne veux pas y penser! Ce serait trop affreux! Etre trahi deux fois dans sa vie dans une affection pareille! et par qui, grands dieux! Ne répondez pas, ne répondez pas, ma chère âme; prenez que je n'ai rien dit! Je ne vous accuse pas, je ne l'accuse pas; je ne sais rien, je ne me doute de rien! Etes-vous contente?" (SV: p. 26). Madame Palazzi, all too aware of the extremes to which Lanza will resort, calmly acquiesces to his wishes.

When Lanza meets Gérasime in an effort to obtain the young suitor's confidence, he assumes a gentle compassionate tone and manages to insert the appropriate questions into the conversation. At one point he says: "Sans doute vous avez gardé un moyen quelconque de correspondre avec la jeune fille? Je ne vous fais pas cette injure de croire que vous négligerez une précaution si nécessaire. C'est d'ailleurs un plaisir si doux! Comment communiquez-vous ensemble?" (SV: p. 34). Candid up to that point, Gérasime is fortunately alert enough to be wary of Lanza's excessive interrogation.

Toward the end of the story the narrator again reappears to interpret Lanza's thoughts. The dying count is so preoccupied with his plotted revenge that he refuses to kiss Madame Palazzi and Sophie. The lengthy funeral orations afford the final portrait of Lanza as seen by the British, Greek, and Italian elements of society.

Sophie Palazzi is an extraordinarily beautiful young girl: "une Vénus antique n'était pas mieux faite" (SV: p. 21). Just as Monsieur Irnois centers his life on Emmelina, so Lanza finds happiness in admiring his natural daughter; "Jérôme, son parrain, restait en contemplation devant elle pendant des heures entières livré à une sorte d'adoration extatique" (SV: p. 22). Sophie's inner strength is first revelaed in her eyes. "Elle avait les yeux de sa mère avec le feu sombre qui manquait à ceux-là" (SV: p. 21).

Sophie's first reaction to love is the gentle, silent giving of her inner self as she hears Gérasime sing in her mother's salon. This state of emotional agitation did not escape the observant Lanza. Sophie's moral force and her powerful self-control come into play the moment she realizes from her mother's conversation that Lanza has forbidden her to see or to communicate with Gérasime. In the face of such an obstacle, Sophie's love requires more of her suitor than physical beauty and social graces. She is inwardly pleased to recive the long letter in which Gérasime promises to vanquish all obstacles to their union. The narrator abridges the eight-page letter and then adds: "bref, Sophie fut contente de Gérasime, se dit mille fois qu'elle était aimée, et ne souffla mot de tout ceci" (SV: p. 31).

Sophie not only inherited her father's energy but also his perceptiveness; realizing from her mother's conversation that Madame Palazzi in no way objects to Gérasime, but that she feels constrained to execute Lanza's directions, Sophie remains silent and takes up her embroidery. Moreover, she knows that Lanza's unhappiness over losing her is secondary to the personal insult which would result from his daughter's marrying the son of his mistress's former admirer. Reconciliation is impossible. Knowing how pitilessly Lanza has dominated her parents' lives and how unfeelingly he had had Gérasime's father assassinated, Sophie feels no scruples about requesting her godfather's death. The dagger and flowers enveloped in the red handkerchief express her desire; as she leaves Mass the slight movement of her eyes unobtrusively designates the victim.

In Sophie these dynamic qualities are complemented by the heritage of ther mother's beauty and sensitivity. She distinguishes herself from Lanza through her generosity: she is able to think of others, to give of herself to Gérasime.

Sophie's characterization is direct and objective. The narrator's comments are limited to a physical description and a single statement concerning her reaction to Gérasime's letter. Sophie's final conversation with her mother is an excellent example of the narrator's utilization of the dramatic technique to characterize his personages.

> Sophie, toujours très occupée à broder son chien vert, dit à sa mère:
>
> —Maman, est-ce que vous n'inviterez pas M. Delfini à venir vous voir?
>
> Mme Palazzi fit entendre une sorte de gémissement:
>
> —Mais tu sais bien, mon enfant, murmura-t-elle, ce que ton parrain m'a dit?
>
> —Est-ce que vous croyez cela? demanda Sophie avec sa candeur habituelle, mais en arrêtant sur sa mère un regard dont la fixité étonnait toujours. Est-ce que vous croyez cela? N'a-t-on pas raconté autrefois des histoires terribles contre mon parrain à propos du comte Tsalla?
>
> —Pauvre Tsalla! murmura la comtesse; et, ce qui ne fut jamais arrivé du vivant de Jérôme Lanza, elle passa son mouchoir sur ses yeux, qui, en effet, contenaient quelques larmes.
>
> —Est-ce que vous croyez que mon parrain avait fait assassiner le comte Tsalla?
>
> —Mon enfant, dit la comtesse, ce sont de ces choses dont il ne faut jamais parler. Tu es jeune, et tu ne sais pas... Jérôme était incapable certainement de rien faire de semblable, et je ne crois pas non plus que Gérasime... Je te jure que je n'ai rien contre ce dernier; si seulement il voulait ressembler un peu moins à sa mère, cette Mme Delfini qui ne valait pas grand' chose, je t'assure; et comme je l'ai dit quelquefois au pauvre Tsalla, il avait bien tort de s'encanailler avec des créatures pareilles. Mais enfin, je te jure qu'j'ai pour Gérasime beaucoup d'amitié, et si tu ne crois pas que ce soit manquer à la mémoire de ton parrain, il me semble que je peux bien le recevoir (SV: pp. 51-53).

Sophie knows her mother's sentimentality and her affection for César Tsalla. Although Sophie is parsimonious with words, her questions are carefully laid out; her eyes alone reveal the suppressed emotion and the force which she will bring to bear upon her mother if need should arise. Sophie easily overcomes the final obstacle to her marriage with Gérasime.

Gérasime Delfini, "un grand garçon, mince et de tournure distinguée" (SV: p. 22), is introduced as a charming young suitor and pleasant addition to Madame Palazzi's salon. His speech is volatile, and by letter he gives exuberant expression to his feelings. Sophie limits her correspondence with Gérasime to the package containing the red handkerchief, but Gérasime first writes an eight page letter in which he paints the state of his passion and then later entrusts an eleven-page declaration of love to Jérôme Lanza. Gérasime gains an inner satisfaction from putting his sentiments on paper. Concerning his second letter, the narrator relates: "Il se méfiait que son confident ne remettrait pas la lettre; il se tenait à peu près sûr qu'en tout cas il la lirait, mais il avait eu à l'écrire un plaisir excessif, et dût-elle ne jamais arriver dans les mains adorées de Sophie, c'était quelque chose que d'avoir pu encore une fois mettre sur du papier ces phrases de roman qui dépeignaient si bien et si agréablement à leur auteur l'état intéressant de son âme" (SV: pp. 36-37).

Gérasime is basically courageous and perceptive. He confides in Lanza because he feels the need to express his emotions and to communicate his distress at being separated from Sophie. Since he knows Lanza to be his aunt's benefactor, he considers him a friend. Suddenly, while talking with the count, however, his suspicions are aroused. "Il [Gérasime] lui trouva, au milieu de ses grimaces sympathiques, un zeste de goguenarderie qui l'épouvanta. Il lui sembla, dans un éclair de soupçon, qu'il marchait sur quelque chose de dangereux, et cette pensée s'empara si bien de lui, que la conversation changea absolument de caractère" (SV: pp. 33-34). He is careful to speak only of his love and conceals the fact that he has communicated with Sophie. When Lanza offers to act as courrier, he hesitates before composing his letter. "Maintenant fallait-il donner une lettre? ne fallait-il pas la donner? Que croire? que penser? qu'imaginer? que résoudre? que faire?" (SV: p. 35). He is cautious not to insert any dangerous statements in his lengthy missive.

His intelligence permits him to interpret Sophie's cryptic package. On learning that Lanza is the designated victim he momentarily fears judicial reprisal, but love vanquishes hesitation. The murder itself is skillfully executed. Gérasime openly leaves for a three-month visit to Naples, thereby creating a strong alibi. In reality his route to Naples goes first via Missolonghi, where he meets Yoryi, and then to Argostoli.

In characterizing Gérasime, the narrator creates an aura of naiveté and ineptitude. Emphasis is placed on the suitor's amorous diatribes and his initial gullibility to Lanza's protestations of friendship. But Gérasime's actions show him to be of sterner mettle. He immediately finds a means of delivering his first letter to Sophie; although open with Lanza, he never reveals compromising details. When asked to assassinate the Count he quickly surmounts his initial cowardice and proceeds with his assignment.

The other characters are of secondary importance. Madame Palazzi is not quite the foolish matron suggested by the narrator's tone. Her love for Tsalla was all too strong, but Lanza has cowed her into obedience. The narrator briefly describes her life after Tsalla's disappearance: "La comtesse Caroline Palazzi resta tout aussi placide qu'auparavant, commença à engraisser, devint très grosse en peu d'années, et persista dans un attachement imperturbable pour le comte Lanza, dont on pretendait qu'elle avait un peu peur" (SV: p. 21). Her love for Tsalla comes to the fore in the final scene; Sophie knowingly plays on her mother's emotions in order to gain parental approval for her marriage. Count Palazzi and his son are only mentioned briefly as being totally under the power of Lanza and never reappear in the narrative.

The unique plot of the narrative is Sophie's effort to marry Gérasime. The narrator first describes Argostoli and then presents Lanza and his family. The first scene takes place in the Palazzi salon the afternoon when Lanza discovers the friendship between Sophie and Gérasime and is informed of the suitor's background. At this point the reader, familiar with Lanza's character, appreciates the danger inherent in the situation.

Gobineau then shifts to a dramatic technique, presenting a rapid succession of scenes linked to each other with a minimum of straight narration:

> Lanza in conversation with Madame Palazzi;
> Madame Palazzi and Sophie;
> the arrival of Gérasime's letter;
> a conversation between Gérasime and Lanza;
> a conversation between Madame Palazzi and her daughter in which the former relates her talk with Lanza;
> Gérasime's reception of Sophie's package and the ensuing interior monologue;
> a short scene at the entrance to the church.

The subsequent interval of a few weeks is merely hinted at. Then the author depicts:

> the conversation between Gérasime and Yoryi;
> the assassination;
> Lanza's deathbed scene;
> the funeral.

The reader briefly wonders whether Lanza's dying request will be carried out, but the ending remains consistent with the body of the narrative. Neither Sophie nor her mother manifests any personality change; the young girl's energy and intelligence easily permit her to control her mother's sentimentality. The initial descriptive presentation and Lanza's death are linked in the person of Yoryi, the brigand who was paid by Lanza to kill Tsalla and then is asked by the latter's son to help plan the assassination of Lanza.

The theme of heredity is hinted at: Sophie owes her energy to Lanza. Similarly Adélaïde received her mother's beauty and tenacity and Emmelina was physically and mentally retarded. Yet in all these cases an element exists which differentiates the child from the parent. Sophie's distinction is her open and generous love for Gérasime.

In "Le Mouchoir rouge" energy and will are not only the prerogatives of the heroine. Like Lanza, Sophie possesses strong passions. These dynamic qualities are not abstractly discussed, but revealed through action. The narrator makes no moral judgment, expresses no scruples. The strong are not afraid of violence.

The setting of the story is not arbitrarily chosen but is of both psychological and intrinsic significance. As we have seen, the action takes place in Argostoli with the exception of a scene in Missolonghi. Zante is mentioned as being Gérasime's home, a trip to Naples is the young suitor's alibi, and the city of Ancona is introduced in the conversation as the city to which Lanza intends to send Sophie and Madame Palazzi, the latter of whom shows her ignorance in assuming that only English is spoken in the Italian port. The description of Argostoli ends with a premonition of the denouement: the wide central boulevard represents "l'élégance et la gaïeté italiennes" while the narrow streets "en figurent l'astuce et les dangereuses réserves" (SV: p. 12). The locale gains importance of its own in that Gobineau wishes to portray the character of a people who do not accept French bourgeois values. His extolling of their energy contains an indirect condemnation of French narrowness and dullness. The Cephalonians resemble their Italian ancestors in character: "Les Vénitiens étaient gens contenus et prudents, et les descendants de leurs anciens sujets le sont de même" (SV: p. 18). Here Gobineau implicitly acknowledges the fact that his protagonists are similar to those portrayed by Stendhal, especially in the *Chroniques Italiennes*.

Gaulmier surmises that in "Le Mouchoir rouge" Gobineau is recording an anecdote: "Il a dû en trouver le sujet dans un 'petit fait' qu'il a appris sur place, pendant la visite qu'il a faite à Céphalonie, ou que lui a raconté un de ses amis grecs" (MR: p. xxxiii). But Stendhal may also be a source. "Le Mouchoir rouge" bears certain striking resemblances to "L'Abbesse de Castro." Stendhal's narrative appeared in 1839 in the *Revue des Deux Mondes* and was republished that same year in book form together with two other stories; in 1855, it was included in the *Chroniques italiennes*. Gobineau in a laudatory article (1844) on the *Chartreuse de Parme* was one of the first critics to praise Stendhal's works. If he did not read the "Abbesse de Castro" when it first appeared in 1839, he probably read it in the collected *Chroniques* of 1855. Even though Gobineau was personally familiar with small German courts, with the Orientals, and with the settlers in Newfoundland, his visit to Cephalonia was brief, and his personal acquaintance with Italy was still very limited in 1869.

Many incidents in the two narratives are similar. Both Hélène de Campireali and Sophie receive letters in the evening on their balconies; Jules proffers his in a bouquet of flowers while Gérasime simply throws his missive tied to a stone. Both young men are quite verbose in expressing their sentiments; Gobineau explains Gérasime's speech as a "mélange très naturel, dans le Midi, de sentiments parfaitement vrais que l'emphase de l'expression rend un peu ridicules pour les gens du Nord" (SV: p. 31). When all other communication fails, both young men realize that they can exchange signs and notes with their heavily guarded mistresses by mingling with the crowds leaving Sunday Mass. In Italy, as on the Ionian Islands, it was an easy matter to hire assassins for a small fee: Jules refuses to spend a few weeks in Rome so that Ranuse can liquidate the Campireali opposition; Gérasime visits Naples while travelling to Missolonghi to request Yoryi's assistance. Violence in the streets is frequent and the citizens when aroused simply observe the scene without interfering. When Jules Branciaforte storms the convent, "quelques bourgeois commençaient à ouvrir timidement leurs fenêtres." [7] Similarly when Lanza is attacked, "... la petite servante eut sa lanterne cassée; mais elle avait eu l'instinct de pousser des cris affreux; quelques fenêtres s'ouvrirent; en voyant ce dont il s'agissait, personne ne se pressa notablement d'intervenir; mais enfin les assassins ayant disparu, on se risqua, on alla chercher le garde, le policeman fut averti, il vint avec son camarade" (SV: p. 47). The national character Gobineau describes in the former Venetian colony of Cephalonia resembles that which Stendhal portrays in the *Chroniques.*

Sophie makes the same resolute decision to have her father killed as did Beatrix Cenci (in "Les Cenci"), who willingly committed patricide in an effort to save her honor and marry her lover. The difference between the *Chroniques* and "Le Mouchoir rouge" lies in the denouement. The tragic element is missing in Gobineau's narrative; the tribunes never suspect Gérasime's participation in the death of Jérôme Lanza and the two young people find happiness in marriage and raising a large family.

The tone of "Le Mouchoir rouge" also distinguishes it from a Stendhalian narrative. Stendhal transcribes the contemporary accounts of his tales, maintaining the terse style of the chroniclers. Gobineau's narrator, too, is direct and avoids flowery circumlocutions, but his is another role. He is evidently a Frenchman who occasionally feels the need to explain his characters' actions and motivations to his compatriots. It is to be recalled that the story appears in a collection entitled *Souvenirs de voyage,* and the narrator is in a sense a traveller bringing back a description of the countries and peoples he has visited. The initial description of Cephalonia is given through the eyes of the narrator who fluctuates between the use of "je" and the more inpersonal "on": "Quand on se promène dans la rue principale d'Argostoli..."

---

[7] Stendhal, *Romans et nouvelles,* ed. H. Martineau (Paris: Bibliothèque de la Pléïade, 1952), p. 618.

and later "Perpendiculairement à cette rue que je décris..." (SV: pp. 11-12). As the plot progresses the narrator occasionally intervenes to explain small details; in regard to Count Tsalla's title, he writes: "... ne vous étonnez pas de tous ces comtes; soit dit en passant, les Vénitiens en avaient peuplé leurs territoires ioniens" (SV: p. 17). Generally, however, the narrator leaves the interpretation of scenes and conversations up to the reader. Knowing Lanza's ego-centered drives, the reader must decipher the hints concerning Lanza's relationship to his goddaughter, his role in Tsalla's disappearance, and must discover what is left unsaid in the conversations.

The narrator here is not omniscient but consistently reflects Sophie's point of view. The only character whose personality is explained is Jérôme Lanza; the only characteristics mentioned and the only actions shown are those which lead the reader to believe that his violent death was merited; Sophie appears to be *de facto* exculpated of any guilt. Early in the narrative, when Lanza inquires about Gérasime's identity, Chevalier Paleocappa replies: "Ne la connaissez-vous pas! C'est Gérasime Delfini, le fils de Catherine Delfini, si revissante il y a quinze ans, qui faisait les beaux jours de Zante, et avec qui notre ancien ami César Tsalla a été si lié. Vous vous souvenez bien de César Tsalla, pauvre diable! dit en terminant l'imbécile" (SV: p. 23). This epithet of "imbecile" reflects Sophie's estimation of any person who, however innocently, would remind Lanza of Tsalla. Sopie, moreover, is the only character who is familiar with all the scenes, either through direct participation or by indirect report from her mother or from Gérasime.

The narrator maintains Sophie's point of view but tempers it with the irony and wit so typical of Gobineau's own conversation. (A contemporary writes: "Son ironie lui suscitait souvent des ennemis mais il ne pouvait s'en défaire!").[8] The examples of this humor are many. The dying Lanza's wish for revenge is termed a "désir bien naturel." The effort of the police to track down Lanza's assailants is described as follows:

---

[8] Marie Dragoumis in her introduction to "Lettres à Marie Dragoumis," *NRF*, XLII (1934), 276.

La justice fit les recherches les plus habiles et les mieux dirigées, mais elle ne decouvrit quoi que ce fût. Quand elle essaya de savoir si le comte Lanza avait quelque ennemi déclaré qui eût intérêt à le faire disparaître, elle ne trouva personne; le comte Lanza n'avait pas un seul ennemi; mais quand elle poussa ses investigations jusqu'à vouloir apprendre s'il était aimé, elle s'aperçut qu'il était détesté universellement, et cette contradiction flagrante brouillant toutes ses cartes, elle fut bientôt obligée de lâcher prise, de s'avouer vaincue; et ce ne fut plus que pour la forme et afin de couvrir sa retraite plus honorablement qu'elle afficha encore pendant quelque temps de s'occuper d'une affaire, où, tout d'abord, elle avait compris qu'elle ne comprendrait jamais rien (SV: p. 51).

The concluding paragraph maintains this witty tone of the narrative. "Quelques semaines après, Gérasime épousait Sophie, ils vécurent heureux et eurent beaucoup d'enfants" (SV: p. 53). We must remember that this has been a tale of passion, energy and violence. If Lanza was a scheming, hypocritical man, Sophie too was unscrupulous. The narrator, however, mimics the typical fairytale conclusion which rewards the virtuous and punishes the wicked.[9] It is precisely this type of humor and irony which distinguishes "Le Mouchoir rouge" from the *Chroniques Italiennes*.

"La Danseuse de Shamakha," which Gobineau lightly refers to as "une machine qui se passe au Caucase" (CB: p. 33), was composed in Stockholm during the early summer of 1872. Originally conceived as part of *Souvenirs de voyage,* the story finally appeared as the opening narrative in *Nouvelles asiatiques*. "La Danseuse de Shamakha" is not so much the struggle between two people as it is the conflict between Omm-Djéhâne and her environment. Accompanied by his friend Assanoff, Juan Moreno, a Spanish soldier of fortune, sets out from the Black Sea port of Poti to join his new Russian regiment in Baku. In Shamakha the travelers are entertained by a group of famed dancers, one of whom is the temperamental Omm-Djéhâne. That evening the young woman gives Assanoff a rendezvous, reveals herself to be

---

[9] See Mistler, p. 260.

his long-lost cousin, and by singing a Lesghy ballad convinces him to desert the troop in order to avenge their murdered tribesmen. After a sobering conversation with Moreno, Assanoff grows less enthusiastic about his recent decision, drinks himself into a stupor, and leaves his friend to handle the explanation in what becomes a violent scene. The young dancer's scorn for her cousin yields to a sudden respect and passion for Moreno, who, unaware of her psychological change, candidly admits his own love for a woman in Spain. Omm-Djéhâne leaves quietly; one winter night she appears on Moreno's doorstep in Baku to die in his arms.

When Gobineau visited the Caucasus in winter 1861, he met Péry, a young Lesghienne girl who had been brought up in the family of a Russian general. Péry became the model for Omm-Djéhâne, while the plot was inspired by a story current in Shamakha; (see NA: pp. xliii-xlv).

Omm-Djéhâne, the central character in the narrative, is no classic beauty, but she radiates a forceful seductive power. "C'était une de ces créatures qui entraînent, qui enivrent, qui ensorcellent, et qui ne vous disent ni pourquoi, ni comment. En vérité, un critique froid n'eût trouvé qu'un seul adjectif à lui appliquer. Il eût dit d'elle: Elle est étrange; mais aucun critique n'eût pu rester froid en sa présence" (NA: p. 38). Her mysterious attraction increases when she performs the Lesghy dance or sings tribal folkmusic. When Assanoff hears her chant, "il était visible qu'il écoutait de toutes ses oreilles et de toute son intelligence, de tout son coeur, de toute son âme!" (NA: pp. 56-57). The young dancer's charms find expression in the art forms of her tribe.

Omm-Djéhâne is a mystic; she guides her actions according to the counsel of her string of prayer beads, her "istikharèh"; "elle mettait une confiance absolue dans les oracles de ses grains de chapelet" (NA: p. 72). She remains in Shamkha where the beads foretell she will see her cousin on whom she has centered her projects for revenge, for a private warfare conducted guerilla style from the Caucasian forests. Omm-Djéhâne possesses "une intelligence merveilleuse" (NA: p. 71) but subjects this faculty to the attainment of her goals. As a young girl, she reads many books concerning supernatural powers with the intention of becoming a sorceress and thus confounding the Russians. However, unable to discover the desired incantations, "... elle ne douta jamais que des maléfices puissants ne fussent au fond de toutes ses affaires; car, d'esprit comme de coeur, elle resta toujours lesghy, et la forme et la nature de son esprit ne changèrent pas plus que ses affections" (NA: p. 71).

Omm-Djéhâne's intense will is directed toward her desire for vengeance. Her determination sustained her as a young child at a time when surrender would have meant death. Omm-Djéhâne narrates: "... j'étais seule au fond d'un bois, accroupie entre des racines d'arbres: je n'avais mangé depuis deux jours qu'un morceau de biscuit gâté, jeté par les soldats au bord d'un campement; c'était l'hiver; la neige tombait sur moi. Je consultais mon chapelet, et le sort infaillible me répétait: Tu le [Assanoff] reverras! tu le reverras! Et, au fond horrible de mon épouvantable misère, l'espérance me soutenait" (NA: p. 68). Omm-Djéhâne's life has been firmly controlled by her will; she has forced herself to stay alive, to wait for the day when she would again see Assanoff, when the two could declare war against the Russians.

Violence fails to intimidate her. At the age of ten she tried to strangle the governess who had called her a little fool. A few months later she slashed the face of her stepsister and almost blinded the girl; at this point her Russian protectors sent her away. The narrator writes: "Omm-Djéhâne n'était pas vicieuse, il s'en fallait; elle était complètement chaste et pure; mais elle n'était pas vertueuse non plus, parce que, si quelqu'une de ses inclinations l'eût commandé, elle eût renoncé à cette chasteté en une seconde, sans combat, sans résistance et même sans le moindre soupçon d'avoir tort" (NA: p. 72).

Omm-Djéhâne had allowed the years to pass without remonstrance, without impatience, guided by the conviction that Assanoff would return. Her first confrontation with reality occurs during the rendezvous with her cousin. She finds him weak and tainted with the vices of civilization, but through music and tales she awakens his racial consciousness and elicits the desired response.

The true recognition scene occurs the following morning in her conversation with Moreno. The future she had in her fantasy constructed around Assanoff's return no longer is possible. The "istikharèh" had promised her that she would see Assanoff, but had failed to describe his weakness. Not only is her whole reason for existence annihilated, but she has, first with Assanoff, and then with a stranger, shattered the shell of silence. She would have murdered Moreno for his part in dissuading Assanoff from his noble resolution, but the Spaniard's reflexes enable him to parry her attack. As the conversation continues Omm-Djéhâne becomes so attracted to Moreno's courage, his forceful logic, and his personality that the vacuum created by the crumbling of her whole carefully projected future becomes filled with admiration and love for this stranger. When Moreno avows his love for another, Omm-Djéhâne, always direct in her thoughts, does not attempt to seduce him. Her hope for revenge destroyed, she is forced to face the present. But for her the present possesses no hope since she is convinced that her love must remain unfulfilled. She allows Grégoire Ivanitch to care for her but desires only death, death at Moreno's doorstep.

Gobineau characterizes Omm-Djéhâne through the use of a technique which he had employed over twenty years earlier with Emmelina Irnois. The heroine, who furnishes the title of the narrative, is first introduced indirectly. Her story is the subject of conversation in the Baku hotel where Moreno spends his first evening in the Caucasus. Then the reader hears about her from Grégoire Ivanitch and from Splendeurs de la Beauté, who directs the Shamakha dancers, as these two and the police chief negotiate a project to sell her to a Trabzon merchant. Finally Omm-Djéhâne enters the scene and astounds Splendeurs de la Beauté by her unexpected acquiescence to the proposed match. Emmelina's eager acceptance of marriage astonishes, for she has never before expressed her will; Omm-Djéhâne's submission is unexpected, since her reputation cannot be characterized as one of docility. The reader grows to understand the Lesghy dancer, first in her scene with Assanoff and then in the one with Moreno. The narrator, however, feels the need to explain Omm-Djéhâne's personality, her inner feelings and motivations, just as the narrator in "Mademoiselle Irnois" feels obliged to "explain" Emmelina.

Assanoff, the center of Omm-Djéhâne's aspirations, is a tall, blond young man with a broad nose and a small, bristling mustache: "Ce jeune homme n'était pas beau, mais leste, découplé, et avait l'air ouvert et cordial" (NA: p. 12). This openness is typical of his entire personality. His enthusiasm is easily aroused. The first manifestation of this trait is in the Poti hotel when Assanof hears of the mysterious seductive power of Omm-Djéhâne; in Shamakha the atmosphere of the dances encourages him to challenge a fellow soldier to a ritual Lesghy dance. His rendezvous with Omm-Djéhâne ends with his determination to wed his cousin and desert the army, but this superficial enthusiasm cannot withstand Moreno's calm logic. Assanoff then turns to the only solace he knows, the bottle. Already in Poti, "L'ivrognerie flagrante d'Assanoff le [Moreno] rebutait" (NA: p. 44).

The narrator's explanation of Assanoff's personality, his lovable good nature, unfortunately coupled with the inability to face up to reality, rests on society's evil influence: "La vérité était que le pauvre Assanoff n'était pas Russe, n'était pas sauvage, n'était pas civilisé, mais de tout cela un peu, et les pauvres êtres, que les périodes et les pays de transition déforment de la sorte, sont fort incomplets, fort misérables et réservés à plus de vices et de malheurs que de vertus et de félicités" (NA: p. 63). Assanoff himself, during an occasional moment of lucidity, realizes his cultural dichotomy. "Quelquefois, parlant de lui-même, il avouait n'être, à son avis, qu'un sauvage mal dégrossi, et, ajoutait-il, assez peu débarbouillé, mais il revenait bientôt sur cette déclaration et se proclamait un gentilhomme" (NA: p. 44).

Assanoff, having escaped the massacre of his tribe at the age of twelve, was sent to cadet school in Saint Petersburg where he grew attracted to all that was French. When speaking to Moreno of the portly Madame Marron he says: "Léocadie n'est ni jeune ni très jolie; mais que voulez-vous faire à Poti? Le diable y est plus malin qu'ailleurs, et, songez donc! une Française, une Française à Poti! Comment voulez-vous qu'on résiste?" (NA: p. 15). On the voyage from Poti to Shamakha, Moreno is charmed by the beauty of the native girls they encounter; as for Assanoff, "[il] les trouvait jolies, mais comme la civilisation le passionnait, il jugeait madame Marron (aîné) douée de perfections d'un ordre très supérieur, bien qu'un peu défraîchie par le frottement des années" (NA: p. 27). Even towards the end of his nocturnal meeting with Omm-Djéhâne, when he has made the decision to elope with his cousin, he tells her in all simplicity: "Tu sais le français? ... Cela nous distraira de le parler quelquefois" (NA:

p. 61). Omm-Djéhâne immediately rejects the suggestion. Assanoff is not only attracted by European "civilization," but the bourgeois moral code has to a great extent become the standard by which he judges himself and others. Assanoff hesitates in his project of marriage and vengeance when Moreno tells him that he would appear ridiculous in the eyes of his friends. "La peur de devenir ridicule le bouleversa" (NA: p. 63). A sense of honor compels him to carry out his promise, but after a few glasses of brandy he decides to slip away unnoticed leaving Moreno to explain his absence to Omm-Djéhâne.

Until meeting his cousin, Assanoff has been a good-natured soldier of unfaltering devotion. When the problems of his daily existence overpower him he turns to alcohol as a panacea; even under stable conditions he is a heavy drinker. His "recognition scene" occurs in Shamakha, first as he performs the violent tribal dance with a fellow Tartar officer, and later in his meeting with Omm-Djéhâne. The power of his race and the exigencies of his background, awarenesses which up to then he has always been able to repress, suddenly emerge and require that he change his life in order to avenge the massacre of his family and tribe. But his will is weak. All his life Assanoff has hesitated to face reality, and hence in this moment of capital importance he is unable to carry out his decision, Nor has he the courage openly to announce his changed intention to Omm-Djéhâne. When he later learns of Omm-Djéhâne's death, he again turns to alcohol and in his despair clings symbolically to France and civilization. "Quand Moreno raconta toute cette affaire à Assanoff, le Tatar civilisé en fut extrêmement ému; il ne dégrisa pas de huit jours, et on le rencontrait partout chantant la *Marseillaise*. Ensuite, il se calma" (NA: p. 78).

In the narrative Assanoff is directly characterized through his actions and words. The reader is introduced to Assanoff before learning his name. From the outset Assanoff is open, exuberant. In his initial conversation with Moreno, Assanoff characterizes himself very succinctly in one long sentence: "Moi, monsieur, je m'appelle Assanoff, c'est-à-dire je m'appelle en réalité Mourad, fils de Hassan-Khan; je suis Russe, c'est-à-dire Tatare de la province de Shyrcoan et musulman, pour vous servir, c'est-à-dire à la façon dont aurait pu l'être M. de Voltaire, grand homme! et dont je lis avec plaisir les ouvrages, quand je n'ai pas sous la main ceux de M. Paul de Kock" (NA: pp. 13-14). His spontaneity is evident in the flow of words and ideas. His Caucasian heritage is revealed in his parentage; but Assanoff considers himself Russian and is proud of his Saint Petersburg education and his rank in the Russian army. The mention of Voltaire as a "grand homme" is almost a cliché; the philosopher was held in great esteem in nineteenth-century Russia.

The key to Assanoff's character, for the reader who is familiar with Gobineau's other writings, is the allusion to Paul de Kock. [10] In a letter to the Comtesse de la Tour written in 1874, Gobineau tells his friend that he finds it not at all surprising that a bourgeois acquaintance of hers would not appreciate the *Arabian Nights*: "Ce monde-là a sa nourriture littéraire spéciale. Il faut la leur laisser: Paul de Kock quand ils sont en belle humeur; les cantiques de Saint-Sulpice quand ils croient élever ce qu'ils prennent pour leur âme; les notes et les rapports sur les céréales, le commerce des fers, les salles d'asile quand ils se prennent au sérieux. Le reste ne les regarde pas." [11] The Tatar Assanoff is enchanted by French civilization. That part of French culture which attracts him most is precisely the part which Gobineau intensely dislikes. Not only is Assanoff's will torn between conflicting allegiances but he is attracted to the weak unimaginative side of civilization. Gobineau considers Paul de Kock suitable for the bourgeois when he is in good humor, and Assanoff is rarely one to be depressed or even overly serious. As Moreno mentioned: "Assanoff avait l'esprit brouillon, mais il avait de l'esprit; il divaguait à l'ordinaire, mais en quelques recontres il montra du coeur" (NA: p. 44).

Only at one point does the narrator seek to explain Assanoff's character to the reader; he presents a justification of Assanoff's lack of will which he links to a condemnation of society for having destroyed the moral strenght typical of the Lesghy without furnishing any positive substitute.

---

[10] Paul de Kock (1794-1871) was a prolific writer who humorously depicted incidents in the lives of the French petty bourgeoisie (*Monsieur Dupont, Georgette*).

[11] J. Mistler, ed., "Lettres de Gobineau à la comtesse de La Tour," *Table Ronde*, no. 28 (avril 1950), pp. 36-37.

The reader learns about the mysterious Omm-Djéhâne and the open-hearted Assanoff through Moreno, the strong sounding board to whom the others reveal themselves. Moreno, a serious individual "d'une humeur assez austère" (NA: p. 11), has been forced to leave Spain for political reasons. "A mesure qu'il s'éloignait de l'Espagne et de la femme qu'il aimait, le découragement des premières heures se transformait en une résignation maladive, qui lui détruisait le prix de la vie. Il sentait que son existence antérieure était finie, et il n'éprouvait aucun désir d'en ressaisir une nouvelle" (NA: p. 43). Thus, when he arrives in Poti he is unwilling to participate in his environment; everything he sees seems to be a dream, "un de ces rêves particulièrement embrouillés où la raison ne se retrouve pas" (NA: p. 44). During the evening in Poti and the ensuing trip to Shamakha Moreno barely listens to Assanof's descriptions, explanations and stories; gradually he breaks his wall of silence to tell Assanoff of his sorrows. The two become friends, even though neither totally understands the other.

In the meeting with Omm-Djéhâne, Moreno is forced out of his own melancholy as he learns of the young dancer's sorrows. Although wounded by her sudden attack with the dagger, he reacts neither with anger nor hatred. "Moreno fut un peu étonné. Il avait des parents dans les montagnes de Barcelone; mais il ne connaissait ni Catalane, ni Catalan de la force de cette petite femme. Pour lui trouver une rivale digne d'elle, il lui eût fallu remonter jusqu'aux Almogavares...." (NA: p. 65). As the interview progresses it is Omm-Djéhâne who becomes impressed with Moreno's courage, generosity and sense of honor. The young dancer's death in Baku moves him deeply. "Moreno eut un chagrin profond. Ce n'était pas raisonnable" (NA: p. 78). During the early years of separation, Moreno still remains faithful to his Spanish fiancée and is sustained by the hope of returning to his country. However, "[son] amour ne lui causait plus le mal irritant des premiers mois; c'était une habitude tendre, une préoccupation mélancolique dont son âme restait comme saturée" (NA: pp. 74-75). When the political reasons which had driven him into exile are resolved, he and his fiancée realize that neither has the money to join the other. "Tout en resta là. Ils ne se marièrent ni l'un ni l'autre, cessèrent avec le temps d'être très malheureux; mais, heureux, ils ne le furent jamais" (NA: p. 75).

Gobineau's avowed objective in the *Nouvelles asiatiques* is the presentation of Asian character. In "La Danseuse de Shamakha," Gobineau wishes to portray Omm-Djéhâne's combination of primitive reasoning and mysticism with her tribal vigor; this strength and energy are contrasted to Assanoff's character which exemplifies the negative elements of civilization. Even though Moreno plays an essential role in the development of the plot, his primary purpose in the story is to afford a point of reference for the reader; Moreno's reaction to certain Oriental customs is the European's reaction; the explanations he receives are also inserted for the benefit of the reader. Through Moreno, the European reader grows to understand and sympathize with Omm-Djéhâne and Assanoff.

Except for the final scene, the presentation of the plot is chronological. The background information about Assanoff and Omm-Djéhâne is woven into the conversations. Towards the end to the narrative Gobineau violates the chronological sequence in order to terminate the Moreno subplot before giving the denouement of the primary plot. Consequently the reader first learns how Moreno's bitter resignation gradually mellows to soft melancholy as he realizes the impossibility of returning to Spain; then in a flashback, Omm-Djéhâne's death and Assanoff's subsequent reaction are dramatized.

The structure of the main plot of "La Danseuse de Shamakha" parallels the dramatic construction of "Mademoiselle Irnois," just as Omm-Djéhâne and Emmelina are presented in a similar manner.

The narrative technique is non-interpretive third person. In this presentation of the Caucasian dancer, Gobineau restrains his wit and humor in order to heighten the effect of the drama. The reader is not required to distinguish between what is said and what is meant. The plot is direct and the characters either speak freely and openly or else say nothing at all. The point of view is that of Moreno; he is either present at the scenes mentioned in the narrative or could easily have been informed of the conversations through Assanoff or through Grégoire Ivanitch who confides in him at the time of Omm-Djéhâne's death. When Moreno is carefree he appreciates the marvelous natural beauty of the Phase valley and its inhabitants. Towards the end of the story, following the emotional scene with Omm-Djéhâne and after the journey to

Baku with the morose Assanoff, the Caspian Sea appears unfriendly.

> Quand la voiture entra à Bakou, l'aspect premier de la ville ne lui [Moreno] rendit pas la gaîté.
> La Caspienne, cette mer mystérieuse et sombre, plus inhospitalière encore que l'Europe, sur les deux tiers de ses rivages, couvrait au loin l'horizon de ses eaux plombées, sur lesquelles le ciel pesait gris et bas. (NA: p. 73)

That this impression reflects Moreno's mood becomes clear when we compare Gobineau's account of his voyage to Tehran via Poti and Baku in winter 1861. In a letter to his sister he notes that he was charmed by the various cities he visited and that he enjoyed crossing the Caspian Sea: "J'ai traversé la Caspienne avec beaucoup de bonheur, un temps magnifique" (EP: p. 7). The narrator, a European who appears to have received the story from Moreno, could be associated with Gobineau himself. Gaulmier prefers to identify Gobineau with Moreno and discovers in the Spanish soldier's feelings toward his fiancée a reflection of Gobineau's melancholy upon being obliged to leave in Paris a woman he loved in order to assume his new post at Stockholm in 1872 (NA: p. xlv).

The locale plays a limited psychological role. In addition to the impressionistic picture of Baku seen by Moreno, there is a description by Omm-Djéhâne as she evokes the tribal village for Assanoff. The elevation of the village is symbolic of the superiority of the Lesghy race: "... tu ne vois pas notre aoûl, notre village, sur son pic de rochers, montant droit au milieu de l'azur du ciel, avec les nuages au-dessous de lui, dans les vallons pleins d'arbres et de pierres? Tu ne vois donc plus le nid ou nous sommes nés, bien au-dessus des plaines, bien au-dessus des montagnes communes, bien au-dsessus des hommes esclaves, parmi les demeures des oiseaux nobles, au sein de l'atmosphère de Dieu?" NA: pp. 53-54).

The colorful pictures of Asian customs and folklore play a double role; first they provide lyric interludes in the narrative, and secondly, they assist in explaining the character of the protagonists. The descriptive passages, far from interfering with the the action, serve as a graceful link between scenes. The brief description of the Phase landscape fills the interlude between Baku and Shamakha; the picture of Baku covers the passage of time which elapses between Moreno's meeting Omm-Djéhâne and her death. The dance performed by Splendeurs de la Beauté is a preface which sets the mood for Assanoff's tribal dance. Assanoff's reaction to the beauty of the Phase Valley maidens, in that he claims to prefer the French charms of Madame Marron, is one of the elements of his characterization. Gobineau avoids gratuitous description and weaves his travelogue pictures into the action of the narrative.

The leitmotif of "La Danseuse de Shamakha" is "civilization," especially the bourgeois aspect of French civilization, and its influence on Assanoff. The narrator, while introducing the latter, comments that the charm and grace of pre-Revolutionary France has been lost: Assanoff's first words were uttered "de bonne grâce, avec cet air sémillant, dont les Russes ont hérité depuis que les Français, qui passent pour l'avoir inventé, l'ont perdu" (NA: p. 13). Assanoff's vices are considered French, whereas the positive traits of his character are traced to his Lesghy heritage. Moreover, Moreno, the exemplary European, is not French, but Spanish. When Omm-Djéhâne excoriates her cousin she calls him a "perfect" European: "méchant, perfide, larron, assassin, sans foi, sans loi, sans Dieu, un pourceau ivre de toutes les ivresses imaginables et roulé dans tous les bourbiers du vice!" (NA: p. 55). To Moreno she later repeats her accusations against Assanoff: "...je vous félicite. C'est un homme encore plus civilisé que je ne le croyais. Il vient de renier son père, il vient de frapper sur la mémoire de la femme qui l'a mis au monde!" (NA: p. 67). The quiet Moreno is not a believer in the progress of civilization; he tells the young woman: "Je suis de votre avis, nous vivons dans un monde fâcheux, et, barbare ou policé, le meilleur n'en vaut rien" (NA: p. 68).

The narration itself to some extent belies these accusations against civilization. Assanoff is in an unenviable position, but he never did possess Omm-Djéhâne's energy. While he was a young cadet in Saint Petersburg his cousin was already constructing projects of vengeance, in spite of her "European" education. Moreno, a product of civilization, never loses his integrity and generosity.

There is also the implicit theme of feminine strength of character. In their conversation, Splendeurs de la Beauté is obviously stronger than Grégoire Ivanitch, and the latter gladly complies with her requests. The narrator gives the impression that women's minds are more active than men's. Speaking of Splendeurs de la Beauté he says: "Il serait hardi de prétendre qu'elle ne pensait à rien. Cet état paradisiaque existe pour les hommes dans beaucoup de pays, mais il est à douter que nulle part il soit accessible aux femmes" (NA: p. 34). In Asia women have the added advantage of social mobility: "...les femmes d'Asie ne sont ni en haut, ni en bas d'une échelle sociale quelconque; elles peuvent tout faire; elles sont femmes ou impératrices ou servantes, et restent femmes, ce qui leur permet de tout dire, de tout faire et de n'avoir aucune responsabilité de leurs pensées ni de leurs actes devant la raison et l'équité" (NA: p. 72). The combination of these feminine qualities with energy gives Omm-Djéhâne a definite superiority over Assanoff, so much so that it seems a bit ironic when she accuses him of being not a man but a woman. (NA: p. 65). The driving force of the narrative is in the hands of Splendeurs de la Beauté and especially of Omm-Djéhâne.

Gobineau has often been compared to Mérimée, with whom he corresponded quite regularly until the latter's death. Young Gobineau, as we have seen earlier, had considered Mérimée a master of the "nouvelle" and had highly praised "Colomba," which in several respects seems to be the prototype of "La Danseuse de Shamakha." Both Colomba and Omm-Djéhâne seek vengeance for the murder of members of their families; both pin their hopes on young men who have been absent receiving a European education. Orso, however, is of stronger character; he did not assimilate the Parisian vices but tempered the Corsican drive for violence with the European notions of calm and order. This latter inclination is further reinforced by Lydia's request that he not kill the Barricini brothers. Both sisters manage to awake the suppressed sentiments of the men on whom they depend. Omm-Djéhâne evokes the Lesghy heritage and the massacre of their tribe: Colomba desfigures Orso's horse and this supreme insult which is attributed to the Barricini family rouses him to action. At this point the two plots separate; Assanoff is unable to implement his decision to desert the regiment and avenge his tribe. The change that is effected in Omm-Djéhâne after her encounter with Moreno, her violent inner struggle and her desire for death, find no counterpart in Colomba, whose personality remains unchanged even in her last scene with the old Barricini. If Gobineau owes his initial inspiration to Mérimée —a distinct possibility— he has none the less created an original work of narrative art.

Certain thematic comparisons can be drawn between "La Danseuse de Shamakha" and other Mérimée narratives. Assanoff's identity is destroyed as a result of the mixture of cultures, the exposure of his primitive Tartar heritage to the degenerate elements of bourgeois society. In "Tamango" Mérimée treated the same moral problem while laying greater emphasis on the misuse of alcohol. The theme of energy, so evident in Mérimée's writings, is explicitly expressed in "La Vénus d'Ille"; the narrator observes the statue in an effort to discover the origin of her seductive powers: "...je me demandais si la supériorité de beauté qu'il fallait bien accorder à la statue ne tenait pas, en grande partie, à son expression de tigresse; car l'énergie, même dans les mauvaises passions, excite toujours en nous un étonnement et une espèce d'admiration involontaire." [12] Gobineau's writings are designed to corroborate this assertion.

Our concluding remarks on narrative technique will focus only on the four latter narratives. "Le Mariage d'un Prince," Gobineau's earliest *feuilleton*, is so inferior to his other stories and received so little attention from the author, that we shall not consider the weaknesses of its construction.

The importance of the female protagonist in each of the four narratives is first indicated in the titles, indirectly so in the case of "Le Mouchoir rouge." The strongest member of the Irnois household was Emmelina; Cabarot was superior to her in intelligence but not in sensitivity. In the other stories, the women set themselves apart in varying degrees from the men who are the objects of their love, hatred, or disdain.

The women are characterized by an intense moral force which manifests itself in will power. The change in Emmelina's soul becomes evident when she unequivocally states her request for

---

[12] *Colomba, La Venus d'Ille, Les Ames du Purgatoire* (Paris: Calmann-Levy, 1927), p. 270.

solitude. All five women, Emmelina, Adélaïde, Elisabeth, Sophie and Omm-Djéhâne, guide their actions by certain ideas which they conceal from their contemporaries. This self-control is a conscious manifestation of their objective appraisal of the situation in which they find themselves; their suppressed energy, however, is revealed in their eyes.

As we have seen, one of Emmelina's distinguishing features was her eyes. Even though physical description plays a very small role in "Adélaïde," the narrator observes the eyes of Elisabeth and her daugter. Both women utilize the severity of their glances, the controlled stare, which betrays hidden resources of energy, to cow Frédéric into submission. When Elisabeth asks for Frédéric's hand in marriage she looks at him "avec des yeux dont il n'avait pas encore vu l'expression âpre et décidée" (A: p. 148). In describing Adélaïde, the narrator mentions repeatedly the unwavering glances directed at one point towards her mother (A: p. 153); at a moment of defeat she stares at the wall (A: p. 167). To gain Rothbanner's acquiescence, "elle regarda fixement Frédéric, car le connaissant comme elle faisait, elle savait quel poignard elle lui enfonçait dans le plus profond du coeur" (A: p. 177).

In "Le Mouchoir rouge" the eyes again are the physical feature which the narrator describes most frequently. Sophie's eyes are characterized by a "feu sombre" (SV: p. 21) which bursts forth in the final scene where through words and glances she obtains her mother's acquiescence. Earlier in the narrative Lanza becomes aware of the tender sentiments which unite Gérasime and Sophie when he notices the former's eyes. As Jérôme Lanza observes his goddaughter that evening his glance is so powerful that it assumes an evanescent existence independent of the count himself:

> D'un regard qui ne pouvait pas se tromper, il aperçut en quelque sorte le coeur même de sa filleule, il le vit battre, il en compta les palpitations précipitées. Sans qu'elle s'en aperçut, tant elle était absorbée, ce regard, le plus incisif et le plus aigu de tous les regards, entra dans ses yeux, et y trouva et y vit des larmes et s'y brûla; il entra dans cette tête charmante, que l'aile de la passion touchait et courbait légèrement du côté de la voix séductrice; il y découvrit, il y saisit en flagrant délit d'existence ce monde de pensées que l'amour demande et que la jeunesse tient toutes prêtes. (SV: pp. 23-24)

The narrator in "La Danseuse de Shamakha" shows a similar awareness. Assanoff's eyes, at the moment he accepts the challenge to perform the Lesghy dance, assume "l'expression à la fois dure et sauvage, mais pleine de flammes" (NA: p. 50). As for the protagonist, Omm-Djéhâne's glances reveal the self-contained force which she employs in an effort to subjugate Assanoff. "On prétend que la fixité du regard de l'homme opère sur les brutes d'une manière merveilleuse, qu'elle les terrifie, les fait reculer et les réduit, en quelque sorte, à néant. Que cela soit vrai ou non, Assanoff ne put soutenir l'expression des yeux que la jeune fille tenait attachés sur les siens..." (NA: p. 67). In all four narratives, the eyes play a double role: they are the unconscious expression of the state of the soul, revealing love, or hate or force; moreover, the energetic heroine employs the directness of her stare as an effective means of attaining a desired goal.

The theme of heredity and the idea of race are subtly introduced into the stories. That Emmelina is mentally and physically crippled can be traced to a combination of the defects of her parents. Adélaïde possesses Elisabeth's beauty, intelligence and will power. Sophie has received her mother's charm and Lanza's acute and perceptive mind. Omm-Djéhâne represents the strength of the Lesghy race. The environment (Taine's *milieu*) appears to have little effect: Emmelina's dull daily life did ot stultify her sensitivity. Adélaïde misguided education led her to develop the project of thwarting her mother's plans but did not change her character; Assanoff's character is ostensibly emasculated through his contact with French bourgeois culture, but he never did possess Omm-Djéhâne's strength. Each character manifests a unique personality which transcends the determining factor of heredity and the lesser influence of environment.

Gobineau employs two distinct plot patterns in these narratives. "Adélaïde" and "Le Mouchoir rouge" depict a clashing of strong wills; the strategy adopted by the protagonists expresses itself in dialogue, in action and even in violence. The plots are tightly constructed and the apparently extraneous remarks are integrated with the action. "Mademoiselle Irnois" and "La Danseuse de Shamakha" present a single individual whose life is changed by the experience of unrequited love, by the giving of self with no tangible return. The heroine manifests such self-control that what she does not do becomes more important than her actions. Loosely connected scenes and incidents are employed to portray the central figures and their environment.

The plots of "Adélaïde" and "Le Mouchoir rouge" can be classified as chronological: the reader is introduced into a complex situation and then desires to learn what happens next." "Mademoiselle Irnois" and "La Danseuse de Shamakha" reveal a causal structure: the reader is presented with an apparently contradictory personality and becomes eager to know "why" a certain decision was made.

The type of plot determines the role of the setting. The action in "Adélaïde" and in "Le Mouchoir rouge" occurs against the backdrop of a salon society; the protagonists are conscious of the impression they convey to others. However, while the former narrative is clearly a psychological study, the latter is concerned with the presentation of Cephalonian character. The descriptions of Argostoli are introduced only as they relate to he characterization of its inhabitants.

The locale is of greater importance in "Mademoiselle Irnois" and "La Danseuse de Shamakha," for even if environment does not determine in an absolute sense the actions and reactions of the individual, it does help explain certain traits and habits. Moreover, the Irnois household defines Monsieur Irnois' personality and, in this sense, Emmelina's heritage. There is no variation, no touch of individuality in the rooms, no sense of lightness or grace. "Toutes les chambres étaient uniformément carrelées de rouge, hors le salon parqueté; toutes les chambres étaient uniformément sombres, hors les chambres à coucher, plus sombres que tout le reste, parce qu'elles donnaient sur la cour" (A: p. 37). In "La Danseuse de Shamakha" the European narrator is conscious of the Caucasian scenery. The descriptions are not gratuitous but generally join together to create the background necessary for an understanding of Grégoire Ivanitch, Assanoff, and Omm-Djéhâne. In describing Moreno's strange reaction to the Caucasus, the narrator explains the role of environment: "Soit résultat des moeurs, soit délicatesse et faiblesse plus grande de l'imagination et du coeur, il existe peu d'hommes aujourd'hui, dont le bonheur et la force vitale ne résident en dehors d'eux-mêmes, dans un autre être ou dans une chose. Presque chacun ressemble à l'embryon: il reçoit ce qui le fait vivre d'un foyer de vie qui n'est pas le sien, et, si on l'en sépare mal à propos, il est douteux, sinon impossible, qu'il subsiste à son aise" (NA: pp. 43-44).

This attitude is similar to the theories Balzac expressed in the *Avant-Propos* (1842) to the *Comédie humaine:* "La Société ne fait-elle pas de l'homme, suivant les milieux où son action se déploie, autant d'hommes différents qu'il y a de variétés en zoologie?" [13] Speaking of his own ambitious project, he states: "Ainsi l'oeuvre à faire devait avoir une triple forme: les hommes, les femmes et les choses, c'est-à-dire les personnes et la représentation materielle qu'ils donnent de leur pensée; enfin l'homme et la vie, car la vie est notre vêtement." [14] It is in this sense that Gobineau focusses on the Asian landscapes.

Narrative techniques also vary. The change towards a more direct presentation is independent of the content of the narratives. The narrator of "Mademoiselle Irnois" is the omniscient *roman feuilletonniste* who acts as a guide interpreting the story and the characters to the reader. The story of Elisabeth and Adélaïde is related by the baron to several guests who are personally acquainted with the Rothbanners. Both accounts contain an equal proportion of actual scenes and straight narration. In "Le Mouchoir rouge" and "La Danseuse de Shamakha" the narrative "je" can be considered a vestige of conversational style. The stories themselves are composed of twice as many scenes as narrative passages. If the stories are considered chronologically, the omniscient narrator of "Mademoiselle Irnois" is replaced in the later stories by a more realistic third-person narrator.

In "Mademoiselle Irnois," "Adélaïde," "Le Mouchoir rouge" and "La Danseuse de Shamakha" Gobineau develops plots which are directed by a dynamic heroine. The degree of energy or will differs with each protagonist; Emmelina's only desire is to protect her own privacy, while Adélaïde and Elisabeth unite to destroy Frédéric's identity. For Omm-Djéhâne and Sophie energy finds its expression in violence. The varying kinds of energy are represented through different types of plots and in a variety of

---

[13] Balzac, I (1953), xxvi.
[14] Balzac, I, xxvii.

settings; different narrative techniques are employed to portray this central theme. Gobineau makes no explicit moral judgment on the means employed by his characters in exercising their wills and, thus, indirectly he reveals his admiration for such energy.

CHAPTER IV

THE POWER OF LOVE

"Die Liebe geht allem vor —dann kommt die Arbeit— und weiter gibt es nichts." [1] In a letter to Prince von Eulenburg-Hertefeld in 1877, Gobineau made this affirmation expressing love's primacy in the hierarchy of human passion and enterprise. Three years previously, while writing to Prokesch, he defined love as "une maladie terrible, telle que les Grecs étonnés l'appelaient *sacrée* et *divine* parce qu'elle était comme incompréhensible"; and he concluded: "... c'est la maladie des âmes fortes et la montrer chez les imbéciles, c'est ce que l'Histoire ne peut pas faire" (CP: p. 381). These statements represent not an abrupt change, but an intensification of Gobineau's ideas and attitudes after 1872, as the result of his friendship with the Countess de la Tour. "Mademoiselle Irnois" and "La Danseuse de Shamakha" depicted the experience of unrequited love and its ennobling effect on the heroine. Gobineau underlines the tragedy inherent in such an experience: once the object of love is removed, the only alternative open to the heroine is death. In "L'Illustre Magicien" and "Les Amants de Kandahar" Gobineau studies the nature and force of reciprocated love. While the total gift of self is a necessary component of this most powerful passion, the ability to receive the love of another is of equal importance.

Already in 1847, in a brief feuilleton entitled "Les Conseils de Rabelais," Gobineau touched on this theme of mutual love. Odet

---

[1] Quoted by Duff (A: p. 7).

de Coligny, Cardinal de Châtillon, requests the advice of Rabelais before renouncing the Catholic faith and seeking exile in England. Although he professes belief in the Huguenot doctrine, his primary consideration is the desire to marry Elisabeth de Hauteville. The narrative is weak. The two parts of the serial are but vaguely linked together and present little dramatic interest; the characters are briefly sketched and the Cardinal's sentiments are never developed. The narrative does, however, present young Gobineau's ideas on love and on society.

In the early part of the sixteenth century, as the story opens, Odet de Châtillon, a man well into his fifties, finds himself attracted by the pure love of a young demoiselle. To Rabelais he explains the difference between mere physical attraction and this more powerful union of souls:

> ... n'avez vous jamais entendu dire ou connu par expérience personnelle qu'il est des amours d'espèces bien différentes? Que tous vous peuvent charmer par leurs dissemblances et que si l'homme libertin, vaniteux, ou inconstant, s'attache pour toute sa vie aux galanteries, voire aussi aux débauches, l'homme dont l'humeur est douce et portée à l'enthousiasme mélancolique, comme vous me savez être, finit toujours par appeler avec ardeur, avec passion, avec grand trouble du coeur, un amour dont le vêtement soit d'honnêteté et la ceinture de chasteté! (CR: [p. 11])

For this love he is willing to sacrifice his faith, his wealth, his country, and his high social position. He spends several years in England with his young wife, and, in the midst of many problems, still firmly believes in the power of their union. He sees only one threat to their love: "celui d'être séparés (CR: [p. 31]). When Odet is mistakenly poisoned by his servants, Elisabeth survives him by only a few weeks. Gobineau depicts Rabelais as the skeptical Renaissance philosopher, whose experiences with society have disillusioned him. In the first part of the narrative Rabelais warns Odet about society's reaction to his project:

> Que les sots vous doivent condamner, vous le savez, et votre tort est de le mépriser, car les sots, c'est tout le monde en un chacun; à eux fut donné le royaume du ciel, comme il est écrit, et mieux encore le royaume de la terre; les sots font la foule, remplissent les rues, les mai-

sons, les couvents, les parlements, les hôtels royaux, parfois même ils occupent le trône; c'est pour leur bon plaisir que l'on juge, ruine et pend; vous avez tort de les dédaigner, ce sont des gens considérables; ... le propre des premiers [gens d'esprit] est de bien connaître les humeurs féroces de la foule et de savoir comme il fait bon cacher la vérité; les gens d'esprit sont donc, par essence, de complexion timide, craintive, poltronne et nullement amie des hasards: tous ils vous abandonneront; les vertueux n'aiment pas le scandale et vous condamneront comme les autres (CR: [pp. 15-16]).

Rabelais' speech reveals many traits characteristic of Gobineau's philosophy. The idea of dividing humanity into four groups becomes one of the themes of *Les Pléiades* over a quarter of a century later: Wilfred explains that apart from the "fils de Rois" the populations of the world are divided into three categories: "imbéciles," "drôles" and "brutes" (P: pp. 22-23), which correspond respectively to the "gens d'esprit," the "vertueux" and the "sots." Gobineau's irony is evident in the pun confusing the latter who are "sans esprit" with the "pauvres d'esprit" of the Sermon on the Mount. Moreover, Rabelais, who paints this depressing picture of society and of the troubles to be encountered by the Cardinal's proposed marriage, belies his exterior pessimism by finally approving of the latter's decision; with tears in his eyes he sees the couple off with the words: "Monseigneur et Madame, soyez heureux autant que vous pourrez... et aussi longtemps que possible!" (CR: [p. 19]).

"Les Conseils de Rabelais" with its faulty organization and lack of unity can hardly, except for its brevity, be considered a short story. However, the work is of documentary interest for it reveals Gobineau's lasting concern with two basic themes; the dichotomy between the elite and the masses, and the power of love.

"L'Illustre Magicien," written in Stockholm in 1873, relates the trials of a young practicing Muslim torn between the love of his wife and the desire for knowledge. On the feast of Ramadan, Mirza-Kassem's house is honored by the visit of an elderly dervish. Fascinated by the ascetic's knowledge and his power over the material world, Kassem resolves to leave his beloved Amynèh in order to become the dervish's disciple. After a day of preparations for departure and a night of tearful farewells, Kassem sets out in search of his teacher. Although his love tends to overpower his thirst for knowledge, the young man perseveres in his quest. At the caverns of Bamyàn, Kassem finds the dervish, who acknowledges the purity of the neophyte's intentions but realizes that the young man has not attained total self-abnegation. Kassem hears his name being called just as the dervish leads him deeper into the cave; after several incantations the latter provokes an explosion in which he himself is buried under a mountain of debris. At the entrance of the cave Kassem discovers Amynèh who had followed him and whose love he acknowledges.

Mirza-Kassem appears in the *Nouvelles asiatiques* as the counterpart to Gambèr-Aly. A member of the upper class, he lives modestly within his revenues and limits his expenditures. His marriage with Amynèh is harmonious, undisturbed by quarrels or drinking. Lacking political ambitions, Kassem feels no desire to enter into the service of the Prince of Damghan. "Ayant ainsi renoncé à devenir premier ministre, et, comme il faut pourtant qu'un homme s'occupe, il avait senti s'éveiller en lui une certaine curiosité pour les choses de l'intelligence" (NA: p. 82). As the learned discussions grow more obtuse, his interest in theology diminishes and he falls victim to laziness and boredom.

Kassem's intelligence has rendered him skeptical about the supernatural claims of wandering magicians. On the evening of Ramadan as he observes the dervish first halt his pulse, then put his hand into hot coals, and finally transform lead to gold, Kassem expresses a mixed reaction of admiration and fright before believing what he has seen. This temptation of material affluence as represented by the power of alchemy is rapidly vanquished, but the young man becomes overpowered by the desire for knowledge. "Kassem venait d'être saisi de la plus dangereuse des convoitises: celle de la science; ses instincts endormis s'éveillaient et ne devaient plus lui laisser un moment de trêve" (NA: p. 93). During a night of contemplation his decision matures; by the time he avows his decision to Amynèh he already considers his pilgrimage a supernatural calling: "Je suis l'élu!" (NA: p. 100).

Once the intellectual decision is made, Kassem discloses the human side of his personality. The thought of indefinite separation makes him realize the desirability of his present position and especially the strength of his love for Amynèh; "l'amour n'avait pas été éteint par la nouvelle passion" (NA: p. 101). However, Kassem firmly believes that his mission is to follow the dervish and study under his tutelage. During the long trip to Bamyàn the conflict between love and duty rages in his mind; he realizes that he will never be able to forget Amynèh nor suppress his love for her. But he also knows that such a passion might, if avowed, destroy the effectiveness of his position as disciple, and he resolves not to reveal his sentiments to the dervish. The denouement is not of Kassem's will, for he would gladly have died with his master. "En vérité, la vie était de toutes les choses celle à laquelle il tenait le moins" (NA: p. 122). Kassem, in spite of his purity, is prevented from becoming a true disciple since his loyalties are divided.

The narrator employs a variety of techniques in characterizing Kassem. First, the protagonist and his moral strength are briefly described. In the subsequent Ramadan bazaar scene Kassem's patience and sobriety are contrasted with the noise and feigned devotion of the majority of the Muslim population of Damghan. The narrator explains:

> Malheureusement, les fidèles observent rarement de façon très exacte le jeûne commandé par la loi dans ce temps consacré. Cependant, il faut aussi l'avouer, il n'est presque personne qui ne tienne à passer pour le faire, et, de cette façon, les apparences du moins sont sauvées. De sorte, que ce sont précisément les hommes sans conscience qui ont mangé leur pilau, tout à l'aise, dans un coin, à l'heure ordinaire du déjeuner, qui, lorsque le soir arrive, sont les plus empressés à se plaindre de la faim qui ne les tourmente pas, de la faiblesse qui ne les envahit guère, et à appeler, avec les cris les plus suppliants, le coucher du soleil (NA: p. 84).

It is during these evening festivities that the dervish selects Kassem to be his host. During the remainder of the narrative Kassem is directly characterized through his thoughts and conversations.

Amynèh, young and pretty, is known in Damghan female society for her laughter, which brightens the conversations; "... elle y apportait une gaïté et un rire si frais, si joli, qu'on en avait fait des chansons qui se répétaient partout: *Le Rire d'Amynèh*" (NA: p. 105). This gentle humor never flowers at the expense of her husband, but is an expression of kindness. Feminine gracefulness pervades her movements and her speech; for example, when learning of Kassem's decision to follow the dervish, she declares her love with delicate simplicity. "Mais ta part [Kassem's destiny] n'est pas si mauvaise, et tu n'as pas raison, en y songeant, de froncer ainsi les sourcils. Ta part, c'est moi, et tu m'as assuré quelquefois, plus d'une fois, et même souvent, que tu n'en demandais pas d'autre" (NA: p. 99). On realizing that Kassem is determined to follow his vocation, she gently requests that he delay his departure by twenty-four hours.[2]

Her love is powerful and unwavering in the face of separation. Since her marriage she has directed her efforts toward assuring Kassem's physical and emotional well-being. Even after the fateful visit of the dervish, she refuses divorce and decides to live at the home of Kassem's sister, Zemroud, while awaiting his return. She enlists the latter's assistance as the last means of deterring her husband's resolution, but this intervention is to no avail. That evening, while acquiescing to Kassem's decision, she assures him: "Non! tu ne me perdras pas. Je serai là, tranquille, chez ta soeur. J'aurai beaucoup de patience... j'aurai beaucoup de courage... Je suis sûre qu'il ne t'arrivera rien, Kassem! Mets encore une fois ta tête sur mes genoux" (NA: p. 110). During their last evening together, she is often the braver.

This powerful combination of love and courage renders the denouement credible. In Persia, Gobineau points out (TA: pp. 419-24), it is very common for both men and women suddenly to leave their homes and set out on a pilgrimage with the assurance of finding food and lodging en route. Amynèh leaves Damghan soon after her husband's departure. "Elle n'avait pas eu le courage de l'attendre. Elle avait marché après lui, elle l'avait suivi; elle le retrouvait, elle le garda" (NA: p. 124). Altough the narrator

---

[2] Gaulmier sees the Countess de La Tour as the model for Amynèh; *Spectre de Gobineau*, p. 147.

states that she had not the "courage" to remain in Damghan, the willingness of a woman to set out alone and unescorted is a virtue rare even in the Orient.

Amynèh is portrayed through direct characterization. Amynèh's feminine charm and devotion to Kassem are first described and then her sincerity is implicitly contrasted with the mundane preoccupations of the women gathered in Zemroud's parlor. The young wife's true love and courage emerge in her scenes with Kassem before his departure and then reappear to dominate the denouement.

The dervish, who furnishes the title of the narrative, attains dramatic importance because of his effect on Kassem. He is a tall, dark, emaciated man, "des yeux flamboyants, l'aspect sauvage, dur et sévère" (NA: p. 87). He has given up riches and political power in India to devote himself to study and subsequently to renounce the material world. In these characteristics he resembles the dervish of an anecdote Gobineau wrote to his sister in 1856 (LP: pp. 38-40) and subsequently developed in *Trois Ans en Asie* (TA: pp. 326-336). The son of Feth Aly-Schah, like Kassem, is visited by a dervish, "... un de ces hommes absolument détachés du monde, complètement voués à la science, et qui, s'enfermant pendant de longues années dans les cavernes pour se livrer sans distraction à la méditation et à l'étude, en sortent un beau jour comme métamorphosés, n'ayant plus d'humain que la forme extérieure, mais tout divins par l'intelligence" (TA: pp. 327-328). In the anecdote the dervish convinces the young prince that the fairy queen wishes to marry him, after he has made the prescribed solitary retreat for several weeks in his sumptuous villa. On the wedding night, he sends away everyone except the dervish; the following morning he awakens from a drugged sleep to find the rooms stripped of their jewels and tapestries and the dervish gone.

The dervish of "L'Illustre Magicien" is not a scoundrel but an ascetic truly devoted to the search for knowledge. After having visited North Africa and the Middle East in his search for a worthy disciple he discovers Kassem. In Bamyàn, however, he realizes that he must proceed alone in his final experiment. To Kassem he explains, "Il faut ici une âme libre; la tienne ne l'est pas. Cependant, tu es bien pur de tout mal; tu étais celui qu'il me fallait..." (NA: p. 123). Knowing that Kassem can no longer serve him, he vents his anger on womanhood: "Maudites soient les femmes! C'est la ruine! C'est le fléau irrésistible! c'est la perte!" (NA: p. 123). Yet before facing the death which will reveal the secrets of the universe, he acknowledges Kassem's passion by taking time to shelter him from the avalanche.

The dervish is consistently portrayed in the manner in which he appears to his disciple. On being accosted in the bazaar, Kassem wonders, "Quel est ce derviche? Il a l'air d'un roi, et plus fait pour commander une armée que pour errer sur les grands chemins!" (NA: p. 89). The reader knows Kassem to be a sober and intelligent person. Thus, as the dervish overcomes Kassem's skepticism with his exhibitions, the reader begins to accept the reality of the dervish's powers. For the reader, as for Kassem, the bar of gold "était la preuve matérielle que tout ce qui s'agitait dans sa tête n'était pas un rêve, mais une franche et ferme réalité" (NA: p. 94). Together with Kassem, the reader accepts the reality of the dervish's powers.

A very secondary role in the narrative is played by Zemroud-Khanoum, or Madame Emeraude, Kassem's elder sister. She has raised him since their mother's death, and it was she who handled his marriage negotiations. Even though Kassem respects her, she is unable to deter him from his decision to follow the dervish. Zemroud is an extremely colorful figure, in many ways similar to Bibi-Djânèm, Gambèr's mother. A strong-willed woman, she dominates her husband to the extent that he is forced to divorce his first wife even though he feels that his social position requires a large harem. Her temper, like Bibi's, is easily aroused. "Sa voix devenait, dans la colère, de beaucoup la plus aiguë du quartier, mais il lui arrivait aussi d'en être la plus douce quand elle se prenait à consoler quelqu'un" (NA: p. 104). Although a minor figure, Zemroud adds zest and humor to the Oriental panorama.

The plot, arranged chronologically, is divided into three parts: the presentation of the characters, Kassem's interior conflict, and the rapid denouement. The first section is almost twice as long as the second, while the conclusion is delineated in a few paragraphs. The third-person narration maintains Kassem's point of view. As for two brief scenes from which he is absent, he could easily have learned from Amynèh what she did at the mosque and at Zemroud's house.

In the first section Gobineau introduces the protagonists and Persian society in a contrapuntal fashion. If we consider Kassem and Amynèh as examples of high moral character and the Persian male and female society depicted in the story as examples of low moral character, with Zemroud midway between the two poles, then the focus of this section of the narrative sways between high and low, from Kassem to male society to Amynèh to female society to Zemroud. Kassem's sobriety becomes more remarkable when contrasted to the boisterous excitement of the bazaar; Amynèh's gentle sincerity is heightened through juxtaposition with the idle chatter of the women gathered at Zemroud's house. The latter's generosity distinguishes her from her guests. These three characters are shown as morally superior to their environment; however, as participating members of society, they do not disdain the weaknesses of their associates. By presenting the characters as part of a culture which is colorfully and convincingly described, Gobineau heightens the credibility, which is of special importance in this story of Oriental magic. Not only does the author paint the encounter of Kassem and the dervish from the point of view of the former, who expresses the doubts and reservations of an intelligent skeptical observer, but he first establishes the sobriety of Kassem's personality.

This careful and lengthy presentation of the characters contrasts with the light irony of the first paragraph: "Le derviche Bagher raconta un jour l'histoire suivante, sur l'autorité d'Abdy-Khan qui, lui-même, l'avait apprise de Loutfoullah Hindy, lequel la tenait de Riza-Bey, de Kirmanshah, et ce sont tous gens parfaitement connus et d'une véracité au-dessus de tout soupçon" (NA: p. 81). Ostensibly the narrator wishes to establish the credibility of his narrative by indicating his sources. But the reader of the *Nouvelles asiatiques,* by now familiar with Oriental speech and manners, immediately doubts the truth of any statement expressed in superlatives. The phrase asserting "une véracité au-dessus de tout soupçon" has the unique effect of arousing the disbelief of the reader. In attributing Kassem's anecdote to the dervish Bagher, Gobineau employs the same method he used for "Adélaïde" in which the baron asserts Frédéric to be the source of a story he has obviously learned from Elisabeth. Gobineau's sense of humor is such that he enjoys encouraging the reader's participation: in one sentence he awakens a disbelief which he requires twenty-five carefully constructed pages to dispel.

The second part of the narrative is a psychological study of the leading protagonist: Kassem is shown suffering from the inner conflict between love and vocation. Although he always remains true to his vocation and never wavers from his decision to follow the dervish, the strength of love varies. In these changes of heart the construction of the second part parallels that of the first part of the narrative: there is a similar sway in the focus which alternates between the strong and weak moments in Kassem's love for his wife. After the evening spent in discussion with the dervish, Kassem informs Amynèh of his resolution. At that point the desire for knowledge is so strong that he is able to intellectualize his feelings, to reassure his wife of his devotion and placidly to suggest divorce. However, as the moment of departure nears, Kassem realizes the power of his love: "... pour bien dire, Kassem était très malheureux, comme on l'est, quand, placé entre le devoir et la passion, on se croit entraîné par le devoir" (NA: p. 110). Due to the novelty of his discipleship, the first days of the pilgrimage are calm and refreshing for Kassem: "Lui-même, il s'étonnait maintenant de la facilité avec laquelle il s'était séparé d'Amynèh, que la veille encore il idolâtrait, et, en se trouvant ainsi, le coeur libre et léger, presque indifférent à la perte qu'il venait de s'infliger, il reconnaissait avec admiration la profonde sagesse du dervich indien. Celui-ci, lorsque Kassem avait insisté sur l'impossibilité de se séparer de sa jeune femme, lui avait prédit absolument ce qui arriverait de l'indifférence qu'il ressentait à cette heure" (NA: p. 113). The monotony of the desert encourages meditation and undisturbed contemplation.

On the ninth day Kassem's passion for Amynèh intrudes on his consciousness and refuses to be silenced. "Il avait cru que ce n'était rien que d'aimer Amynéh et de la quitter. Mais l'amour s'était joué de lui... qui était le maître en lui-même? L'amour ou lui? C'était l'amour!" (NA: pp. 115-16). Kassem never falters in his vow to follow the dervish, but gone are his enthusiasm, his joy. He realizes that the only means of achieving tranquility is to forget his wife, but this he refuses to attempt: "C'était se renoncer soi-même, s'anéantir et faire place à un nouveau Kassem qu'il ne connaissait pas et haïssait profondément" (NA: p. 117). Victim of two equally matched, equally exalted passions, love and learning, Kassem surrenders to melancholy; he asserts, "ayant touché le fond de mon infortune, j'y suis comme prosterné et je ne songe pas même à m'en retirer jamais!" (NA: p. 120) This, then, is the point of equilibrium between the two passions which gnaw at his soul. Kassem offers the dervish the complete fidelity of heart and will which are required, but only momentarily, for he is no longer master of the love.

The brevity of the conclusion increases its dramatic effect. Amynèh's presence was already prepared in the first part of the narrative where Kassem, explaining his vocation, carefully describes his itinerary in terms of his master's plans: "Il est parti pour le Khorassan, il va traverser Meshed, Hérat et le pays de Kaboul; je le retrouverai au plus tard dans les montagnes de Bamyân (NA: pp. 99-100). The Persians are a mobile people. Amynèh knew where Kassem's pilgrimage would lead him; her appearance at the end of the narrative is unexpected but understandable.

The death of the dervish is also prepared so as not to disrupt the tenuous level of credibility established in the course of the narrative. During the first visit into the caves Kassem feels the heat of the walls, "la roche vive" (NA: p. 122), warmed through the proximity to an active vein of the dormant volcanic formation. Later he notices that the dervish is attempting to dislocate rocks on the ceiling of the cave. Indirectly Gobineau introduces a natural explanation for the sudden earthquake which buries the dervish and demolishes part of the cavern.

The first theme, which the dervish represents, is that of the power of knowledge. This supreme force does not reveal itself in material possessions, as the dervish explains to his disciple: "La puissance, à vos yeux, s'annonce par un grand appareil; ... Vous pensez comme tout le monde sur ce point" (NA: p. 90). He then demonstrates his power over his own body, his power over fire, and his power over men as expressed by his ability to create gold, while adding: "... la puissance n'est pas dans ce qui s'affiche, mais uniquement dans l'autorité des âmes fortes, ce que le vulgaire ne croit pas!" (NA: p. 92). True knowledge requires study and renunciation. The dervish, however, in all his perfection needs a disciple to attain the ultimate: the individual by himself cannot surpass a certain level of knowledge. For the dervish this search for a disciple has intensified his scorn for the average man: "Il n'a partout vu que des gens d'un esprit borné ou d'un coeur irrésolu. La plupart l'écoutaient avec complaisance, tant qu'il leur parlait des moyens de faire de l'or; mais quand il voulait élever leurs esprits, plus de ressort!" (NA: p. 100). His disdain is so contagious that Kassem begins to look upon his former existence with disgust: "Que valait le monde au milieu duquel il avait vécu jusqu'alors? Rien, rien absolument; c'était de la fange au physique, de la fange au moral; en un mot, néant" (NA: pp. 97-98). Kassem undertakes the search for wisdom wich will enable him to separate himself even more distinctly from the society to which he is already superior.

The second theme to be introduced is the reciprocated love of Amynèh and Kassem in which all experiences are shared. For example, Kassem announces his decision to follow the dervish by referring to the intimate tie which links Amynèh's heart to his own: "... ce coeur saigne; il va affliger son compagnon (NA: p. 99). While traveling across the deserts Kassem meditates not only on the power of knowledge but also on the nature of love. He regards the search for wisdom as his personal "kismèt" or destiny, but he learns to appreciate the magnitude of human passion. He realizes that Amynèh is not merely a symbol of former happiness but an essential part of his existence, "la source de sa vie" (NA: p. 116). For Amynèh, her love leads to an understanding of her husband, to a sublime generosity, "ce sentiment si fin, si tendre, si divin qui appartient, en tous pays, aux femmes, quand elles aiment et qui seul suffirait à en faire les êtres vraiment célestes de la création" (NA: p. 110). The woman's concern is for the man, but the man is primarily concerned with himself. Kassem never wonders whether he is the source of Amynèh's life, but he knows that without her presence he is unhappy.

The narrative itself is constructed around the conflict of these two themes. Love and the desire for knowledge are well-matched rivals.

> Exaltation pour exaltation, frénésie pour frénésie, celle de l'une vaut celle de l'autre; il y a, de part et d'autre, autant d'abnégation, autant de discernement, peut-être autant d'aveuglement; et si l'amour peut se vanter d'emporter au-dessus des vulgarités de la terre l'âme qu'il transporte

> dans les plaines azurées du désir, sa rivale, celle-là précisément qui tenait l'âme de Kassem en même temps que l'amour, a le droit de répondre d'une manière assurée qu'elle n'exerce pas un pouvoir dirigé vers des buts moins sublimes. (NA: p. 119)

Although for Kassem the love for knowledge is apparently the stronger passion, the dervish is mistaken in believing that it can totally destroy human passions; he claims, "... quand on met violemment le pied dessus, elles [human passions] gémissent d'abord, puis se taisent, et, comme des ombres qu'elles sont, finissent bientôt par s'anéantir devant la volonté inexorable" (NA: p. 113).

Since the dervish and Kassem, both of whom are considered as "âmes fortes," hold contrary opinions on the nature of human love, Gobineau tries explicitly to resolve this difference. The dervish is referred to as representative of the supernatural; for example, in order to explain Kassem's hestitation on meeting the dervish in the Bamyân, the narrator adds, "Il n'était pas là en présence du monde, mais en présence d'un redoutable infini" (NA: p. 123). Already in the desert Kassem had recognized the sublimity of his teacher: "Il est déjà Dieu; moi, hélas! hélas! que suis-je?" (NA: p. 120). Although this question is left unanswered, the response is obvious: Kassem is not a saint, but a mortal. By equating the desire for knowledge with the divine, the narrator seems to imply that human love is the inferior passion. Yet, here again Gobineau inserts an interpretive element. Kassem, whose point of view the narrator assumes, appears to assert such a hierarchy of passions. But the moving denouement of the narrative itself induces the reader to conclude that love is the human passion, that through love man can most perfectly realize his potential. To deny love is to deny the true nature of man.

Schemann considered "L'Illustre Magicien" the finest story in the *Nouvelles asiatiques,* "freilich die Krone der Sammlung und eine der schönsten Schöpfungen Gobineau." [3] It is true that the narrative demonstrates Gobineau's mastery of the genre.

---

[3] Schemann, p. 41.

"Les Amants de Kandahar," an Afghan variation of the Romeo and Juliet theme, is the only narrative of the *Nouvelles asiatiques* whose scene is laid in a country which Gobineau had never visited. He was, however, indirectly acquainted with the country through the reports of travelers and citizens whom he had met in Tehran. The protagonist is modeled after Myr-Mohammed-Elèm-Khan, an Afghan prince, "jeune homme de vingt-quatre ans, d'une beauté remarquable, d'une rare distinction de formes et d'esprit, et sachant beaucoup" (TA: p. 454). The young noble died in 1857, while leading a valiant attack against enemy forces which greatly outnumbered his own. Gobineau composed his story in Stockholm in the late summer of 1872.[4]

Mohsèn Ahmedzyy, upon officially attaining manhood at age seventeen, makes three resolutions: first, he will kill his cousin Elèm to avenge an insult to his father by the latter's brother; second, he will assassinate Abdoullah Mouradzyy whose family is an hereditary enemy of the Ahmedzyys; and third, after these exploits he will become a cavalier of the Prince of Kandahar. One evening, as he enters his uncle's house with the intent of murdering his cousin, he is met by the latter's sister Djemylèh, who barters her love against her brother's life. Mohsèn, overpowered by Djemylèh's charm and beauty, renounces his planned vengeance. Subsequently reduced to a state of extreme depression by mentally exaggerating the impossibility of seeing Djemylèh again and by doubting the reality of her love, Mohsèn finds his strength restored by the arrival of his fiancée. The two escape together pursued by the wrath of the young girl's family. As the

---

[4] Mistler gives a different date of composition and quotes a letter written to Zoé Dragoumis on November 1, 1872, in which Gobineau speaks of his stories: "Il m'en reste quatre à faire" (Mistler, p. 19). Since two of the stories, "La Danseuse de Shamakha" and "L'Histoire de Gambèr-Aly," were definitely finished by August 1872, Mistler concludes that "Les Amants de Kandahar" must have been written after November 1. However, an examination of the correspondance between Gobineau and Prokesch-Osten reveals that "Les Amants de Kandahar" was composed by mid-September. On September 23, 1872, Gobineau wrote Prokesch: "Il y en a trois de faites" (CP: p. 358). Mistler's misinterpretation arises from the fact that he counted only the six narratives which appeared in the *Nouvelles asiatiques*. In November 1872, Gobineau still intended to write seven stories for that volume (CP: p. 361) and had finished three of them.

couple is ambushed, Mohsèn courageously fights off his uncle's men. The two lovers are saved by the intervention of a young noble who identifies himself as Akbar, son of Mohammed Mouradzyy. Mohsèn conceals his identity until he has gained asylum in the Mouradzyy harem. When for political reasons Mohammed plans to violate the strict dictates of Afghan hospitality by releasing his guests to the Prince, Akbar escapes with the young couple to a distant summer villa. The three die defending their retreat against the royal soldiers of Kandahar. The entrance of love into Mohsèn's young life has modified his earlier resolutions: the insult to his father is sufficiently avenged by his elopement with Djemylèh, his sense of honor prevents him from assassinating his protector, and death renders his third project impossible.

Mohsèn, whose name signifies the handsome one, possesses a physionomy hinting at a strong pride and passion. The actions of an Afghan noble are motivated by a sense of honor which is stronger than familial ties (NA: p. 245). Mohsèn has grown up with his cousin Elèm, whom he loved dearly; but the insult to his father makes him resolve to kill his friend. "L'honneur parlait, il fallait que l'honneur et seulement l'honneur fût écouté" (NA: p. 244). Mohsèn's decisions are further tempered by the sentiment of pride; not only does he want to be worthy of the love of his parents but he wishes to gain the esteem of the Prince and Kandahar society.

After his meeting with Djemylèh, all Mohsèn's former considerations are subordinated to his nascent passion. "Mohsèn donna sa vengeance, donna l'idée qu'il se faisait de son honneur, donna sa liberté, se donna lui-même, et, instinctivement, chercha encore, dans les plus profonds abîmes de son être, s'il ne pourrait donner plus" (NA: p. 250). When Mohsèn is separated from Djemylèh, doubts enter his mind: on giving up his plan for vengeance in an effort to please his love, perhaps he has lost the respect of his loved one. Perhaps Djemylèh has betrayed him by lying in order to save the life of her brother. His own passion is so overpowering that he begins to question whether his generosity is reciprocated. He has given all to his passion, so that, once the object of his love is removed, his inner resources vanish and he succumbs to a delirium from which only Djemylèh's presence can rouse him.

Reinforced in his love, Mohsèn rediscovers his courage. He realizes the dangerous implication of Djemylèh's flight and prepares for the inevitable battle. "La dernière trace d'abattement avait disparu. S'il avait la fièvre, c'était une fièvre d'action. L'enthousiasme éclatait sur sa figure" (NA: p. 254). His courage weakens only momentarily late that evening when he discovers that Iousef-Beg, at whose home the two were to find refuge, has left Kandahar: he fears not for himself but dreads the thought of Djemylèh's being physically harmed. The young girl revives his spirits, and from that moment his courage never falters. He carefully keeps guard over the hiding place where he and Djemlylèh have sought refuge, and the attack of his uncle's men finds him prepared. "Rien qui ressemblât à de la peur ne toucha son courage, dur comme l'acier" (NA: p. 26). At the end of the narrative this same bravery is still with him; he ceases fighting only to die in Djemylèh's arms.

Mohsèn's straightforward personality is characterized in the opening paragraphs. His passion, his despair, and his courage hide no complexity. When young Mohsèn is initially presented the narrator stresses his physical beauty, his pride, and his sense of honor. Love diminishes the latter two qualities, but helps to develop a heroic Afghan courage which until that time had remained latent. This love and courage characterize Mohsèn's death.

Djemylèh, or the charming one, matches her lover in youth and beauty. Only fifteen years old, she gladly forfeits the concept of family honor first to save Elèm's life and later to reanimate Mohsèn who would have died without her presence.

Her love lacks Mohsèn's fever and passionate excess; her actions are continually those of submission and devotion. The simplicity of her affection manifests itself in her explanation of the elopement: "[if I had not come] je serais couverte de honte à mes propres yeux, lâche, fausse, odieuse à ce qui aurait pu deviner mon crime, meurtrière de ma tendresse, traîtresse au maître de mon âme" (NA: pp. 281-82). For Djemylèh, Mohsèn is not only her master but an integral part of her being. During their flight she asks Mohsèn: "Pourquoi veux-tu rejeter de ton être ce morceau qui en est, qui est moi, et qui ne peut ni vivre ni mourir sans toi?" (NA: p. 282).

Djemylèh knows her power over Mohsèn. At their first fatal meeting she symbolically places her foot on his shoulder as he kneels at her feet. Yet she never seeks to exploit this domination and apparently realizes that aggressiveness would stifle the femininity which forms the foundation of her charm. In times of danger it is usually Djemylèh who possesses the required imagination and foresight, yet never does she directly tell her fiancé what should be done. Rather she suggests a solution and remains confident that his intelligence will allow him to discover the wisdom in her proposal. As Osman and his men are storming Mohsèn's house, Djemylèh is the one who notices a curious noise and notifies her fiancé of the flank attack. When Mohsèn is overcome with depression at finding that Iousef cannot shelter them, Djemylèh manages to renew his strength with gentle reassuring words and an embrace; when he wonders where to go she replies: "... je ne sais pas: mais tu le trouveras, j'en suis sûre! tu vas le trouver tout à l'heure dans ta tête; parce que, toi, tu es brave, tu ne trembles devant aucun péril, mon cher, cher Mohsèn, et tu sauveras ta femme!" (NA: p. 26). This expression of encouragement rebuilds Mohsèn's confidence and he leads Djemylèh to shelter. After the rescue by Akbar, the two are again in danger of death, this time at the hands of the hereditary enemies of their families; deception would only postpone their fate. As Mohsèn contemplates the dilemma, it is again Djemylèh who finds the solution: "Une inspiration singulière était dans ses beaux yeux. Elle ne dit pas un mot, il la comprit" (NA: p. 268). On arriving at the Mouradzyy residence the two find sanctuary in the harem. Throughout the narrative, Gobineau depicts Djemylèh as the ideal woman, quiet and reserved, yet ready in time of danger to offer moral assistance and intuitive inspiration.

Djemylèh's characterization is direct. The narrator never explains her motivations, never analyzes her actions. The reader perceives her as Kassem does: he sees her charming eyes, hears her gentle conversation, feels her gentle devotion. Djemylèh herself explains her motivations and, since she is presented in a non-interpretive manner, her own self-analysis is accepted by the reader as an unbiased view of her character.

The third protagonist, Akbar-Khan Mouradzyy, represents Afghan nobility. Young, handsome and arrogant, his actions are ruled uniquely by the sentiment of personal and family honor. Although he would not have flinched at killing Mohsèn, the moment the two young lovers have acquired the protection of his mother he realizes, even before his father, that the Afghan code of hospitality is inviolable. He admires Mohsèn's courage but refrains from any demonstrations of friendship "Ainsi, le protecteur et l'obligé, au milieu de démonstrations assez solennelles d'un mutuel dévouement, maintinrent intacts les droits imprescriptibles de l'animosité ancienne et se les reconnurent l'un à l'autre" (NA: p. 274). Akbar loves his wife and respects his father, but the call of honor transcends both personal inclination and love. When in the villa he learns that his father has ordered the arrest of Mohsèn and Djemylèh, Akbar refuses to comply and exclaims: "Alors Abdoullah-Khan est un chien et je n'ai pas de père!" (NA: p. 288). Similarly Mateo Falcone, in Mérimée's *nouvelle,* places the sacred law of Corsican hospitality above family ties and feels constrained to kill his son.

Akbar is initially introduced as he appears in Mohsèn's eyes. An entire paragraph is devoted to a detailed description of his rich dress and bejeweled arms, features which impress Mohsèn since he is quite conscious of his poverty. As Akbar enters the fray, "sa physionomie revêtit une expression arrogante et terrible" (NA: p. 265). In the subsequent scenes, the narrator maintains Mohsèn's point of view; thus, as the latter grows to know and respect his protector, Akbar's positive qualities are emphasized. The manner of his death remains consistent with his character and concept of Afghan honor.

The parents of the three protagonists contribute to the devevopment of events but fail to influence the resolutions and actions of their children. Djemylèh and Akbar actively defy their fathers' projects; Mohammed would have preferred a different wife for his son, but he stands behind his son's decision. The two Ahmedzyy govern their actions according to the concept of honor, but Abdoullah Khan has lost the ability to live by his conscience. His primary concern has become the preservation of his social and financial position in the Kandahar court. When compromise becomes unfeasible, when he is forced to choose between his comfort and the protection he had so grudgingly granted, his allegiance unfalteringly remains with the former.

The dramatic plot is related in chronological order with the exception of one flashback necessitated by the complexity of the events. First Osman's nayb or lieutenant gives his report concerning Mohsèn, and then the narrator recounts the details of the lovers' flight.

From the outset of the tightly constructed narrative, the death of the three young protagonists is prepared. The verb in the first sentence is in the imperfect: such a reference to Mohsèn in the past tense indicates to the reader that the end will be a tragic one. The description of Afghan character several pages later reinforces this presentiment: "Ils sont rares les hommes de cette race, qui, avant quarante ans, n'ont pas reçu le coup mortel à force d'avoir atteint ou menacé les autres" (NA: pp. 246-47). During the scene in which Mohsèn is fighting Osman, the narrator intervenes to inform the reader in advance that although Mohsèn's capture is imminent, the young combattant will escape such a fate: "Par bonheur, un incident, sur lequel personne ne comptait, vint changer bientôt la face des affaires" (NA: p. 264). Subsequently the details of the combat and the arrival of Akbar are depicted. The actual events leading to the denouement are prepared by the careful delineation of personalities during the harem scene. Just as Akbar is quick to bow to the requirements of Afghan hospitality, so is the prompt in upholding this hospitality, even unto death. Abdoullah-Khan, however, must exercise great self-restraint to prevent harming his avowed enemies; when forced to choose between self-interest and honor, especially when that honor means protecting two young people towards whom he feels no sentimental attachment or obligation, he hesitates only momentarily before ordering the release of the young couple to Osman.

The narrator relates the story in an objective fashion. He does not interpret the events, but neither does he strive to efface his presence. Throughout the account, the initial conversational style is maintained. The narrator directly addresses the reader as if he were obliging the latter's curiosity by giving the details of Mohsèn's death. The story begins in this manner:

> Vous demandez s'il était beau? Beau comme un ange! Le teint un peu basané, non de cette teinte sombre, terreuse, résultat certain d'une origine métisse; il était chaudement basané comme un fruit mûri au soleil ... Il était grand, vigoureux, mince, large des épaules, étroit des hanches. A personne l'idée ne fût venue de s'enquérir de sa race; il était clair que le sang afghan le plus pur animait son essence et que, en le contemplant, on avait sous les yeux le descendant authentique de ces anciens Parthes, les Arsaces, les Orodes, sous les pas desquels le monde romain a frémi d'une juste épouvante. (NA: p. 241)

It would not be inappropriate to identify the narrator with Gobineau himself, who was known for his conversational talents. This concept of race becomes a leitmotif for the narrator. When he introduces the royal doctor of Kandahar his first comment is: "Ce n'était pas un Afghan de race, mais, seulement, ce qu'on appelle un Kizzilbash, descendu de colons persans, quelque chose d' analogue à un bourgeois" (NA: p. 277). Purity of race is the requisite for nobility of feeling.

The primary theme is the power and magnificence of total love. "La beauté est belle; la passion, l'amour absolu sont plus beaux et plus adorables" (NA: p. 282). This epitome of love can exist only when nourished with the unreserved gift of self; all other human considerations must be of secondary importance. The narrator never tires of emphasizing the necessity of total abnegation: "Quand on aime, on ne fait qu'aimer" (NA: p. 280). "L'amour demande à chacun le don de ce qu'il a de plus cher; c'est là ce qu'il faut céder; et, si l'on aime, c'est précisément ce que l'on veut donner" (NA: p. 249).

Such an absolute love fortifies both lovers. when young Mohsèn is near death, Djemylèh's arrival reanimates him immediately, "comme une lampe presque épuisée dans laquelle on verse de l'huile" (NA: p. 253). The consuming flame of the lamp symbolizes human love which cannot develop in a vacuum but requires nurture and sustenance. The choice of the simile maintains the literary tone, for the oil-burning lamp is a typical Oriental form of illumination.

Those in love attain a degree of mental communication incomprehensible to the observer. This magnetic influence allows lovers to exchange ideas without recourse to spoken language and permits an intimate sharing of pain, happiness and courage. For such a love the prime enemy is not death, because death represents union. The prime enemy is separation. Nascent love withers when the loved one is absent; for mature love such separation causes suffering, but not despair.

The secondary theme is the concept of honor. The Afghans, who live by honor, realize the possibility of imminent death, but enjoy tranquility of conscience. Other Oriental tribes, such as the Persians, the Kurds, and the Uzbeks, lead a carefree, boisterous existence. "La vie est bien différente, en effet, pour eux.... Ils peuvent rire: rien que les coups ne les blessent ou les affectent" (NA: p. 308). The Afghan sentiment of honor distinguishes Akbar and Mohsèn from the characters of the other *Nouvelles asiatiques*. Mohsèn, on accepting Djemylèh's love, renounces specific projects of vengeance, but not his honor which distinguishes the young noble from the bourgeois and from the corrupted courtesan.

In composing the narrative, Gobineau created a unified work of art. The opening sentence prepares the tragic denouement, which in turn becomes the culmination of the themes of love and honor. The descriptive passages are subordinated to the dramatic plot and create the uneasy atmosphere typical of nineteenth-century Kandahar. According to Alain, Gobineau in this story shows himself to be "fort et éternel encore une fois." [5]

"La Cour d'Amour" is an unfinished narrative which Gobineau had intended to include in his projected *Nouvelles féodales*. The lengthy fragment, edited by René Béziau, appeared for the first time in the *Mercure de France* in 1963. Although the ending was never written, the extant portion of the narrative is extensive enough to merit attention. [6]

Enguerrand Havot, orphaned at a young age, entered into the service of the Countess de Champagne. When he was twenty, he declared his devotion to Aliénor de Foy, one of the maids of honor in the court and received the permission to plant a kiss on her forehead. Two years later, as Enguerrand is about to leave

---

[5] Alain, p. 208.
[6] See René Béziau, " 'La Cour d'Amour,' dernière nouvelle de Gobineau," *RHLF*, LXIII (1963), 652-666.

Champagne to go to the defense of Normandy, he publicly avows his love for Aliénor and asks to kiss her a second time. Upon hearing her refusal, he requests the Countess to call a session of the Cour d'Amour to try his case. Victor, he is alloved to maintain his favored position as her "serviteur." That evening Enguerrand knocks out Aliénor's fiancé, Jacques de Bévannes, who has made mockery of the Cour d'Amour. The manuscript comes to an end after Enguerrand offers to defend his honor in a duel and Jacques de Bevannes is contemplating the murder of his adversary.

Enguerrand Havot, one of the distant ancestors whom Gobineau had included in *Ottar Jarl,* is the ideal hero of the courtly romance. Were it not for his impoverished condition, he would be one of the most brilliant members of the Court of Champagne:

> Aucun de ses compagnons ne maniait l'épée mieux que lui. Il était cité comme la meilleure lance de la Cour, personne ne manégeait un cheval comme il le savait faire. Il parlait le picard comme pas un et savait par coeur une quantité de poèmes qu'il récitait aussi bien que le plus éloquent des ménestrels; la comtesse aimait à lui faire chanter devant des seigneurs dont elle faisait cas, des parties de la chanson des Lohérains; il disait bien de même les sirventes en langue d'oïl qu'il connaissait à merveille; on lui avait appris aussi beaucoup de passages sinon toutes les Histoires de la Table Ronde et il comprenait le breton; il pouvait aussi savoir les beautés des poètes tyois qui écrivaient vers Strasbourg et les dames le priaient de chanter des renouveaux et des ballades car il tirait du rebec des sons merveilleux; mais ce qu'on louait surtout en lui c'était sa courtoisie qui n'avait pas d'égal. (CA: pp. 264-265)

At twenty, he realizes that, for his honor he must devote himself to the service of a lady. His conscious choice of Aliénor brings into the open the attraction he had already felt towards the young maid of honor; however he hesitates to declare himself until one afternoon the Countess chides him for not being in love. Enguerrand replies: "J'aime et je ne peux rien dire et je ne vous dirais rien que ceci seulement: celle que j'aime n'a que quatorze ans; je ne lui demande rien; je ne lui ai même jamais dit que j'étais son serviteur. Maintenant, je vais le dire, puisque vous pensez qu'il me convient d'aimer. Mais le dire c'est tout ce que j'oserai et tout ce que je voudrai" (CA: p. 268). After his conversation with the Countess, Enguerrand meets Aliénor in the garden, makes his declaration, and places a kiss on the young girl's forehead. Thereafter, Enguerrand seeks no interviews and requests no favors; he transforms his sentiments into poetry and song keeps the entire court wondering about the identity of his lady.

Two years later, having proven himself in battle, Enguerrand takes leave of the court and publicly affirms his devotion to Aliénor: "... Je m'en vais demain, peut-être ne vous reverrai-je jamais, car je ne peux trop dépenser mon revenu, dont je n'ai rien, à faire de longs voyages, pour venir savoir souvent combien vous vous faites belle et parfaite. Je vais donc vous donner le baiser dont j'ai coutume, peut-être ce sera le dernier et vous ne m'oublierez pas dans vos prières" (CA: pp. 276-277). Enguerrand's "grain de fierté de trop" (CA: p. 276) which triggered the public avowal of his love, is entirely absent when the Cour d'Amour hands down its decision in his favor. He tells Aliénor: "Ce que vous ordonnerez, demoiselle, sera très bien et je ne demande rien davantage mais qu'on sache seulement que je vous ai bien aimée et que pour rien au monde je ne voudrais vous faire la moindre peine" (CA: p. 288). After his brief encounter with Jacques de Bévannes, Enguerrand still outwardly maintains Aliénor's total freedom to marry whom she pleases: "Je ne réclame rien, je ne m'oppose à rien, je ne contredis rien et je ne ferai rien, on peut en croire ma parole, pour ne troubler en rien un mariage que l'on a bien le droit de conclure sans m'en demander mon avis" (CA: p. 295). But tears stream down the young man's face as he demands the right to a duel.

This interpretive third-person narrative reflects the point of view of Enguerrand. The lyric style and restraint are both qualities of the young hero and contribute to the effectiveness of the characterization. The apparent two dimensional portrayal of Enguerrand is deceptive; gradually the reader grows aware of greater depths of psychological complexity which the narrator is at great effort to hide. Enguerrand's tears are the only visible sign that the young man is hurt by Aliénor's choice of the unworthy Jacques de Bévannes. One question remains. Does the racist element in the story stem from Gobineau's desire to write a "pièce à these" or should it be considered a rationalization on the part of Enguerrand who inwardly needs to prove his superiority over those who scorn his poverty and the decisions of the Cour d'Amour?

Aliénor is much more sketchily portrayed. The narrator first emphasizes her eyes; "Elle avait les yeux bleus et Enguerrand n'imaginait pas que le ciel lui-même fût plus pur, mais aussi plus vivant, plus charmant, plus séduisant, plus candide et plus éclatant de divine lumière que ces yeux-là" (CA: p. 266). [7] The old knight who pleads Enguerrand's case before the Cour d'Amour underscores "[la] noblesse du sang, la beauté du corps, la grâce de l'esprit de demoiselle Aliénor de Foy" (CA: p. 286). But Aliénor was very young the first time Enguerrand asked to be accepted as her "serviteur" and unsure of her feelings:

> Oui, lui dit-elle; mais elle ne savait plus ce qu'il disait, encore moins ce qu'elle répondait. Il faut se rappeler qu'elle n'avait pas quatorze ans. Elle le voyait beau comme il l'était, et savait bien comme on parlait de lui. La veille, un oncle qu'elle avait, vieux chevalier, avait dit d'Enguerrand qu'il serait le plus noble chevalier du temps qui allait venir et une voix lui disait au fond de sa poitrine: qui ne m'enviera un tel serviteur; elle le regardait donc bien doucement et lui ne se trouvait pas mal reçu, comme assurement il ne l'était pas. (CA: p. 270)

She refuses his parting kiss two years later, because she is afraid that she is losing a love she never really experienced (CA: p. 277). But she openly admits her error at the Cour d'Amour and concludes: "Ce qui vous paraîtra le meilleur, je suis toute prête à le donner mais je vous en prie, ne dites pas que je vous ai fait un tort quelconque, car rien n'est plus loin de ma volonté" (CA: pp. 287-288).

Since the last part of the narrative was never written, the reader can but speculate on the final outcome of the action. Will Aliénor remain the undecided young girl and divide her sentiments between Enguerrand and Jacques de Bévannes or will she discover the energy to refuse her fiancé and find fulfillment in Enguerrand's

---

[7] Gobineau places importance on eyes, as we noted earlier (Chapter III).

devotion? Will Enguerrand's possible violent death bring about a transformation in her? It is impossible to tell whether Gobineau intended Aliénor to remain a secondary figure, beautiful but weak, or whether he intended to make of her a heroine equal in determination to her "serviteur." The latter conclusion appears more appropriate, because of a comment the narrator makes after having described the kiss with which Enguerrand sealed his declaration: "Elle avait pris sa vie et le monde entier s'était ouvert devant eux" (CA: p. 271).

The three predominant themes of honor, love and race are intermingled in the narrative. Enguerrand is of Germanic origin and consequently concerned with his honor and sensitive to the refinements of courtly love. He also possesses the Gobineau tendency to show anger when aroused: "... colère, il l'était et ne raisonnait pas trop avec ses comportements" (CA: p. 278). Jacques de Bévannes claims a Roman consul in his family tree, but Roman blood is a sign of degeneracy. Member of an inferior race, Jacques is by nature incapable of appreciating the Cour d'Amour, which he severely mocks in Enguerrand's presence, and shamelessly considers murdering his rival.

The narrator makes it evident that only those of Nordic background can appreciate the concept of honor. The institution of courtly love and Enguerrand's defense of his position stem from his preoccupation with honor. In making his first declaration to Aliénor, Enguerrand states: "Je vous jure, demoiselle, que personne plus que moi ne désire de gagner de l'honneur et de le mettre à vos peids" (CA: p. 270). He rests his entire defense, before the Cour d'Amour and in regard to his fight with Jacques de Bévannes, on the phrase "je ne laisserai pas dire... que j'ai manqué d'honneur" (CA: p. 295).

Gobineau had intended this narrative as "le pendant des *Amants de Kandahar,*[8] and both stories stress the interrelationship of honor and love. The difference in the two works resides principally in the concept of love; Enguerrand is told: "Aimez seulement...; vous faites assez et tout ce qu'un amour sincère peut persuader de grandes choses, vous les saurez faire ainsi et

---

[8] Béziau, p. 268.

mieux que si vous n'épousez jamais votre belle" (CA: p. 268). Courtly love demands honor and respect, but not fulfillment. It is a delicate sentiment accessible only to the chosen few.

"La Cour d'Amour" is the only narrative in which Gobineau so emphatically and so obviously stresses his racist feelings. In certain passages he even becomes heavily didactic: "La population d'origine romaine devenant de jour en jour la plus nombreuse et la plus forte, établit de plus en plus sa domination dans le droit comme elle l'établissait dans la langue. Le sang frank, le sang normand, le sang visigoth et le sang burgonde allèrent de plus en plus disparaissant du français, en même temps et pour les mêmes causes qui firent disparaître dans le droit les principes de la liberté et de l'honneur germanique" (CA: p. 282). Gobineau returns to this racist position in describing the Cour d'Amour:

> A juger les choses comme on pourrait le faire aujourd'hui, les mauvais plaisants et les rieurs devaient abonder, surtout si l'on tient compte de ce qui a été dit plus haut que les gens de race romaine devaient être de beaucoup les plus nombreux. Ils l'étaient en effet et leurs physionomies variées, généralement brunes, à cheveux bruns ou noirs, crépus ou emmêlés, leurs nez aquilins ou aplatis, leurs grosses lèvres ou quelquefois aussi très fines, le montraient assez... Mais il y avait aussi bien des laboureurs, bien des ouvriers, bien des marchands de taille plus grande, aux yeux bleus, aux cheveux blonds ou rouges, qui avaient un autre sang dans les veines... (CA: p. 284).

The directness of this elevation of the Aryan race and the downgrading of Latin elements, probably the preoccupations of an aging and bitter man, seriously alienate the modern reader.

Throughout his life Gobineau was preoccupied with the idea of love. In all four narratives, "Les Conseils de Rabelais," "L'Illustre Magicien," "Les Amants de Kandahar," and the fragment "La Cour d'Amour," love is depicted as a sentiment accessible only to an elite. The ability to experience love becomes a symbol of nobility, a curious return to the doctrine of "l'Amour Courtois" of the Middle Ages.

"Les Conseils de Rabelais" emphasizes the primacy of love over the demands of society. Although the narrative itself is weak, the theme, for Gobineau, is of utmost importance.

"L'Illustre Magicien" and "Les Amants de Kandahar" depict two aspects of the most powerful human sentiment: love. For Gobineau the following poetic description of Mohsèn and Djemylèh's spiritual union is applicable to any couple united by a total passion: "ces amants planaient ensemble dans l'éther du plus absolu bonheur que l'homme le plus fortuné puisse respirer jamais!" (NA: p. 360). This apogee of human experience is open to the intellectual and the non-intellectual. Kassem tries to reason out his destiny and erroneously puts his vocation before his love. Mohsèn's reaction to passion is complete unreasoning acceptance; he automatically considers Djemylèh more important than his projects of revenge and advancement. Kassem places his self-fulfillment over and above his devotion to Amynèh; Mohsèn is more generous. But these two different heroes, with opposing attitudes, both assert that love is the greatest human passion and leads to the greatest human happiness. Such a passion apparently cannot exist side by side with strong political ambition or intellectual striving; it is an absolute which requires the suppression of all desires and values not directly related to its attainment.

Although Mohsèn and Kassem are of contrasting personalities, Amynèh and Djemylèh possess similar traits. Both are beautiful, both know how to attract and soothe their lovers, how to encourage them in times of stress. Even when their intuition is responsible for the inspiration of the moment, they are experienced in the art of suggestion and submission. They are of delicate frames but strong constitution. Djemylèh endures the two strenuous flights at Mohsèn's side without a word of complaint. Amynèh undertakes the project of following Kassem on his pilgrimage, leaving the easy luxury of life in Damghan to assume the privations and hardships of desert travel. Apparently, for Gobineau, the ideal female companion must combine charm and femininity with intelligence, capability, and moral strength.

"La Cour d'Amour" resists complete analysis because the denouement was never written. Enguerrand finds himself in a more fortunate position than either Kassem or Mohsèn for he experiences no conflict between love and other desires. In fact, for Enguerrand, love and honor are synonymous. The core problem of the narrative resides in Aliénor's youth and uncertainty. She, too, is as beautiful and charming as Amynèh and Djemylèh, but while the latter are women, she is but a child. Whether the unwritten part of the narrative was to have described Aliénor's blossoming into womanhood and her acceptance of Enguerrand's devotion is a question that can never be answered.

Love, for Gobineau, is not a sensual passion, but an expression of total generosity.[9] In this respect it is of interest that the three latter narratives were written after Gobineau's first meeting with the Countess de La Tour who became the passionate love of his last years. The platonic nature of their relationship could account for the lack of sensuality in the stories and the emphasis on delicacy and sensitivity.

The narrative techniques differ in each story. "L'Illustre Magicien" in presenting the vacillations of Kassem's intentions relies on an initial series of descriptive scenes and a subsequent lengthy interior monolog: only the denouement can be classified as dramatic. Mohsèn is basically an emotional individual who rarely suppresses his sentiments; "Les Amants de Kandahar" discloses a dramatic construction in which simple narration is limited to the opening and closing paragraphs. The body of the narrative is a mosaic of scenes bordering on the melodramatic. Enguerrand is a musician and poet, lyric passages abound and conversations are but briefly (and poetically) recalled. Even Enguerrand's act of violence in knocking Jacques de Bévannes unconscious is described as a graceful ballet sequence. Thus in the three latter narratives Gobineau patterns the dramatic technique on the character of the central figure.

Similarly, the treatment of the locale varies. In "L'Illustre Magicien" Persian society is directly contrasted with the protagonists; the desert plays a catalytic role in enabling Kassem's ideas to transcend the occupations of daily life and consider the nature of love and knowledge. In "Les Amants de Kandahar" the locale is

---

[9] See Louis Tenenbaum, "Love in the Prose Fiction of Gobineau," *MLQ*, XVIII (1957), 110.

employed to explain the character of the protagonists. Race assumes excessive importance in "La Cour d'Amour" and medieval courtly society reflects the inevitable conflicts between the Nordic and the Latin elements. The implicit conclusion to be drawn from these three stories is that even though man and societies differ, human passion is a sign of aristocracy and must be regarded as the supreme expression of man's potential.

Chapter V

THE CONFRONTATION OF CULTURES

"Au rebours de ce qu'enseignent les moralistes, les hommes ne sont nulle part les mêmes" (NA: p. 6). Such a theory can be dramatically illustrated by placing a representative of one society in a foreign milieu and then emphasizing the areas of discord and conflict. Gobineau used such a confrontation of cultures as the core of three narratives: "La Chasse au caribou," "Akrivie Phrangopoulo," and "La Vie de voyage." Each story concerns two different societies: a Parisian playboy makes a voyage to Newfoundland, a British captain visits the Greek island of Naxos, and a young Italian couple tours the Middle East. Yet, although the themes are similar, Gobineau has created three highly disparate narratives.

In "Adélaïde," as we noted in Chapter III, Gobineau criticizes the superficiality of many members of society by comparing them to tricycles: "... ils ne roulent que sur les trottoirs; hors des trottoirs, ça tombe. Moi, j'aime mieux les gens qui sont gênés sur les trottoirs, mais qui peuvent très bien marcher dans les bois" (A: p. 166). A year earlier, in the narrative "La Chasse au caribou," Gobineau had given life to his simile in the person of a Parisian playboy, Charles Cabert, whom he sends on an excursion to Newfoundland.[1] In contrasting the flightiness of European society

---

[1] The exact dates of composition are unknown. However, on September 25, 1868, Gobineau makes a reference to the story in a letter to Zoé Dragoumis and it would appear that the young lady had already seen the man-

with the solidity of a pioneer country Gobineau has created a humorous tale which in its irony condemns the superficiality of nineteenth-century "civilization."

In order to dramatize the melancholy resulting from his broken liaison with a French actress, Charles Cabert decides to hunt caribou in Newfoundland. After a brief stay in Saint John at the home of the Dutch consul general, Anthony Harrisson, Cabert sets out by ship with the pioneer Georges Barton for the latter's homestead, which is to serve as a center of operations for the hunting expeditions. Cabert's dismay at finding himself so completely isolated from society is counteracted by the presence of Barton's daughter, Lucy. Cabert, who had already shown himself to be totally insensitive to the manners and customs of the inhabitants of Newfoundland, commits the more serious error of expressing his devotion to Lucy in flowery salon phraseology which the young girl understands to signify a marriage proposal. The misunderstanding is finally straightened out and Cabert returns to Paris without having seen any caribou.

Charles Cabert, son of a wealthy entrepreneur, is a young man of slight build with fine blond hair and a light mustache. Cabert has a high opinion of his physical elegance and, even though discouraged upon arriving at Mr. Barton's island, "... il se secoua, et commença sa toilette avec l'intention charitable de montrer à ses malheureux hôtes ce que c'est qu'un homme élégant, afin qu'ayant joui une fois dans leur vie de cette brillante apparition, ils pussent ne l'oublier jamais" (SV: p. 195). Cabert is equally convinced of his general merit and attractiveness: "Un Parisien orné de ses grâces, perfectionné par la vie élégante, connaissant à fond les passions, ayant le revenant bon de ses expériences, une pareille perle échouant sur les rives sauvages de la Baie-des-Iles, quelle merveille...!" (SV: p. 207). The egotism so evident in the above two passages is indicative of Cabert's character and pervades the entire narrative.

Basically Cabert is unsure of himself. When Jenny Harrisson's fiancé O'Lary demonstrates his affection by carrying him on his shoulders from Harrisson's house to Barton's boat, Cabert has

---

uscript; in "Nouvelles Lettres athéniennes," ed. J. Mistler, *RdDM*, CXXIV (1954), 420. "Adélaïde" was written in December 1869.

recourse to the childish expedient of kicking in a futile attempt to have the Irishman put him down. The moment of crisis occurs when Cabert is confronted with Barton and his son Patrice, who accuse him of breach of promise. Cabert, whose language usually reflects the polish and refinement of elegant conversation, finds himself unable to compose his thoughts: "Je ne lui ai pas dit que je comptais... D'ailleurs, vous savez, dans tous les cas, il faudrait que je prévinsse mon père, et, sans son aveu, je ne saurais réellement... Il y a des résolutions graves que... Certainement, j'ai pour Mlle Lucy une admiration... Mais je croyais que l'usage de ces îles..." (SV: p. 218). The superficiality of his self-confidence and of his assurance becomes evident when his position is challenged.

Since Cabert subconsciously desires to protect himself from being judged by others, he finds protection behind the screen of ironic speech. Occasionally his lack of comprehension leads him to sarcasm, as when he comments on the fact that Gregory had four children before being sacramentally married. Lucy in her simplicity interprets Cabert's manner of speech as indicative of unquestionable superiority and is enchanted by "l'accent un peu aigre de la voix, le plus souvent timbrée par l'ironie" (SV: p. 204). Barton takes Cabert's remarks at face value and fights them directly; only Monsieur John, the teacher, understands the weakness of the Parisian tourist.

Cabert, who prides himself on his exquisite social graces, is singularly unperceptive of others and their feelings: "L'idée de ménager les sentiments d'autrui parut... singulière à Charles" (SV: p. 181). The young man immediately ridicules new customs, or comments on them in a sarcastic fashion, since he fails to understand their background. He purposely misinterprets the actions of Barton and Harrisson and mistakes hospitality for rudeness. Cabert's inability to communicate reaches a climax in the two scenes with Monsieur John. The devoted schoolteacher had been educated in European society and had travelled extensively before coming to Newfoundland. He attempts to give an indirect explanation of Newfoundland manners, but Cabert cannot understand the subtleties of the schoolteacher's warning. Monsieur John suggests:

> —Monsieur, ... dans votre intérêt, je vous engage à ne pas vous croire ici dans un salon d'Europe.
>
> —Je ne m'y crois pas non plus, Monsieur! repliqua Charles avec cet accent d'ironie qu'il maniait à la perfection. Il me faudrait une puissance d'illusion que je ne possède pas!
>
> —C'est donc à merveille, repartit froidement M. John; buvez, mangez, chassez, amusez-vous de ce qu'on vous offre, mais ne commettez pas de méprise, vous n'en comprenez pas les conséquences.
>
> —Ce que je ne comprends pas, c'est votre discours... (SV: pp. 209-210)

In this scene, too, Cabert's first reaction is irony followed by a slight burst of anger. Utterly impervious to Monsieur John's counsel, Cabert bandies words with Lucy and would have been forced into marriage by Barton had Monsieur John not arrived in time to offer a gentle explanation of the misunderstanding. Yet Cabert is unable to realize that he owes his freedom to Monsieur John's intervention; upon returning to the ship which will take him to Halifax he still finds only one adjective to qualify the schoolteacher: "odieux."

Both Charles Cabert's character and the narrator's opinion of the protagonist are established in the short first paragraph:

> Charles Cabert était fils d'un homme devenu passablement riche dans les affaires où il était question de zinc. Il avait été élevé au collège comme tout le monde, en était sorti sans plus de science que ses camarades, et, en garçon distingué, s'était fait recevoir membre d'un club ou il perdait assez d'argent pour être traité avec considération. Ses amis lui firent connaître des dames, et afin de ne pas se singulariser, il se résolut un matin à épouser une figurante. (SV: p. 157)

For Charles the only important consideration is his social standing. Having finished his education with the equivalent of a "Gentleman's C," he spends his days in the clubs and salons of Paris without distinguishing himself in any way. In fact, the subservience of personal identity to "group" membership has become his goal in life. Evidently such a person will judge people and their actions by the strict code which condemns any deviation from established forms and customs.

The story is fundamentally told from Cabert's point of view; thus, terms such as "en garçon distingué" parallel the young man's opinion of himself. Cabert considers his ironic and even sarcastic comments to be the expression of a refined sense of humor. Cabert's account is transformed by a narrator, perhaps Gobineau himself, who lets it be known that he finds Cabert's position ridiculous and considers Cabert the typical representative of a degenerate salon society. The first sentence of the story reveals the attitude of Gobineau-narrator. Cabert pictures himself the heir of a highly successful zinc entrepreneur. The narrator shows his disdain by inserting the adjective "passablement" before "riche" and by subsequently assuming an air of naiveté concerning the nature of the business, "les affaires où il était question de zinc." In the second sentence the narrator gives a negative twist to his explanation of the results of Cabert's education; the latter would obviously have stated "avec autant de science" rather than "sans plus de science." In the third sentence the phrase "afin de ne pas se singulariser" again reflects the attitude of the narrator who wishes to indicate his low opinion of Cabert and his comrades. Were Cabert directly narrating the events he would have referred to Coralie not as a mere "figurante" but as "cantatrice" or "actrice." Thus the events are seen through Cabert's eyes, but his version of the story is related by an unsympathetic narrator. Throughout the narrative this dual level of narration is maintained: Cabert is characterized through his own words and thoughts, and secondarily through the irony of the narrator.

Lucy Barton, in spite of her hard labor on the homestead, possesses innate feminine charm and grace. Even Cabert, appalled as he is by her unflattering work clothes, notices her beauty: "... les yeux étaient splendides, les couleurs d'une fraîcheur nacrée et rosée incomparable, les cheveux du blond le plus avenant et d'une opulence magique, et tous les mouvements empreints de cette grâce parfaite qui ne s'apprend pas et que la nature seule peut donner aux êtres heureux auxquels elle a accordé une taille sans défauts" (SV: p. 193). The explanation of Lucy's gracefulness originates with the narrator; where harmony exists it is not the product of society but rather a natural phenomenon unrestricted as to country and era. Cabert is more impressed with Lucy that evening when she wears an elegant dress patterned after the most recent London fashions.

In Newfoundland it is customary for the young girl to assume the initiative in the courtship. When Lucy meets Cabert she is attracted to him and subsequently determined to maneuver an engagement. At this point the narrator, having presented an unflattering portrait of Cabert and a delightful picture of Lucy, feels obligated to explain the latter's infatuation. "Comme Cabert ne ressemblait en aucun point aux hommes qu'elle avait pu voir jusqu'alors, il représentait pour elle, à un degré suprême, cette apparition de l'inconnu, toujours si puissante sur les imaginations féminines" (SV: p. 204). Lucy appreciates Cabert's qualities and at the same time is conscious of her own value: "... elle se savait digne d'être acquise: belle, courageuse, dévouée, tendre, fidèle comme de l'or" (SV: p. 206). Thinking that Cabert will simply indicate his refusal if he is uninterested in marriage, Lucy orients the conversation by asking, "Est-ce que vous aimiez quelqu'un?" (SV: p. 208). With the same directness Omm-Djéhâne had asked Moreno, "Aimez-vous une femme dans votre pays?" (NA: p. 69). Lucy receives a more encouraging answer than Omm-Djéhâne did, and after a brief conversation with Cabert she misinterprets his "Mon destin est fixé à vos pieds" as a marriage proposal.

Lucy Barton is completely candid: life on a Newfoundland island allows no place for dissimulation and feigned emotions. That evening, believing herself to be engaged, she is unable to conceal her happiness. The following morning when Cabert informs her that she misinterpreted his words, she is stunned and, gradually understanding Monsieur John's explanation, breaks into tears. Courageous Lucy is unable to bear this one scene in which she must avow her error to the detriment of her personal pride and also see the ruin of her dreams for future happiness.

Lucy is characterized from Cabert's point of view. For him she is first a name mentioned by Barton. Later, as she comes out to meet the boat, Cabert hears Barton's enthusiastic praise of his daughter. "C'est Lucy, ... et si vous en trouvez une autre comme elle pour aller au large, par une bonne brise, aussi tranquille qu'au coin de son feu, faire son chargement de harengs, là où mes hommes ne prennent rien, je lui tirerai mon chapeau à celle-là!" (SV: p. 192). Such a eulogy has a negative effect on Cabert, who none the less is soon forced to acknowledge Lucy's beauty and grace. During the evening conversation the narrator feels obligated to interrupt his assumed point of view in order to interpret Lucy's reactions. She is last seen, again by Cabert, sobbing and running out of the Barton living room.

George Barton is physically an imposing man of great stature. Through the eyes of slender Cabert, he appears as a giant: "... un gaillard large comme est long un enfant de huit ans, avec une tête monstrueuse, couvert d'une forêt, de cheveux bruns à demi gris, bouclés dru les uns sur les autres, et qui, enveloppé, Dieu sait comme! d'un habit noir dont on eût pu habiller quatre personnes raisonnables" (SV: p. 166). It is not until the second part of the story, the boat trip and the visit to his homestead, that Barton begins to reveal the basic generosity of his character.

Barton himself is extremely independent; he has settled his island in a search for autonomy. For him democracy means freedom, as he explains to Cabert: "... je ne connais ni rois, ni empereurs, ni ducs, ni présidents, ni magistrats. Je suis mon magistrat à moi-même! Je paie ce que je dois, je prends ce qui m'appartient; si l'on m'attaque je me défends, et j'ai des bras pour m'en servir. Voilà ce que j'appelle un vrai démocrate!" (SV: p. 201). The straightforwardness evident in his business affairs also distinguishes his dealings with people. Eeager to give part of his fortune to Cabert as dowry for Lucy when he believes the two to be engaged, he is equally direct about his threat to drown Cabert when he considers the latter a seducer. His last words with Cabert are indicative of his personality: "Monsieur Cabert, lui dit-il, je vous demande pardon. Cette petite fille s'est trompée et m'a trompé moi-même. Voilà tout ce que je peux vous dire; mais comme, franchement, nous ne sommes pas faits aux belles manières, et que ma Lucy aurait de la peine à vous voir désormais, vous m'obligeriez si vous vouliez vous en aller, je ne vous le cache pas" (SV: p. 223). Barton has none of the inhibitions of social pride; beneath his brusque speech is an open heart willing to confess an error, but, for that, no less sensitive to the needs of family harmony. He politely asks Cabert to leave, giving the real reason for such a request: Lucy would be upset by his continued presence. His hospitality is all the warmer in that he invites only those people whom he truly desires as guests.

Harrisson, the Dutch consular agent, is a large man with an incredibly strong handshake. When Cabert first meets him in the warehouse the latter is unwilling to be interrupted at his work. That evening, however, he invites the young tourist to his house and even organizes a large party in his guest's honor. Other characters such as O'Lary show this same directness coupled with warm hospitality. The life in a small North American community in which the citizens work together in order to dominate nature and thus secure their lives tends to encourage direct and open negotiations.

The one figure who contrasts with the husky pioneers of Newfoundland is Monsieur John. The thin, ascetic Englishman is modelled after a schoolteacher whom Gobineau had met in Sydney on his Newfoundland mission and whom he briefly described in his *Voyage à Terre-Neuve:* "... c'était un gentilhomme anglais qui, à la suite de malheurs d'une nature très-poignante, avait quitté le service, était venu s'établir dans le désert, et sous l'impression d'idées religieuses, s'y était dévoué à l'éducation des enfants" (VTN: p. 80). The narrator breaks the point of view in order to devote two pages to the teacher's background. Hector Latimer, after a period of debauchery following his wife's infidelity and elopement, came to Newfoundland. "Cherchant un moyen aussi humble, aussi abaissé que possible d'expier ses fautes et celles des autres, il se fit maître d'école sous le nom de M. John, et rendit de grands services à la population abandonnée de chasseurs et de pêcheurs établie dans cette contrée" (SV: p. 199). In "La Chasse au caribou" Gobineau develops in greater detail this figure whom he had briefly mentioned in an earlier work. Since Gobineau generally follows his models very closely, we could almost assume M. John's background to be an exact reproduction of the "malheurs d'une nature très-poignante" hinted at in the earlier work.

Gobineau dramatizes the general theme of the narrative, that is, the artificiality of Parisian salon society, by introducing Cabert to the pioneers of Newfoundland and allowing the reader to draw the appropriate conclusions as to the relative merits of the two cultures. As we have seen, Cabert's egoism and lack of sensitivity are sharply contrasted with the generosity and fundamental honesty of Barton and Harrisson. Cabert's polished manners and the Newfoundland "boorishness" are both shown to be a mere coating from which it is impossible to judge the merits of the true personality. Gobineau even tends to suggest the conclusion that manners are a sign of degeneracy while directness is indicative of honesty and manhood. Such a conclusion, however, would not be in accord with Gobineau's other works, such as "Akrivie Phrangopoulo," where extreme formality is considered a virtue.

French society is more directly criticized by the inhabitants of Saint John. The Irish bellhop is especially outspoken and tells Cabert: "Harrisson?... c'est un homme comme vous ne devez pas en avoir beaucoup dans votre sale Europe" (SV: p. 164). Harrisson himself maintains North America's superiority over "cette misérable Europe, accablée en ce moment sous le fardeau de son ignorance, de sa misère, de son asservissement!" (SV: p. 170). Even Barton, who is usually generous and direct, modifies Europe with the adjective "pourrie" (SV: p. 189).

For the reader the Newfoundland invectives lose some validity in their overstatement. Although Cabert's portrait exaggerates the failings of Parisian society, it is nevertheless effective in pointing up the weakness of the European bourgeoisie. The criticism stems not so much from the direct remarks as it does from the irony. Moreover, it is this irony which ties together the diverse incidents and unifies the narrative.

The plot focusses on the person of Cabert who left Paris with the express intention of encountering new experiences whose description would astound the members of his social circle. Cabert's stay in Newfoundland is cut short after ten days: thirty-six hours in the town of Saint John, eight days on Barton's boat, and twenty-four hours at the Barton home. The people and their customs are shown through the eyes of Cabert and directly through conversations.

The majority of the incidents are adapted from *Voyage à Terre-Neuve*. Monsieur Harrisson's welcome party recalls the ball given by the colonial secretary Monsieur K *** where the French were greeted with eloquent toasts. Gobineau had complained about the exaggerated patriotism of the Newfoundlanders and the false idea they had of their local importance (VTN: pp. 241-242); Harrisson's toast expresses the hope that Cabert may understand "la supériorité de nos institutions et la grandeur de notre avenir" (SV: p. 171). Gobineau had commented that the mother of the family passes unnoticed; similarly, Madame Harrisson, seated in a corner, does not participate in the conversation except to complain of a toothache. The nature of politics, the power of the bishop, the role of the economy, all are discussed at the Harrisson dinner table.

In the years which had passed between his trip and the composition of "La Chasse au caribou" Gobineau's opinions mellowed. Certain customs which had surprised and even shocked him are presented in a matter-of-fact way as the manners of a vigorous, dynamic country. In this respect it is interesting to compare the two accounts of unchaperoned walks (VTN: p. 296; SV: p. 183), the courtships (VTN: p. 295, SV: p. 205) and the belated marriages (VTN: p. 202, N: p. 203).

Most of the descriptions of scenery and of domestic life are directly drawn from accounts of *Voyage à Terre-Neuve*. A complete study of all the similarities could be accomplished only in a dual edition with the text of the narrative on one side and the appropriate sentences from the travelogue on the other. In general Gobineau greatly abridged the exterior descriptions while enlarging the characterizations, as in the case of M. John. Irish strength and petulance are assigned to O'Lary, Irish reasoning and philosophy of love to O'Callaghan. The travel journal presented general observations. In the narrative these broad traits are particularized in individuals creating a panorama which permits the reader to formulate a general impression of Newfoundland.

"Akrivie Phrangopoulo," a lyrical "souvenir" of Naxos, is considered by many critics to be Gobineau's finest *nouvelle*. Schemann

THE CONFRONTATION OF CULTURES   141

and Reinhold Falk single out this story for special mention.[2] Among the French critics, Seillière considers the narrative "l'ouvrage littéraire le plus achevé du comte."[3] Many later critics give the narrative particular praise,[4] but the most generous comment occurs in an essay by Paul Colin who asserts that "Akrivie" and "La Chasse au caribou" are "... peut-être les nouvelles les plus parfaites que le XIXe siècle français ait vu naître."[5] It remains to be seen if a detailed analysis of the story bears out such generous laudatory remarks.

Although "Akrivie Phrangopoulo" is dated Patissia, August, 1867, a careful reading of Gobineau's correspondence would indicate that the narrative was written in Rio de Janeiro in early fall 1869.[6] On September 27 of that year Gobineau confided to Zoé Dragoumis:

> Je vais avoir fini peut-être la semaine prochaine *Akrivie Phrangopoulos*. Je pense que cela vous plaira et l'adoration de Naxos n'a jamais été poussée si loin ni dans les temps anciens ni dans les temps modernes. Je parle aussi d'Antiparos et de Santorin. Au fond ce n'est autre chose que la description du voyage que j'ai fait sur le *Racer* pendant que vous étiez à Corfou. Mon héros ressemble un peu à Brine, mon héroïne est la charmante fille que nous avons vue là; la partie romanesque n'est pas autre chose que les rêveries que Brine [et moi] avons faites sur le bonheur de vivre dans une pareille île sans avoir plus rien de commun avec le monde. Enfin le sentiment général est cette

---

[2] Schemann, Ludwig, *Gobineau und die deutsche Kultur* (Leipzig: Teubner, 1934), p. 41; Reinhold Falk, *Die weltanschauliche Problematik bei Gobineau* (Berlin: Norm-Druck, 1936), p. 82.
[3] Seillière, p. 302.
[4] See Souday, pp. 23-24; Dreyfus, pp. 268-269; Rowbotham, p. 85.
[5] "L'Ame de Gobineau," *Europe*, III, no. 9 (1923), 32.
[6] Jean Mistler believes that August 1867 indicates the time at which the story was conceived or rapidly sketched out, rather than when it was established in its final form (Mistler, p. 16). Gobineau made his first voyage to the Cyclades in February 1866, but it was on his second voyage in October 1867 that he met Captain Linday Brine. Must we consider the Patissia notation on the manuscript as an inadvertent slip on Gobineau's part? There is another explanation: Gobineau abbreviated the month of December as "Xbre" and probably noted October as VIIIbre; an editor must have deciphered the notation as August whereas Gobineau had intended to write "Pâtissia, octobre 1867."

passion violente que j'ai pour la Grèce et qui, de loin peut-être, ne lui voit plus le moindre défaut. (LDA: pp. 117-18)

(Gobineau deleted the final *s* of the heroine's name before the story was published.)

The narrative describes the brief sojourn of the British captain Norton on the island of Naxos while his ship was undergoing minor repairs. Norton is attracted by the simplicity and Homeric beauty of Akrivie and finally decides to renounce his naval career and take the young girl as his wife.

The narrator's attention centers on the rapid transformation of Norton's personality. Thirty-three-year-old Henry Fitzallan Norton enjoys his sea-faring life and passes his time in thought rather than in conversation. His mind is highly receptive to new and different experiences; he is fascinated by paradoxes in that they present a challenge to his intelligence. "C'était un homme logique et suprêmement maître de lui" (SV: p. 107). Moreover, Norton was not at all naive in love, but his previous affairs or engagements had all dissolved at the instigation of one or both parties.

On seeing Akrivie as she enters from the balcony, he falls in love at first sight: "... lorsque la jeune demoiselle, ayant atteint le bas de l'escalier, traversa la longue salle pour venir s'asseoir à côté de sa mère, le commandant jugea nécessaire d'appeler à son secours toute la roideur civilisée afin de couvrir son émotion, et il s'imposa un air froid et compassé digne du pavillon britannique" (SV: p. 90). Disappointed at not having noticed any similar emotion expressed by Akrivie, Norton spends the following night in contemplation. The fact that even his dog Didon, who disliked all strangers, spent the afternoon at the charming girl's feet, confirms for him the power of her attraction. He gradually defines his feeling toward Akrivie as the concretion of an innate longing for the purity and simplicity of Homeric times. This new emotion surprises him, for until then he had always been attracted to contrary qualities: brilliant conversation, social graces, sparkling vivacity. However, several months before arriving in Naxos, Norton has already become conscious of a deep-seated disenchantment with the emptiness of his present life. After his first meeting with Akrivie he would gladly give up his naval career, but his logical mind demands that he await the dissipation of the initial effects of his romantic meeting and of the calm night on the deck of the ship.

Subsequent meetings and especially the two-day cruise to the neighboring islands of Santorin, Paros, and Antiparos confirm Norton's decision to renounce his previous life and to ask for Akrivie's hand. After an unsuccessful conversation with the young girl, he comes to the realization that custom demands he first speak with her father. The technicalities are resolved, Norton resigns his commission and the two are happily married.

The narrator presents Norton as representative of that branch of the Aryan race which became established in Great Britain. After describing Norton's initial meeting with Akrivie, the narrator defines the heritage which has a determining influence on the captain's character. "Cette race normande, la plus agissante, la plus ambitieuse, la plus turbulente, la plus intéressée de toutes les races du globe, est en même temps la plus portée à reconnaître et à pratiquer le renoncement aux choses" (SV: p. 106). In this statement the narrator allows the reader to anticipate the denouement. Just before giving an account of Norton's wedding proposal the narrator reintroduces the same racial theme: "Je conclus en répétant que ce goût pour l'exil et le renoncement est si fortement prononcé chez cette race à personnalité puissante, qu'il atteint même les femmes.... Norton était donc en plénitude de ses facultés anglaises" (SV: p. 146). Norton's definitive return to Naxos is prepared from the outset of the narrative.

Norton's point of view is maintained throughout the story. On two occasions Norton expresses his ideas and feelings directly through an interior monologue. The transcription of Norton's thoughts during his first meeting with Akrivie is striking, for the light critical comments made in a humorous tone contrast sharply with the tone of previous pages fluctuating between lyricism and straightforward narration. "Je suis fou ou occupé à le devenir. Elle [Akrivie] ... est fagotée comme on ne l'est pas! ... Je crois entendre d'ici les bonnes remarques de lady Jane. Quel massacre! Et puis, d'ailleurs, quelle éducation a reçu cette malheureuse enfant? Elle doit être sotte à plaisir! Il faut que je la fasse causer" (SV: pp. 91-92). In the midst of the formality of the Naxiote family, Norton in his mind reverts to the conversational tone of a British salon. He assumes the perspective of a disinterested spectator who plans to narrate his adventures in London as a humorous diversion during an evening's conversation. (In this his reaction is identical to that of Charles Cabert during the latter's visit to Newfoundland.) Familiar with Norton's character, the reader is able to interpret the psychological significance of these verbalized thoughts. The denigrating tone of the monologue indicates that Norton is subconsciously striving to counteract the powerful emotional effect of Akrivie's entrance into the salon. During the ensuing conversation Norton's premonitions as to the scantiness of the girl's education are borne out, but she manifests such clear judgment and vigor that his defenses are overridden. "Norton ne put réussir à la trouver sotte. Il arriva même tout le contraire" (SV: p. 95).

The second interior monologue occurs just after Akrivie has refused his proposal and sought refuge in her cabin.

> Si elle m'aimait... elle ne serait pas ce que j'aime en elle, la fille de l'antiquité et de la vie simple, étrangère aux orages du sentiment. Akrivie ne doit aimer que ses parents, son mari et ses enfants; hors de là le monde n'existe pas pour elle... L'épreuve où je viens d'échouer, loin de me détacher de ma résolution, doit m'y confirmer davantage, car je vois plus que jamais à quel point le trésor découvert par moi est pur et sans mélange. Je ne prétends pas chercher les agitations d'une tendresse à l'européenne; ce sont les éléments d'une vie spéciale que je recueille. (SV: pp. 147-148)

By this point Norton is in full possession of his faculties and his discourse reflects his predominantly logical nature. He is impressed with Akrivie's Grecian beauty, but his love is directed not towards her as a person but rather towards that which she symbolizes for him: a return to the purity of human nature unspoiled by the superficialities of modern civilization.

Akrivie Phrangopoulo, since she is characterized uniquely through the eyes of Norton, is presented in simple lines. Her most obvious trait, the one which first arouses the interest of the British captain, is her classical beauty. From afar he first notes the extreme simplicity of her muslin dress and the smallness of her waist. As she approaches his attention is attracted to her face: "...des yeux merveilleux, brillants comme des saphirs bleus et de la même transparence que ces pierres, et une chevelure mordorée, épaisse, abondante, tordue et, semblait-il, avec quelque impatience de la peine qu'elle donnait pour la soumettre, bien que plus fine que la soie et souple à miracle; la bouche la plus rose, le sourire le plus épanoui, les dents les plus dignes de la comparaison ancienne avec un rang de perles" (SV: pp. 88-89). As was noted in Chapter III, Gobineau's attention is first drawn to the eyes, and then extended to include other features. This description is in accordance with the simplicity of Akrivie's dress; she has no need for jewelry since her features emanate the splendor of sapphires and pearls. When Norton analyzes his overall impression he finds that Akrivie resembles the beautiful maidens depicted on Athenian vases.

Akrivie's beauty is coupled with a purity and artlessness which are a direct product of the isolation of her Grecian island. Akrivie's intelligence is such that she rapidly learns English and masters the art of reading. But she prefers the simple refreshing life of Naxos and is extremely bored by her brief visit to Britain.

Akrivie's sentiments and feelings are never presented, since Norton was attracted to her not for herself but rather for what she represented. In many ways Akrivie does not understand Norton, but she is convinced of one thing: "la supériorité absolue de son mari sur le reste de la chrétienté" (SV: p. 153).

The secondary characters are important only to the extent that they influence Norton's ultimate decision to give up his naval career and to retire to the island of Naxos with Akrivie. The first persons whom Norton encounters upon landing in Naxos are Dimitri de Moncade, the British consular representative, and Nicolas Phrangopoulo, agent for the Hanseatic league. These two gentlemen are first seen through the eyes of Norton, as they greet the incoming vessel. The two men, one thin and the other stout, wear the formal dress of several decades previous. Hence, even before setting foot ashore, Norton feels that he is entering an older era. He is consequently not too surprised to find that the women of the island evoke a bygone simplicity. The greeting by the two officials initiates a regression in time which leads Norton eventually to compare Akrivie to a Homeric creation.

Monsieur de Moncade and Monsieur Phrangopoulo maintain the politeness and manners of the eighteenth century. The reliance on prescribed forms is not a false exterior but becomes the expression of racial purity. This same formality, which surprises Norton at the beginning of the narrative, serves to reinforce his decision to marry Akrivie, since it is precisely the sentimentality and frivolity of British society which he desires to give up. For Norton, and consequently for the reader who receives Norton's point of view, Monsieur de Moncade and Monsieur Phrangopoulo are symbols of an ancient aristocracy whose purity and simplicity Norton desires to espouse.

Charles Scott is briefly sketched. Even though the narrator digresses to furnish the family background for the young junior officer, Charles never assumes a reality of his own. He is introduced into the narrative only because of his affection for Akrivie, or more precisely because of the effect of this affection on Norton. "Norton s'apercevait qu'il avait un rival; mais il n'en était point inquiet, et loin d'en concevoir de l'humeur, il sentit augmenter sa sympathie ancienne pour l'audacieux, son protégé de tout temps" (SV: p. 122). The fact that his favorite experienced the powerful attraction of Akrivie's beauty and simplicity reinforces the captain's intention to establish himself in Naxos.

In "Akrivie Phrangopoulo" Gobineau demonstrates his capacity for detailed psychological analysis and precise characterization. Although related in the third person, the narrative maintains Norton's point of view. Throughout his conversations and thoughts the captain manifests a pronounced degree of egotism and vanity. Consistent with this attitude, the other characters are depicted only to the extent that they play on his consciousness. They tend to become symbols or even caricatures because such is the transformation they undergo in Norton's mind.

The primary theme is the contrast between the life on the island of Naxos and the civilization of Western Europe. Generally the contrast is implicit; Norton is presented as an intelligent and sensitive Englishman and his gradual decision to take up residence in Naxos must be interpreted as a value judgment concerning the relative merits of European society and the primitive life of a Grecian island. Occasionally the narrator becomes more explicit in his theme. The inhabitants of Naxos are envied as a people "qui se permet de vivre au dix-neuvième siècle dans une sorte d'état paradisiaque" (SV: p. 77). The direct speech and stiff manners, which at first had shocked Norton, cease to appear strange: "... il n'apercevait plus en eux [the inhabitants] que leur exquise politesse, leur désir de se rendre agréables, la distinction vraie et la noblesse native de leurs manières" (SV: p. 81). For Gobineau this "noblesse" is the trait which distinguishes the elite from the mediocre masses.

The rare mentions of British society are couched in a tone of light irony. After Norton's first conversation with Akrivie, the narrator remarks that the captain found her to be quite ignorant. "L'esprit lui parut singulier; il n'y vit rien de ce qui orne l'imagination d'une jeune demoiselle dans les pays heureux où fleurissent les bonnes éducations et les salons distingués" (SV: p. 93). This same irony is evident near the end of the narrative: Akrivie, when invited to a Yorkshire manor during her visit to England, becomes the subject of an amorous adventure. "Un délicieux jeune homme lui avoua la vérité vraie sur lui-même; il passait les nuits à pleurer le triste sort d'une femme si supérieure unie par un destin toujours barbare et aveugle à un homme incapable de la comprendre. Il n'est pas sûr en effet qu'Akrivie comprit très bien Norton, mais il est incontestable qu'elle comprit encore moins le délicieux jeune homme, et elle s'ennuyait tellement en Angleterre et d'une manière si visible, que Henry, ne s'y amusant pas beaucoup lui-même, la ramena tout droit à Naxos" (SV: pp. 152-153). For Gobineau the temptation to introduce a witty touch into the last page was apparently so strong that he broke the point of view he had maintained so carefully. The first sentence of the quotation evidently reflects the attitude of the suitor: he considers himself as "délicieux," as coveted by women. The phrase "la vérité vraie" is a redundancy typical of his vocabulary, and the epithets "barbare et aveugle" again form part of his speech, not Norton's. The young suitor, both in his own traits and in his humorous presentation, appears as the British counterpart of Charles Cabert, the protagonist in "La Chasse au caribou." Thus, even in a psychological narrative in which the lyrical element dominates, Gobineau cannot refrain from introducing light irony when speaking of those aspects of Western society which he finds ridiculous.

The confrontation of the two cultures is carried out along lines established by the pre-Romantics: the sensitive European, critical of "civilization," becomes attracted to the pure beauty of "nature." The narrator emphasizes the poetic descriptions of the setting and the innate wisdom of the Naxiotes. Akrivie, however, is not the noble savage, but rather the reincarnation of a Homeric heroine. The narrative is founded neither on the conflict between two societies, nor on the discord arising from misinterpretation, but depicts the attraction of the simple island life on an Englishman who has not been tainted by the degenerate features of the European bourgeoisie.

A secondary theme, that of love, is closely woven into the primary one since the object of Norton's affections is as much Akrivie's way of life as it is Akrivie herself. The narrator occasionally intervenes to philosophize on the nature of love. Concerning the possibility of love at first sight, he writes: "Il semblerait pourtant qu'il en doit être de l'amour ainsi que de la mort, plus faible que lui, au dire du livre saint. Quand on n'est pas tué dès la première atteinte, c'est que l'on a été mal navré; mais le coup qui vous jette à terre pour toujours aurait pu se passer de ceux qui l'ont précédé" (SV: p. 89). Gobineau later adds that most Europeans are unwilling to admit loving a woman for her physical qualities. "On n'aime plus aujourd'hui une femme uniquement parce qu'elle est belle; cela arrivait autrefois, dans les temps antiques, dans les temps barbares, mais ne saurait plus se produire chez des esprits aussi raffinés que ceux de l'époque actuelle" (SV: p. 101). After the cruise Norton realizes that what he loves in Akrivie in addition to her beauty is precisely her simplicity and the pure life she personifies.

Gobineau, while respecting the chronological order of events, has divided the plot into four parts:

>Norton's arrival in port, 8 pages
>the first two days in Naxos, 46 pages
>the visit to the other islands, 35 pages
>the engagement and denouement, 6 pages.

The anticipatory remarks are few. As a transition from the calm description of the *Aurora*'s approaching Naxos to the sudden accident which necessitates the ship's prolonged stay in that harbor, the narrator writes: "L'*Aurora* continuait à s'avancer avec lenteur vers cette rive hospitalière, quand survint un incident sur lequel on ne comptait pas, et qui faillit changer du tout au tout le caractère paisible de cette arrivée" (SV: p. 64). This conversational technique of giving advance indication of a climax is often employed by Gobineau. A less direct anticipation of the denouement is offered as Norton catches his first glimpse of the Phrangopoulo manor: "... le voyageur anglais eut l'impression que c'était une sorte de Rubicon qu'il allait franchir, et qu'il laisserait sur une rive sa vie ancienne pour, sur l'autre, recommencer une nouvelle existence" (SV: p. 84). The narrator goes on to explain that such premonitions are generally never confirmed, but ends with the comment that it would be superstition to assume that such impressions are always deceptive.

The locale plays varied roles. At the beginning of the narrative the setting creates the mood. The opening sentence reads: "Les Cyclades sont un des endroits du monde au quel [sic] l'epithète de séduisant s'applique avec le plus de vérité" (SV: p. 57). There the narrator, while speaking of the physical setting, introduces the motif of the entire narrative: the attraction of Akrivie and the life she represents for Norton. The idea of seduction is maintained in the imagery used to describe the landscape: feminine beauty and precious jewels. Speaking of the Greek Islands the narrator writes: "La lumière qui les inonde au milieu d'une atmosphère sans tache, et les flots d'azur qui les enchâssent, en font, suivant les heures du jour, autant d'améthystes, de saphirs, de rubis, de topazes.... Les Cyclades donnent l'idée de très grandes dames nées et élevées au milieu des richesses et de l'élégance" (SV: p. 57). The rising of the sun is equated with "une charmante fille" who opens the doorways of the day. The sea too is presented as a woman, "non ridée mais plissée coquettement pour faire miroiter sur son sein les faisceaux de la jeune lumière" (SV: p. 62). Just as the ship approaches the island the imagery is carried one step farther in an anticipation of the denouement: the town of Naxos is shown "blanche comme une fiancée" (SV: p. 63). These themes of feminine beauty and jewelry are again united, as we have seen, in the first description of Akrivie.

The narration of Norton's first two days at Naxos combines scenes and conversations with numerous descriptive passages concerning primarily the daily life and the philosophy of the inhabitants. These descriptions often become rather lengthy, as in two pages on the various ancestries of the inhabitants, one page on the infrequency of the mail boat, three uninterrupted pages on the urban and rural scenery of the island. While providing the curious reader with a description of the physiognomy of the setting, these passages also interpret Norton's impressions, the things he saw and learned during his first few hours on Naxos. In this manner, they are related to Norton's personality and their combination is relevant to an understanding of the captain's decision to remain on the island.

The third part of the narrative describes the cruise to the islands of Paros, Antiparos and Santorin, a cruise on which Monsieur de Moncade, Monsieur Phrangopoulo and Akrivie are guests of the captain. The pleasure trip is of importance in that Norton is given two or three days in the company of Akrivie to ruminate his decision. During the short voyage the secondary character, Charles Scott, is introduced. The bulk of the section, however, is devoted to lyrical descriptions of the diverse islands, including the descent into a limestone cave and the visit to the Santorin volcano. These lengthy accounts are of documentary interest, but scarcely related to the plot. The engagement and marriage are briefly related, with a minimum of description. On subsequent rereadings of the narrative the reader finds himself omitting many pages which increasingly seem to interfere with, rather than assist in, understanding Norton and his relationship with Akrivie. Curiously enough, Gobineau himself expressed boredom while composing the narrative: "*Akrivie Phrangopoulos,* la nouvelle naxiote, est presque terminée; mais c'est une chose merveilleuse comme je suis ennuyé d'écrire de la prose; on dirait que je ne l'ai jamais fait ou que je l'ai trop fait. La plume me tombe des mains à tous moments et cela fait l'effet de n'avoir ni forme ni couleur." [7]

---

[7] Quoted by Duff (A: p. 20).

The overemphasis on lyrical descriptions in the third part of the narrative spoils the unity of plot and thus undermines the effectiveness of Gobineau's excellent characterization of Norton. Gobineau had written *Trois Ans en Asie* before composing his *Nouvelles asiatiques*; *Voyage à Terre-Neuve* preceded "La Chasse au caribou." Gobineau never composed a travel diary narrating his mission in Greece and his visits to the Greek islands and, therefore, seems not to have previously purged himself of his tendency toward colorful accounts of his experiences. In the third part of the narrative he often digresses from the central plot and introduces incidents which would properly be placed in a travelogue. Mère Bénédicte, Gobineau's sister, interpreted this section of "Akrivie" as a personal account of her brother's experiences. On October 4, 1872, she writes him: "Les descriptions du volcan de Santorin et de la grotte d'Antiparos sont admirables; mais celle de la grotte surtout m'a beaucoup amusée, tu t'y peins toi-même avec ton aversion pour l'obscurité et les entreprises hasardées" (CB: I, 42). Had Gobineau found an earlier occasion to commit his Grecian impressions to paper, "Akrivie" might well have acquired a tighter construction and been worthier of the praise it has so often received.

"La Vie de voyage," written in Stockholm in 1873, was published as the final story of the *Nouvelles asiatiques*. Its position in the book is significant, for the story itself may be considered as a distillation of Gobineau's Persian experiences as they are related in his correspondence, in *Trois Ans en Asie*, and in the preceding *Nouvelles asiatiques*. The primary theme is the introduction to the Near East of a young Italian couple, or more specifically of the young wife who had never travelled much outside of Naples.

The narrative is a description of Lucie Conti's reaction to the culture of the Orient and the subsequent effect of this exotic culture on her psychological well-being. Lucie and Valerio have been married but a week when the bridegroom learns of his financial ruin; the only prospect for advancement lies in a voyage to Constantinople where he expects to find employment. Lucie refuses to leave her husband and asks to accompany him on his voyages; Valerio acquiesces. In Constantinople, the Count P. accepts Valerio into his service and sends him as his emissary to chart the natural resources of Turkey, Iraq and Iran. The mission is stated in very indefinite terms, and the young couple are permitted to travel wherever they desire. After many weeks with a caravan en route for Tehran, a period of time filled with new adventures and new acquaintances, Lucie is overpowered by a melancholy curable only by their return to European civilization where she feels herself less a stranger.

The only character to undergo psychological transformation is Lucie Conti. The eighteen-year-old bride is beautiful and charming; her love for Valerio is so great that the idea of separation revolts her. On hearing of Valerio's travel plans she tells him: "Il faut que je te suive, il faut que je vive auprès de toi; le reste n'est rien" (NA: p. 291). The journey through the Near East acquires the nature of a honeymoon or, more specifically, a sojourn in Eden. "Comme ils vivaient! Comme ils s'aimaient! Et rien ne les empêchait de s'aimer! Aucun souci ne frôlait de son aile grise ou noire l'épanouissement de leur tendresse et, au sein de la vaste nature, ils étaient aussi libres de s'abandonner à leurs sentiments simples et grands comme elle, que jadis, à l'aurore des âges, l'avait pu faire, avant la période de la chute et du travail asservissant, le couple heureux du premier Paradis" (NA: p. 300). Lucie also possesses a high degree of sensitivity. She travels with an open mind and open eyes. Easily enthused, she enjoys the novel experiences which await her in the Near East. "...Lucie sentait par instinct le prix de ce qui a du prix; elle en devinait la valeur cachée au moins aussi bien que Valerio, peut-être avec plus de délicatesse encore, et elle était avide d'explications" (NA: pp. 293-94). Nor does she blindly accept all that she sees: her critical judgment allows her to classify the value of the exterior world. Some things she appreciates, some awaken her disgust.

After many weeks of love, of joy, of excitement, one night suddenly brings on a negative reaction. Without any explicable stimulus, Lucie is invaded by great sadness and awakes sobbing. In an effort to explain her tears she develops a series of images before acquiring the perspective which enables her to analyze the reason for her uneasiness. First she considers herself in a prison, then in a desert, then in a tomb. She continues: "...je me sens prise..., je viens de m'apercevoir que nous sommes seuls, absolument seuls, au milieu d'un monde qui nous est étranger" (NA: p. 335). In the long conversation which follows she defines her uneasiness and concludes that she is basically Italian: "Je voudrais me retrouver dans un autre pays, dans le nôtre, dans celui que nous avons contemplé toute notre vie, qui n'a pas de mystère et d'inconnu pour nous; pour lequel nous sommes faits" (NA: p. 336). Although her love for Valerio makes her try to accept his reassuring words, she is overpowered by a melancholy which does not depart until she learns that the two will join the next caravan in the direction of Bagdad and the Mediterranean.

Gobineau reveals his careful command of female psychology in his portrait of Lucie and her reaction to the Orient. Lucie's naive enthusiasm, while typical of her good intentions, is at the same time evidence of her weak will; in this she resembles Assanoff. When the feeling of an undefined fear awakens her that evening she finds herself unable to control her emotions. Yet she possesses the lucidity to analyze her reactions even though she is unable to dominate them. She believes firmly that her role as a wife means that she should please her husband; but in this instance she cannot find the control manifested, for example, by Amynèh and Djemylèh. Once she knows that she will return to Europe, her good humor comes back just as rapidly as it disappeared and she is sincerely unhappy to leave the friends she has made on the caravan. The final scene of the narrative is also consistent with the body of the story. From the perspective and distance of the Berlin salon, she selectively recalls the colorful aspect of her Oriental travels. To her listeners she explains that if it were not for her husband's mission in Germany, "...je serais encore dans cet Orient, que j'ai trop rapidement traversé, et qui éveille au milieu de mes souvenirs les sensations les plus heureuses, les plus brillantes, les plus inoubliables que j'aie jamais éprouvées" (NA: p. 340). This is not a conscious distortion of the truth; Lucie, once away from the caravan, remembers only the joys of her first weeks with Valerio and has forgotten her feeling of loneliness.

The narrator allows Lucie to characterize herself through her conversations and reactions to the varied experiences of her travels. As we have seen, it is Lucie who tries to define the reasons for her uneasiness. Only after the reader has grown to know Lucie does Gobineau introduce an explanation for her reactions. "Elle était en proie à une réaction qui se produit assez ordinairement en Asie chez les gens, peu ou mal trempés. On voit de ceux-ci, pris subitement, et sans autre cause qu'un travail intérieur de leur conscience, par des paniques qui, en s'accumulant les unes sur les autres, s'exagèrent et s'exaspèrent, arriver à la veritable folie" (NA: p. 336). Gobineau's reasoned explanation is much less effective than Lucie's effort at self-examination.

Valerio Conti plays a minor role in the narrative. He is an intelligent Italian, twenty-six years old at the time of his marriage. "Il était homme actif, d'esprit, de science et de mérite" (NA: p. 291). Having travelled extensively in the Near East, he is able to serve as guide for his young wife. He is deeply in love with Lucie, but lacks the experience which would enable him to interpret her reactions. His counsel comes from the leader of the caravan who, having escorted many European women on his journeys, is familiar with their reactions to the strangeness and hardships of travel.

In spite of his merits or perhaps because of them, Valerio becomes the least interesting character of the narrative. He tends to play the role of an inanimate sounding board. When in Naples Lucie decides to accompany him, he accepts her proposal with little argument; when the leader of the caravan counsels him to return to Europe, he acquiesces without explaining his own opinions. He encourages the various secondary characters in Constantinople and on the caravan to relate their tales and their philosophies, but never does he seriously question what these other people tell him. To Kerbelay-Houssein, the caravan leader, he says: "... vous êtes un digne homme...; je vous écoute avec toute attention et une confiance entière" (NA: p. 307). When Sèyd Abdourrahman finishes his tirade against the Europeans, "Valerio ne vit aucune raison d'argumenter contre lui et on parla d'autres choses sur lesquelles on pouvait être mieux d'accord" (NA: p. 326). Valerio's only distinctly positive action accurs in Trabzon; the members of the caravan represent many races and nationalities, but they all join together in persecuting a man of the Shemsiyèh religion. Valerio intervenes in this scene of violent intolerance and takes the victim into his service.

The weakness in Valerio as a dramatic personage lies in his impeccable character. He is obviously created to resemble Gobineau, the observant voyager. Gobineau rightfully feels that anti-European sentiment will be less effective coming from the mouth of an Italian; therefore Valerio is introduced into the narrative to encourage the Oriental voyagers to state their opinions. The end effect of this is that the reader looks upon the Orientals as curiosities and tends to identify himself with Lucie rather than with Valerio.

In addition to the main characters, Gobineau introduces a series of secondary characters and colorful descriptions. The many facets of these vignettes produce Lucie's overpowering feeling of uneasiness. The primary purpose, however, is to place before the reader a panorama of Oriental scenery and customs.

The most prominent of the secondary characters is Kerbelay-Houssein, the leader of the caravan. The first comment of the narrator on introducing him is: "Il n'y avait qu' à le considérer avec un peu d'attention pour reconnaître immédiatement dans son visage les signes de l'intégrité native." (NA: p. 304). This trait is of greater importance than either his enormous physical strength or his obstinate will, for the entire economic system of the Near East relies on the honesty of the caravan masters.[8] Since it is considered an insult for a merchant to ask for receipt either for advance payment or for goods, the integrity of the caravan master is an essential factor in the economic system. Kerbelay-Houssein appreciates Valerio's decision to engage the Shemsiyèh in his service even though his own primary concern is the maintenance of order. Kerbelay shows his affection for Valerio by designating a gentle mount for Lucie and later by giving him advice concerning his wife's uneasiness. The master of the caravan is a very proud individual; he allows no one to contradict his decisions and offers advice with the knowledge that it will be accepted.

---

[8] Gobineau had pointed out this feature in *Trois Ans en Asie* (TA: pp. 123-127).

In Erzeroum, Lucie and Valerio are welcomed by Osman Pacha, the governor of the city. An Asian who had received a European education, Osman has attained an equilibrium between his native instincts and his acquired tastes. Little concerned for the welfare of his people, he directs his activity toward improving his own financial and social position and rendering his private life as comfortable as possible. His wife, Fatmèh-Hanoum, has acquired European habits, speaks fluent French and is only unhappy that Erzeroum offers no fancy balls and no theater. "Bref, Osman Pacha se montrait homme de goût, avec quelques défectuosités; la dorure n'avait pas pénétré dans l'intérieur du métal kurde" (NA: p. 302).

The Shemsiyèh whom Valerio hired as his servant, is depicted as a sincere individual unwilling to deny his allegiance to one God. He has been working in Erzeroum in order to buy the necessary medical supplies for his sick wife and is now returning home to Avadjyk.

Madame Euphémie Cabarra, a native of Trieste, is a middle-aged widow who has been spending her life travelling with caravans, engaging in petty commerce, and hiring out her services as a cook. She hopes to achieve immortality through an autobiography which shows her to have preserved her moral integrity throughout the most dangerous adventures. [9]

Another voyager is a young Swiss poet, whose verses are as weak as his constitution. An admirer of Thomas Moore, he hopes to complete a pilgrimage to Persia in an effort to attain sublime inspiration. Before reaching the Persian border he dies of tuberculosis and his grave is marked with a simple tombstone.

Redjèb-Aly and his young wife have joined the caravan to accomplish a pilgrimage to Kerbela in order to thank the holy Imams for their happy marriage. Redjèb has already completed the same pilgrimage twice previously, once to fulfill the vow of the dervish who cured his dying fiancée and a second time in gratitude for his wife's miraculous recovery.

---

[9] The model for Madame Euphémie Cabarra appears in *Trois Ans en Asie*: "Sa grande préoccupation dans son livre, écrit d'un style très-prétentieux, est de prouver au monde qu'elle a toujours servi Dieu dévotement, et à travers mille périls, conservé intacte sa vertu" (TA: pp. 220-221).

One day as these friends were conversing in Valerio's tent Sèyd-Abdourrahman introduces himself. This erudite voyager explains his philosophy at great length, emphasizing "le néant de toutes choses" (NA: p. 321). Having found that the most rewarding existence lies in being a perpetual traveller, he has travelled widely in Asia and Africa while avoiding Europe. He vigorously expresses his anti-European sentiments without any challenge from his listeners.

Many of the vignettes depict scenes, the most pervasive picture being the colorful description of the caravan. The movement, noise and hidden order in this slowly moving city of two thousand people make a great impression on European travellers. "C'était un spectacle très beau et très grand" (NA: p. 312). The narrator describes it in greater detail:

> On voit cette masse, et les chameaux, et les chevaux, et les mulets, et les ânes, et les chiens, et les gens refrognés, et les élégants, et les prêtres, et les musulmans, et les chrétiens, et les juifs, et tout, et le tapage on l'entend. La foule marchait en avant, marchait avec lenteur, mais, en même temps, semblait constamment tourbillonner sur elle-même; car les piétons surtout, en agitation perpetuelle, allaient de la tête à la queue du convoi et de la queue à la tête pour parler à quelqu'un, rencontrer quelqu'un, amener quelqu'un à quelqu'un, c'était une agitation permanente et un bouillonnement qui ne s'arrêtait pas. (NA: pp. 312-13)

In this description Gobineau employs the rhythm of the sentences to portray the movement of the caravan. The series of nouns each joined to the following with the word "et" not only gives a verbal impression of the size of the spectacle but also evokes the jerky rhythm of this moving mass. The obvious noise of such a large body of thronging people and animals is accentuated with the inverted word order which terminates the first sentence: "... et le tapage on l'entend." The second sentence emphasizes the inner movements of the convoy with the varied repetitions of the word "quelqu'un." The narrator subsequently digresses to insert Lucie's impression of this novel experience and then concludes: "C'est ... là, dans ce vagabondage organisé, que se développe le plus à l'aise le caractère et l'esprit des Asiatiques" (NA: p. 313). The spirit of this Oriental caravan pervades the narrative.

The small descriptive paragraphs, which are interspersed between the portraits of the fellow travellers, may be compared to scenic twentieth-century postcards. Lyric passages portray the trip which takes Valerio and Lucie to Constantinople, then from Constantinople to Trabzon "la porte de l'Asie," to the valleys of the Taurus, to Erzurum, and to the mountains of Armenia and Kurdistan. The narrator is most enthusiastic about the natural scenery and the native inhabitants. The cities themselves are of little interest: "Trébizonde n'a en soi rien de bien curieux" (NA: p. 299). "Erzeroum n'est pas une ville attrayante" (NA: p. 303). But as for the untamed natural beauty of the mountains and valleys and the ruins of Byzantine fortresses, "L'Europe n'a jamais connu rien de pareil" (NA: p. 300). This final phrase is indicative of Gobineau's attitude throughout the narrative: since he feels that Europeans generally travel to find what is similar to their culture elesewhere, he purposely emphasizes only those aspects which are not common to Occidental culture and landscape.

The selection of the descriptive passages and the personalities to be included in the narrative apparently was governed by the relation of those vignettes to two predominant themes: the art of travel and the criticism of the European bourgeois and his culture.

The art of travelling with any degree of perception is a gift reserved for the chosen minority. After a brief dramatic introduction the narrator explains: "Savoir voyager n'est pas plus l'affaire de tout le monde que savoir aimer, savoir comprendre et savoir sentir" (NA: p. 292). For those who instinctively know how to appreciate the landscapes they visit and the people they meet, the highest degree of pleasure is to be found in travelling. The Count de P. explains the charms of the errant life to Valerio and Lucie as he sends them on their mission: "Pendant quelques mois, vous n'aurez rien à faire qu'à marcher devant vous, où vous voudrez, comme vous voudrez, vite ou lentement; rien ni personne ne vous presse. J'ai connu cette vie; et je la pleure éternellement. C'est la seule et unique qui soit digne d'un être pensant" (NA: p. 297). The traveller Sèyd-Abdourrahman is even more categorical in praise of his kind of life. When questioned as to the fruits of his many exhausting journeys he replies: "...d'abord j'ai évité les fatigues bien plus grandes de la vie sédantaire, un métier, la société permanente des imbéciles, l'inimitié des grands, les soucis de la propriété, une maison à conduire, des domestiques à morigéner, une femme à supporter, des enfants à élever. Voilà ce dont je suis quitte; n'est-ce rien?" (NA: p. 322). The silent acquiescence of his interlocutors seems to confirm the justice of Sèyd's position. The traveller is constantly broadening his horizons without the daily worries which accompany the establishment of a fixed household.

Especially turbulent and exciting is the participation in an Oriental caravan. Towards the end of the narrative Gobineau concludes this theme as follows:

> On peut donc s'expliquer que lorsque les hommes ont goûté une fois de ce genre d'existence, ils n'en peuvent plus subir un autre. Amants de l'imprévu, ils le possèdent, ou plutôt s'abandonnent à lui du soir au matin, et du matin jusqu'au soir; avides d'émotions, ils en sont abreuvés; curieux, leurs yeux sont constamment en régal; inconstants, ils n'ont pas le temps même de se lasser de ce qui les quitte; passionnés enfin pour la sensation présente, ils sont débarrassés à la fois des ombres du passé, qui ne sauraient les suivre dans leur évolution incessante, et encore bien plus des préoccupations de l'avenir écrasées sous la présence impérieuse de ce qui est là. (NA: p. 333)

In this well-balanced paragraph Gobineau sums up the qualities which he admires and which he probably feels to be his own. The eager and happy traveller is then one who lives in the present, a kind of dilettante eager for new sensations and new discoveries, and not overly reluctant to leave one revelation to uncover another.

The corollary to this theme is an expression of scorn for those who are unable to appreciate this type of errant existence: the European bourgeois. The narrator first introduces this secondary theme, which is subsequently picked up by the various members of the caravan. As the narrator describes the ship which takes Valerio and Lucie from Naples to Constantinople, he is unable to conceal his disdain for the other European passengers, "...un bon groupe de ces excellents animaux, que la mode chasse tous les printemps de leurs étables, pour les emmener faire, comme ils disent, un voyage en Orient. Ils vont en Orient et ils en reviennent, ils n'en sont pas plus sages au retour... Les paysages ne ressemblant ni à la Normandie, ni au Somersetshire, ne leur paraissent que ridicules" (NA: p. 292). Kerbelay-Houssein, the caravan master, criticizes the Europeans for their dishonesty: "Il paraît que vous autres Européens, vous êtes de grands voleurs, car vos négociants se demandent constamment des gages les uns aux autres" (NA: p. 306). By mocking Western business methods Kerbelay indirectly praises his own probity; similarly he defends the Oriental *laissez-aller* by accusing the Europeans of constantly rushing about. He is very critical of European women who are unable to adapt themselves to the exigencies of caravan life. One mule, he explains to Valerio, serves as a mount for two Asian women and half a dozen small children. "Mais vos femmes sont trop raffinées; vous leur apprenez tant de choses, vous les gâtez si fort, qu'il est impossible de les traiter de cette façon-là" (NA: pp. 307-08).

Kerbelay's criticisms arise from the practical view-point of his position as caravan master. The comments of the philosophic Sèyd, comments which Valerio never strongly refutes, are much more serious. Sèyd explains that he has never visited the countries of Europe, "ces pays du diable" (NA: p. 324), because Western society has no place except prison for the penniless traveller. In order to prove Asian superiority he makes the following statement which Valerio finds quite accurate: "Je ne me suis jamais étonné, effendum, de voir ce que vous avez dû observer comme moi, vu que ceux de vos Européens qui viennent demeurer au milieu de nous, ne peuvent plus s'en détacher, prennent vite nos habitudes et nos moeurs, tandis qu'on n'a jamais cité un des nôtres qui eût la moindre envie de rester dans vos territoires et de s'y établir" (NA: p. 325). Although no reservation is expressed, Sèyd must be referring to the rare Europeans who know how to travel, for the narrator has previously indicated that the large majority of Europeans are incapable of appreciating the customs and culture of the Near East. Sèyd categorically condemns all Europeans as incapable of art, philosophy and literature: "De tout ceci il résulte que l'Europe ne saurait exercer aucun attrait sur les natures délicates, et c'est pourquoi je vous répète que jamais un galant homme n'y met les pieds" (NA: p. 326). Even though Sèyd has been introduced as a wise man, his lack of tolerance and his blanket statements diminish the force of his arguments.

The story line, chronologically presented, is extremely simple: Valerio and Lucie Conti join a caravan in order to carry out a mission for a Byzantine prince; after several weeks Lucie's psychological crisis makes their return necessary. The point of view is consistently that of Lucie; she is present during all of the scenes except those between Valerio and Kerbelay-Houssein and she probably obtains an account of those conversations from her husband.

This plot occupies six out of forty-five pages, the remainder of the narrative consisting of the numerous vignettes of personalities and scenes. At this juncture a serious question must be raised: does such a minimal plot allow the narrative to be actually considered as a *nouvelle,* as a short story? Complexities of plot do not determine literary genre: the significant factor is the harmony of the artistic whole. The travelogue is a non-fiction form in which the narrator relates his experiences as a traveller; here the only unity required is in the person of the narrator even though the narrator himself and his reactions do not furnish the central point of interest. The short story, generally limited because of its length, focuses on a unique point of interest: either a plot, a character, an emotion, a locale or a strictly unified combination of these characteristics. Gobineau attempts to give this type of essential unity to "La Vie de voyage," thus distinguishing the story from his *Trois Ans en Asie,* through the invention of the character of Lucie (who probably owes many of her traits to the young Mrs. Gobineau who accompanied her husband on his first mission to Tehran). But even though Lucie is present as a quiet spectator during most of the narration, she is never directly tied into the "vignettes." Her crisis at the end of the narrative appears rather to have been added as a convenient means of terminating the story. Thus, structurally speaking, "La Vie de voyage" must be classified as a fictionalized travelogue rather than as a unified short story.

"La Chasse au caribou," "Akrivie Phrangopoulo," and "La Vie de voyage" exemplify three highly distinct methods of treating the same theme: the visit of a European to a foreign country. Not only do the countries differ, but the reaction of the European representative determines the tone of the narrative.

In each narrative the foreign cultures, though different, are presented in a favorable light. The Greek society of Naxos is characterized by extreme formality and reserve. The closeness of the family group is in no way violated by the generous hospitality of the inhabitants. Altough the people of Newfoundland manifest a similar warmth in hospitality, the dynamism of the pioneers contrasts sharply with the calm aristocracy of the Greeks: heavy-set, vociferous Barton is the direct opposite of thin, quiet Monsieur Phrangopoulo. The Near East caravan is composed of a variety of characters, varying from the outspoken Kerbelay to the reserved Redjèb.

Just as Gobineau is generous in praise of other cultures, he is quick to criticize the French. The British and Italian, represented by Norton and Lucie Conti, are able to appreciate the attractive features of the lands they visit. Lucie's melancholy is a psychological reaction; during the entire journey she eagerly observes and learns about the customs of the Orient. Charles Cabert, whose position in the narrative is that of an anti-hero rather than a hero, typifies the Europeans whom the narrator of "La Vie de voyage" ridicules by comparing them to "animals" on an annual migration. Norton's reaction to Naxos and its people is one of attraction and love. Lucie appreciates the Near East, while acknowledging the existence of a certain mystery. Cabert sees only the superficial differences and completely lacks comprehension.

The technique of the narratives is basically similar in that all three incorporate a number of observations and excursions made by Gobineau the traveller. In "Akrivie Phrangopoulo" and "La Chasse au caribou" the protagonists discover the qualities of society incorporated in a lovely girl. The respective plots begin with an initial meeting scene in which the girl is observed from a distance. Subsequently the narrator transcribes direct conversations terminating in an engagement scene. Akrivie, who misinterprets Norton's request for her hand as a literal invitation to shake hands, runs away when she realizes the import of his statement. Lucy Barton misinterprets Cabert, but in the opposite sense, by giving deeper meaning to his words than is intended. In each case a brief denouement resolves the confusion.

The three narratives may be distinguished from each other mainly through their tone, which in a sense also reflects the personality of the protagonist. "La Chasse au caribou" is permeated with two levels of irony which correspond to Cabert's attitude towards America and to the narrator's opinion of Cabert. Norton's sentimental attraction to the simplicity and natural beauty of Naxos is reflected in the lyrical tone of "Akrivie Phrangopoulo." "La Vie de voyage" is predominately descriptive, for Lucie was interested in novelty. Of these "La Chasse au caribou" is the story in which Gobineau, by avoiding an oversaturation of the travelogue form, created a fictional work which could stand on its literary merits as well as its documentary value. Only minor inconsistencies, such as the shifting point of view, bar the story from being considered a masterpiece among the French ironical short stories.

Chapter VI

A PERSIAN "CANDIDE"

In "La Guerre des Turcomans" Gobineau experimented with a type of story he had never before considered: a highly interpretive autobiographical narrative. Certain stories, such as "Adélaïde" and "Le Mouchoir rouge," did require some interpretation on the part of the reader. All the stories were told by a narrator who was never totally absent from his narration. But not until 1874 in Stockholm, where Gobineau composed the final stories for his *Nouvelles asiatiques,* did he combine these two techniques, interpretive style and first-person narration, with undeniable efficacity. The feigned naiveté of the narrator and the simplicity of the style have led critics to compare this story to a Voltarian philosophic tale.[1] Gobineau himself, though flattered by such criticism, was not altogether pleased. In a letter to Marie Dragoumis he mentions the comparison and adds: "Ce sont de grands mots, mais je n'y tiens pas dans l'idée que ce que je fais m'appartient à moi seul, bien et mal compris" (LDA: p. 189).

Ghoulam-Hussein, more familiarly known as Baba-Aga, marries his cousin Leïla and leaves the small village in the Khamsèh province to establish his household in the capital city of Zendjân. Since he finds himself without a protector, he is soon pressed into military service. Sadly he arranges a divorce with Leïla and leaves for Tehran to join his regiment. Aga and his

---

[1] For example, see: Alain, 206; Seillière, p, 4; Souday, pp. 19, 22; Charles Vildrac, "Sur les 'Nouvelles asiatiques,'" *Europe,* III, no. 9 (1923), 97.

fellow conscripts, having discovered the pleasant features of sedentary military life, are quite reluctant to leave their post and engage in an expedition against the Turkomans. Lacking provisions and leadership, those troops which do not perish of malnutrition or under enemy fire are captured. Eventually the Persian authorities ransom Aga and his regiment, but once repatriated the soldiers are put in chains. At the end of the narrative, Aga optimistically reports that he is anticipating a promotion to the rank of major, or perhaps colonel.

Baba-Aga, who narrates the story, possesses many of the character traits of Gambèr-Aly, traits typical of the lower classes of Persian society. Both protagonists manifest the same attitude towards money, the same lively imagination and tendency towards exaggeration, and the same propensity for oaths and colorful speech. In Zendjân, when Aga discovers the magical charms whose presence explains his infatuation with Leïla, he is especially upset about the loss of the money he earned as a hunter: "... je regrettais amèrement mes trente tomans dont il ne me restait guère, et cela me rendit songeur et morose." (NA: p. 189) Not only does he value his own possessions, but he exhibits no scruples in falsely obtaining money from others. En route to Tehran he and two friends pose as tax collectors to pocket bribes from the peasants. Once in the capital he learns to lend small sums at a high rate of interest. He himself explains his system: "Je n'accordais que des prêts très petits et je voulais des remboursements très prompts. Tant de prudence était absolument nécessaire, elle me réussissait assez. Cependant, il m'arrivait aussi d'avoir affaire à des débiteurs dont je ne pouvais rien obtenir; pour contrebalancer ces inconvénients, j'empruntais moi-même et ne rendais pas toujours" (NA: p. 199). This concept of finance reveals a kind of detachment incomprehensible to an industrialized society; each Persian tries to obtain what he can, and wealth is the result of ingenuity. Towards the end of the narrative, Aga explains how the released prisoners were forced to repay their ransoms; he concludes: "Seulement, il fallait que chacun de nous prît garde à ses petites recettes, car soit nous-mêmes, soit not soldats, nous ne pensions naturellement qu'à nous emparer de ce qui n'était pas à nous" (NA: p. 231). Thus Aga expresses a Persian philosophy of life which was only hinted at in "Gambèr-Aly."

Aga exhibits less gratuitous imagination than Gambèr, but a similar tendency to exaggerate. When he wishes to borrow Kérym's "koulydhèh" or embroidered tunic he laments: "... je suis un homme perdu, ruiné, abondonné de l'univers entier et sans personne qui prenne le moindre souci de mes peines" (NA: p. 193). In an effort to obtain charity as a released prisoner, he cries out: "J'ai une pauvre mère aveugle, les deux soeurs de mon père sont estropiées, ma femme est paralytique et mes huit enfants expirent de misère" (NA: p. 232). On meeting his cousin Souleyman in Meshed, Aga passes himself off as a captain rather than a simple enlisted man; later when the cousin introduces him to several friends he presents Aga as "major du régiment de Khamsèh, un héros des anciens temps" (NA: p. 210). This desire to acquire increased social stature in the eyes of others parallels a penchant for amplifying one's emotions. Aga's protestation of love tends toward the ridiculous: "... je souffre, j'expire, je meurs, je suis mort, on m'a enterré, tu ne me verras plus!" (NA: p. 186). [2]

Like Gambèr, Aga expresses no compunction or guilt about making false promises. While trying to borrow Kérym's outfit he swears, "Par ta tête! Par mes yeux! Par la vie de Leïla! Par mon salut! Puissé-je être brûlé comme un chien maudit pendant toute l'éternité, si tu n'as pas ton habit avant même de l'avoir désiré!" (NA: p. 193). Here Aga manifests what in Gobineau's eyes is a characteristic Persian attitude: oaths are not really taken seriously, for often religion has ceased to be matter of conscience.

Aga, however, differs from Gambèr in that he is more generous and correspondingly less egocentric. He prefers the company of men to that of women; his friendship with his male cousins transcends momentary feelings of jealousy over Leïla. When Kérym slashes him across the face during a dispute, he refuses to let the police seize his cousin. He explains: "J'aimais beaucoup Kérym et infiniment plus que Leïla, et j'aurais été désolé qu'il lui arrivât malheur pour une méchante histoire..." (NA: pp. 189-

---

[2] His words echo Harpagon's monologue in *L'Avare* at the moment when the miser discovers the loss of his strongbox: "C'en est fait, je n'en puis plus; je me meurs, je suis enterré!" (Molière, *Théâtre complet*, ed. Robert Jouanny, Paris: Garnier, 1960, II, 302).

90). In Meshed he comforts Souleyman by inventing touching details concerning Leïla's supposed death. Aga, moreover, does not exhibit Gamber's cowardice; during the battle with the Turkomans he stands his ground and only surrenders upon realizing that failure to conclude a truce would be pointless suicide.

Aga's fluctuating attitude towards women gives an added dimension to his personality. Since many of his statements about women, and especially about Leïla, appear to be contradictory, the reader must interpret Aga's real feelings. His pessimism is the result of deceived idealism, for as a young man he found himself truly in love with his beautiful cousin. In retrospect he considers his emotional involvement with an air of bitterness: "J'aurais donc été un homme extrêmement content de son sort... si, tout à coup, je n'étais devenu amoureux, ce qui gâta tout" (NA: p. 185). He endeavors to explain that his infatuation was the effect of colored threads which Leïla had sewn in his cap; once he has destroyed the talisman he relates: "... je ne me souciais pas plus de Leïla que de la première venue" (NA: p. 189). The derogatory remarks, however, are outweighed by Aga's positive statements; upon considering her financial maneuverings he exclaims: "La vérité est que c'est la perle des femmes" (NA: p. 188). At the moment of his forced divorce even though he realizes that Leïla is also attracted to his other cousins, and they to her, he writes: "La vérité est que Leïla et moi nous nous adorions, et jamais le Dieu tout-puissant n'a créé et ne saura créer une femme plus attachée et plus fidèle" (NA: p. 192). Returning to Tehran in chains, Aga is freed by Leïla's generosity. He learns that she has now married his cousin Abdoullah, a successful merchant, and that he must henceforth consider her only as a relative. Aga adds: "Pour mon malheur, je la trouvai plus jolie que jamais, plus saisissante, et j'avais des larmes qui me gonflaient le coeur" (NA: p. 234). Much as he tries to denounce Leïla, much as he strives to convince himself that his love died once the talisman was removed, he unconsciously allows his true sentiments to appear. Far from denigrating love, he even pities the Turkomans who have never experienced such a passion. These complex attitudes render Aga a much more convincing person than Gambèr.

The contemporary psychologist might classify Aga's personality as a variant of the authoritarian syndrome. His view of society is definitely hierarchial. He is submissive toward authority and tries to ingratiate himself with his commanding officers: "Je prenais soin de me rendre agréable à mes supérieurs; je me présentais quelquefois chez le colonel; je me montrais empressé auprès du major; j'étais, j'ose le dire, l'ami du sultan; le nayb me faisait des confidences; je cultivais constamment la bienveillance du vékyl, à qui je présentais souvent des petits cadeaux...." (NA: p. 199). He believes in a Supreme Being whose ways are often inexplicable. He demonstrates disdain and insolence towards those he considers his inferiors, for example, the Turkoman women: "Ces femmes sont stupides, méchantes, brutales et ne savent que travailler, mais aussi on les fait travailler comme des mules, et on a raison" (NA: p. 222). Yet, in spite of such characteristics, it would be premature to classify Aga as an authoritarian. He does apparently manifest many traits of such a submissive personality; but here, too, it must be remembered that the narrative is an interpretive one. It is rather to be surmised that Aga is trying to create a deceptive impression of himself, for he is an intelligent, clever fellow. He tries to please his superiors so that he can lead his own life without interference. A hedonist rather than a rebel or reformer, his belief in Allah frees him of any responsibility for striving to better his own situation and the position of his countrymen.

Since Aga is narrating this autobiographical sketch, it is he who characterizes himself. Gobineau has maintained a strict first-person point of view; the other characters are presented only as they appear to Aga. As we have already seen, Aga wishes to give the impression of extreme simplicity, through statements and tone. Speaking of his love for his cousin he employs the unsophisticated device of simple repetition: "... je pensais tant et tant et tant à Leïla" (NA: p. 185). When accepting the truce offered by the Turkomans he naively expresses the assumption that his company will be permitted to return to Meshed. Later, when the ransomed prisoners are about to enter that city, the soldiers request them to put on chains in order to excite the pity and charity of the populace; Aga writes: "Nous trouvâmes cette idée excellente et nous en fûmes charmés" (NA: p. 228). Apparently he wishes the reader to believe that not one of the ex-prisoners imagined that the chains were of a more permanent nature. This interpretive narration allows Gobineau to attain a high degree of humor and irony.

Leïla is introduced at the age of fourteen as she is encouraging Aga's love in order to obtain a marriage proposal. However, her affection is not reserved uniquely for Aga, but is also directed towards her other cousins, Kérym, Souleyman and Abdoullah. Only Aga possesses the necessary dowry, so she chose to marry him: a Persian woman gains her independence through marriage. When Aga finds himself conscripted, she accepts the divorce and marries Kérym. Kérym, falling victim to a propensity for "raky," often termed "thé froid," finds himself unable to support a wife; consequently Leïla marries her cousin, Abdoullah, by then a successful businessman. She later explains to Aga: "J'avoue que je t'ai beaucoup aimé et que je t'aime encore; mais aussi je n'ai pas été insensible aux bonnes qualités de Souleyman; la gaîté et l'entrain de Kérym m'ont ravie, et je suis pleine d'estime et d'attendrissement pour les mérites d'Abdoullah. Si l'on me demandait de déclarer quel est celui de mes quatre cousins que je préfère, je demanderais que des quatre on pût faire un seul homme; et celui-là, je suis bien sûre que je l'aimerais passionnément et pour toujours" (NA: pp. 234-235). Although Leïla thinks primarily of her own material comfort, she does not wish to hurt any of her cousins. Marriage for her is an economic bond and not primarily a sentimental one. In Persia divorce was a simple matter; one had only to declare before the mullah his intention to separate from his wife and the marriage was thereby terminated. When Leïla is married to Aga she invites Kérym to live with them; when she sees Aga in chains she encourages Abdoullah to pay the necessary ransom money. Leïla appears as a woman concerned with her own welfare, a woman susceptible to comradeship but incapable of passion.

Leïla is characterized through Aga's inconsistent comments and through transcribed conversations. The first conversation takes place in the forest where Aga accuses her of dalliance with the other cousins. Leïla kisses him and replies: "Pardonne-moi, ma lumière, j'ai eu tort, mais je te jure par tout ce qu'il y a de plus sacré, par Aly, par les Imams, par le Prophète, par Dieu, par ta tête, que je ne recommencerai plus, et la preuve que je te tiendrai parole, c'est que tu vas tout de suite me demander en mariage à mon père! Je ne veux pas d'autre maître que toi et je serai à toi, tous les jours de ma vie" (NA: p. 186). When Gambèr and Aga reinforce a statement with a series of oaths, they generally have no intention of keeping their word. Leïla's conversation also follows this pattern. She is attracted to Aga for economic reasons, because in Persia it is the young man who offers a dowry to the bride's father. When Aga asks if his uncle would accept a promissory note, Leïla replies: "Comment veux-tu que mon père donne pour rien une fille aussi jolie que moi? Il faut être raisonnable" (NA: p. 187). This egotism revealed in her words is complemented by a sharp business acumen. Leïla explains to Aga how to handle the dowry: "... Maintenant va trouver mon père et demande-moi à lui. Tu lui en promettras sept [tomans], et tu lui en donneras cinq, en lui jurant que tu lui apporteras les deux autres plus tard. Il ne les verra jamais. Pour moi, je saurai bien lui en arracher deux que je te rapporterai et, de cette façon-là, je ne t'aurai coûté que trois tomans" (NA: p. 188). In this first conversation Leïla is so well characterized that later conversations and the final scene in which she explains her affections are effectively prepared.

Aga's cousins exhibit an innate kindness and generosity of sentiment. Kérym is a humorous fellow who relinquishes his new tunic to Aga even though he himself had planned to wear it to his wedding. Souleyman welcomes Aga into his home when the latters is ragged after the long march from Tehran; later, he generously contibutes to Aga's ransom upon seeing his cousin in chains. Abdoullah is a meticulous businessman but gladly furnishes the money necessary to free Aga. In spite of a mutual love for Leïla the cousins suppress jealous feelings and retain a vigorous sentiment of family unity.

Into the narrative are woven a variety of themes: a portrait of Persian society, a caricature of its army, and a light anti-European sentiment, all tempered with a happy-go-lucky philosophy.

In "La Guerre des Turcomans" the Persian middle-class so colorfully described in "L'Histoire de Gambèr-Aly" acquires the added dimension of the military. As Aga sets out for Tehran the sergeant whom he encounters en route explains to him the financial position of the simple foot soldier. "Fais-toi maçon; il est forgeron, notre ami Khourshyd; moi, je suis cardeur de laine. Tu me donneras un quart de ta solde; le sultan aura la moitié, en sa qualité de capitaine; tu feras de temps en temps un petit cadeau au nayb ou lieutenant, qui n'est pas trop fin, mais non plus pas méchant; le colonel, naturellement, prend le reste, et tu vivras comme un roi avec ce que tu gagneras" (NA: p. 194). Aga accepts this condition philosophically: "Ce n'est rien que de perdre sa solde, et, au fond, puisque les vizirs mangent les généraux, j'avoue qu'il me paraît naturel que ceux-ci mangent les colonels qui, à leur tour, vivent des majors, ceux-ci des capitaines et les capitaines de leurs lieutenants et des soldats" (NA: p. 195). The financial structure explains many events of the narrative, for both Aga's moments of happiness and his days of physical suffering indirectly stem from this aspect of Persian political and military life.

Aga is forced into service, which in Persia is a lifetime occupation, because he has no protector to influence officials in his favor. Once in Tehran he avoids training periods, drills and guard duty by bribing and flattering his superiors. Conversely, the march to Meshhed is rigorous; mules and soldiers die of hunger and thirst. Aga comments: "Il serait injuste de cacher que l'auguste gouvernement nous avait annoncé que nous serions fort bien nourris pendant toute la campagne. Mais personne n'y avait cru. Ce sont de ces choses que les augustes gouvernements disent tous, mais qu'il leur est impossible d'exécuter. Le général en chef ne va jamais s'amuser à dépenser, pour faire bonne chère aux soldats, son argent qu'il peut garder dans sa poche" (NA: pp. 204-205). During the march many soldiers become so weak that they throw away their packs and munitions; consequently at Meshed the men must take up a collection to appease the major and to buy additional arms. During the actual battle conditions are worse. "Pour la poudre, la question restait difficile. En partant de Meshed, on ne nous en avait guère donné. Les généraux l'avaient vendue" (NA: p. 215). After three days of fighting the remaining troups capitulate to the Turkomans. Learning of the defeat, the Shah accuses the generals of incompetence and threatens to have them executed. However, "... le Roi eut des présents magnifiques, et il fut résolu que les chefs rachèteraient tous les soldats captifs chez les Turcomans, et les rachèteraient à leurs frais, puisqu'ils étaient cause du malheur arrivé à ces pauvres diables" (NA: p. 227). Once the soldiers leave the Turkoman camp they are kept in chains until they are able to solicit not only the ten tomans paid to their captors but also an additional five tomans. Aga adds: "... la charité des Musulmans nourrissait les pauvres captifs mieux qu'elle ne l'avait fait jadis pour les soldats du Roi" (NA: p. 231).

Guided by such financial matters, the generals manifest little interest in their profession. Many are mere adolescents, the sons of influential families. They possess no concept of the methods of warfare and are present only to review the troops. Aga describes the "état-major" in this manner: " 'Tamasha,' comme on sait, c'est tout ce qui sert à faire un beau spectable.... De très jolis jeunes gens, habillés le mieux possible, montés sur de beaux chevaux, se mettent à courir ventre à terre, de tous les côtés; ils vont, ils viennent, ils retournent; c'est ravissant à voir" (NA: p. 202). During the actual encounter, however, the commanding officers remain in Meshed. Aga comments: "Il paraît que c'est absolument nécessaire ainsi; parce que de loin on dirige mieux que de près. Les colonels avaient imité les généraux, sans doute pour la même raison. En somme, nous avions peu d'officiers au-dessus du grade de capitaine, et c'est très à propos, attendu que les officiers ne sont pas faits pour se battre, mais pour toucher la paye des soldats" (NA: p. 211). Despite the incompetence of generals and the lack of discipline among the troops, the Persian Army is not totally ineffective. As would be expected, many do flee at the first sign of battle and are quickly captured by the enemy. Those who stand together are able to resist the attack, for what the soldiers lack in training they offset with enthusiasm: "Nous étions au comble de la joie; nous étions délivrés et nous n'avions peur de rien" (NA: p. 213). That evening the seven hundred soldiers remaining out of the seven thousand who set out from Meshed discover a natural fortification and prepare to withstand attack. When the lieutenant and sergeant who take command are killed the second day, Aga assumes command. The soldiers would readily have given their lives to defend the promontory, until they realize the irrationality of such a stand.

The Persians, especially the simple footsoldiers, manifest a strong national spirit. When Aga is a prisoner, he exclaims: "Je sais bien qu'il se passe assez de vilaines choses dans l'Iran, et qu'on y trouve bien du mal; pourtant, c'est l'Iran, et c'est le meilleur, le plus saint pays de la terre. Nulle part au monde on n'éprouve autant de plaisir ni autant de joie. Quand on y a vécu, on y veut retourner; et quand on y est, on y veut mourir" (NA: p. 225). [3] For Aga this nationalism is coupled with a sentiment of xenophobia; the Turkomans are considered heretics and "chiens maudits" (NA: p. 213).

The criticism of Europeans generally bears on their methods of developing an army. Not only does European discipline make of the soldiers "des bêtes de somme" but drill is such that men are reduced to the status of machines (NA: p. 196). The Europeans are criticized for insisting that the enlisted men stay in the barracks at night and that they relieve each other at guard duty at regularly established intervals. "Ils ne savent qu'inventer pour tourmenter le pauvre soldat" (NA: p. 196). Admittedly the European methods can win a war, but for Aga the freedom of the soldier is more important.

After explaining how he tricks his Turkoman mistress, Aga comments: "J'ai toujours remarqué que les gens les plus forts sont toujours les moins intelligents. Ainsi voyez les Européens! On les trompe tant que l'on veut, et, partout où ils vont, ils s'imaginent qu'ils sont supérieurs à nous, parce qu'ils sont les maîtres; ils ne savent pas et ne sauront jamais apprécier cette vérité que l'esprit est au-dessus de la matière" (NA: p. 223). When Aga explains the Persian etymology of the word "état-major" or "tamasha," he digresses to denigrate the Europeans, "dont les langages sont aussi absurdes que l'esprit" (NA: p. 202). Aga expresses his gratitude for this lack of intelligence: "Heureuse-

---

[3] *Romans et contes*, ed. Henri Bénac (Paris: Garnier, 1958), p. 141.

ment le ciel, en les créant très brutaux, les fait au moins aussi bêtes, de sorte que, généralement, on leur peut persuader tout ce qu'on veut. Gloire à Dieu, qui a donné ce moyen de défense aux Musulmans!" (NA: p. 196). Aga's only word of praise for European methods concerns guaranteed wages, but the inconveniences of discipline, in his eyes, render this too large a price to pay for such small benefits.

Aga's fellow Iranian officer, who has received his degree from Saint Cyr, understands the basic reason for the conflict between Europeans and Persians. Concerning the former, he states: "... ce sont des niais, ils ne comprennent pas que tout chez nous, les habitudes, les moeurs, les intérêts, le climat, l'air, le sol, notre passé, notre présent rendent radicalement impossible ce qui, chez eux, est le plus simple" (NA: p. 236). Aga himself fails to realize that the Persian system would appear equally ridiculous to a European.

The motif which unifies the narrative is Aga's straightforward philosophy. Realizing that all is not perfect in the world, he loves Iran in spite of the many aspects which displease him. This generosity toward country and countrymen permeates the narrative. As a youth, Aga in all simplicity offers his love to Leïla. Later in Tehran he studies under a philosopher, whose lectures he interprets as follows: "... je commençai à comprendre, ce que je n'avais pas fait jusque-là, que tout va de travers dans le monde. Il est incontestable que les empires sont gouvernés par d'horribles coquins, et si on mettait à tous ces gens-là une balle dans la tête, on ne ferait que leur rendre justice; mais, à quoi bon? Ceux qui viendraient après seraient pires. Gloire à Dieu qui a voulu, pour des raisons que nous ne connaissons pas, que la méchanceté et la bêtise conduisissent l'univers!" (NA: p. 200). This is the pessimism of a disillusioned idealist, of a Candide, but a pessimism tempered with Oriental submission to God's will. The narrative resounds with ejaculations praising God's foresight, and submitting to his will. The first paragraph ends with a statement of confidence in Allah: "Mais Dieu dispose de tout ainsi qu'il lui plaît!" (NA: p. 184). Aga terminates his story with the Persian qualifying phrase "Inshallah! Inshallah!" (if God be willing), a phrase which often recurs during the narration. Aga does not conscientiously practice his faith, but he would never deny that his Islam religion represents a distinct part of the Persian cultural heritage.

Consequently, even though God's will appears absurd, even though life is far for from what he would desire, Aga rarely complains. When first drafted into service he explains: "... je réfléchis que je ne pouvais pas échapper à mon destin, et que, mon destin étant d'être soldat, il fallait s'y résigner et faire bonne mine" (NA: p. 191). He learns to adapt to life's vicissitudes and to discover the advantages of his present position without lamenting the loss of previous comforts.

During his first visit to Persia, Gobineau studied the attitudes and daily occupations of people in all walks of life; subsequently these observations were collected together in *Trois Ans en Asie* to form the basis of the chapter, "L'Etat des personnes." The lot of the soldier is briefly described:

> Jamais, au grand jamais, à moins d'événements extraordinaires, le soldat persan ne touche le solde que l'État est censé lui allouer... Mais le soldat, d'autre part, n'est pas astreint à beaucoup de fatigues. Il ne va guère à l'exercice, l'été parce qu'il fait trop chaud, l'hiver parce qu'il fait trop froid... il s'installe dans son corps de garde à demeure et en est absent à peu près toute le journée... S'il sait un métier, il l'exerce et sur ses gains prélève de quoi faire des cadeaux à ses officiers...; enfin, dans la mesure de son intelligence, il s'organise une position aussi agréable que possible. (TA: pp. 406-407)

In time of combat, however, the pleasant situation of the soldiers disintegrates, "leur sort devient bien triste" (TA: p. 408). Gobineau explains: "L'intendance n'existant pas en Perse, ils n'ont ni chaussures, ni vêtements, ni armes, ni vivres. Souvent ils sont réduits à manger l'herbe sur la route, là où il y a de l'herbe" (TA: p. 408). In "La Guerre des Turcomans," written fifteen years later, Gobineau develops these aspects of Persian garrison life and of the military campaigns in greater detail by letting Aga narrate his experiences in a spirit of total detachment. Aga himself fits Gobineau's description of the typical Persian soldier: "Il est toujours doux, timide et gai. Qeulquefois, quand il souffre trop, il s'insurge; mais pour peu qu'on donne satisfaction à ses exigences, le plus souvent très-justes, il rentre aussitôt dans le devoir. Il est admirable d'intelligence, et je dirais aussi de courage..." (TA: p. 408).

The materials concerning the wars against the Turkoman tribes were collected during Gobineau's second mission in Tehran as Minister. In his official dispatches to Paris he describes the nature of the campaign. In 1863, an unsuccessful expedition against the invading tribes was undertaken in the vicinity of Meshed; although the incompetence of the commanding officers was responsible for the defeat, Gobineau remarks: "On se bornera, probablement, à exiger du général prisonnier qu'il se rachète lui-même avec ses soldats" (DD: p. 261). The narrative differs from the historical conflict in that the generals of Aga's expedition did not even accompany the troops. Details concerning the condition of the Persian army are scattered throughout the dispatches. Before the Meshed defeat, Gobineau had told the Shah "que l'armée persane, sans chefs, sans souliers, sans pain, sans armes, n'était pas une armée mais un ramas de mendiants" (DD: p. 222). The untrained soldiers generally fled without resistance and were immediately taken prisoner. Gobineau adds: "Je ne crois pas qu'on puisse estimer à moins de 12 millions de francs le taux des rançons payées aux Turcomans depuis... deux ans" (DD: pp. 261-262). The officers are usually young and inexperienced; Gobineau even recounts an unsuccessful maneuver conducted by a thirteen-year-old colonel (DD: p. 217).

Gobineau describes the Turkomans as essentially agricultural peoples who engaged in slave trade merely out of luxury rather than as a means of subsistence. Before the unsuccessful expeditions of Merv and Meshed, Gobineau in his dispatches mentions the existence of a simple means for suppressing the invaders: "Si par une opération que tous les renseignements montrent facile, la Perse coupait leurs canaux d'irrigation, ils seraient obligés de se rendre à merci" (DD: p. 174). It is probably to such a plan that allusion is made in the final scene of the narrative; the Saint-Cyr officer laments that he lives "sous le poids d'une suspicion incurable, parce qu'[il sait] comment on mène des troupes et ce qu'il faudrait faire pour venir à bout en trois mois des Turcomans de la frontière" (NA: p. 237).

In his dispatches Gobineau had also commented on the mutual distrust between the Persians and the Europeans. In 1862, he wrote: "Les Européens sont ici pour la plupart souvent hautains, toujours rapaces au-delà de toute expression. Les Persans leur opposent leur légèreté et leur improbité de détail ordinaires. Ils se plaignent becaucoup les uns des autres et ont, je crois, raison des deux parts" (DD: p. 170). Thus not only the events but also the attitudes find their models in Gobineau's diplomatic experience.

Of lesser degree and import are certain literary influences. As a young man, Gobineau had written an article praising Stendhal's *Chartreuse de Parme*. He especially singled out Stendhal's technique in describing the Battle of Waterloo through the eyes of Fabrice. For Aga, the "état-major" is a group of men galloping on horseback, just as colorful as the escort of Marshal Ney, but less effectual. The actual encounter with the Turkomans is narrated from the point of view of Aga, an individual participant.

The resemblance of "La Guerre des Turcomans" to a Voltairian *conte* has often been alluded to but never discussed in detail. The most evident similarity is the tone of detachment employed by both Aga and the narrator of *Candide*. Both cheerfully accept the miseries of malnutrition, the exaggerated physical punishments meted out by those in power, the injustices showered on the weak and defenseless. The experience of death is related just as impassively as any other event of human existence. For example, in describing the review of the troops in Tehran, Aga fails to differentiate between the colorful spectacle and the human tragedy: "Quand le Roi se fut amusé quelque temps à considérer ce tamasha, on voulut lui montrer comment on allait traiter les Turcomans, et pour cela on avait préparé une mine que l'on fit sauter. Seulement, on ne se donna pas le temps d'attendre que les soldats, aux environs, fussent avertis de se retirer, de sorte qu'on en tua trois ou quatre; sauf cet accident, tout alla très bien et on s'amusa beaucoup" (NA: pp. 203-204). The combat losses are also reported without emotion. In *Candide*, Voltaire writes: "Les canons renversèrent d'abord à peu pres six mille hommes de chaque côté; ensuite la mousqueterie ôta du meilleur des mondes environ neuf à dix mille coquins qui en infectaient la surface. La baïonette fut aussi la raison suffisante de la mort de quelques milliers d'hommes. Le tout pouvait bien se monter à une trentaine de mille âmes." [3] Aga narrates: "... nous vîmes qu'en tout nous pouvions être à peu près au nombre de 7 à 800. Ce n'était pas beaucoup sur 6 à 7.000 qui étaient sortis de Meshhed" (NA: p. 214).

Both works treat an identical theme: the inhumanity of warfare. As a corollary, both authors include humorous accounts of military training. Candide was forced into the Bulgarian army and heavily disciplined; Aga when conscripted manages, through his ingenuity, to avoid physical punishment: "On me jeta sur le dos; deux ferrashs, prenant les bouts du bâton me sountinrent les pieds en l'air, deux exécuteurs brandirent, d'un air féroce, chacun une poignée de verges et ils administrèrent au bâton auquel j'étais attaché une volée de flagellations, parce que je leur avais, en tombant, glissé à chacun un sahabgrân dans la paume de la main" (NA: p. 190). Once in the regiment Candide participates in military drills: "On le fait tourner à droite, à gauche, hausser la baguette, remettre la baguette, coucher en joue, tirer, doubler le pas...." [4] Aga complains about the methods of military training employed by the Europeans: "... ils nous feraient tous, sans distinction, venir sur la plaine au soleil l'été, à la pluie l'hiver, pour quoi faire? Pour lever et baisser les jambes, agiter les bras, tourner la tête à droite ou à gauche" (NA: p. 196). It is the narrator's tone of detachment and the ridiculing of European military discipline which have led to the frequent allusions to a similarity between Voltaire and Gobineau.

However, although Aga might be considered a Persian Candide, [5] he is not conceived in a truly Voltairian spirit, for in his story Gobineau expresses a greater love for his characters and creates a greater illusion of reality. Abel Bonnard considered "La Guerre des Turcomans" to be almost "... Voltaire en Asie, s'il [Gobineau] ne mêlait pas à sa curiosité malicieuse une sympathie pénétrante que Voltaire n'éprouva jamais." [6] This is a debatable

---

[4] Voltaire, p. 140.
[5] Janine Buenzod, "Gobiniana," *RHLF,* LXI (1961), 599.
[6] Bonnard, p. 206.

point since Voltaire did foreshadow Aga's gentle philosophy of acceptance in *Le Monde comme il va* (1748) published eleven years before *Candide*. At the end of the former tale, the angel Ituriel decides not to destroy Persepolis, "car, dit-il, *si tout n'est pas bien, tout est passable.*" [7] When Aga relates the rigorous march to Meshed during which many soldiers died, he adds: "Cela ne nous empêchait pas de chanter; car s'il fallait se désespérer des maux inséparables de la vie, mieux vaudrait n'être pas au monde, et, d'ailleurs, avec de la patience tout s'accommode" (NA: p. 205). The essential difference between the stories of Voltaire and "La Guerre des Turcomans" may be found in the realism of the latter. Aga is neither a symbol nor the representative of a given philosophical system; he is characterized as a unique individual. Moreover, unlike the characters in *Zadig*, Aga cannot be considered a European in Oriental disguise. Voltaire purposely destroys the illusion of reality in his tales so that the reader will become primarily concerned with its philosophical implication. Aga colors his narrative with light irony and feigned naiveté, but his story remains credible. As such it must be considered a realistic, rather than a philosophical tale.

"La Guerre des Turcomans" discloses a humorous portrait of nineteenth-century Persia, while reiterating a positive philosophical attitude. Aga is like Gobineau: behind his irony lies his love of Persia, behind his pessimism lies his love of life. The careful construction and consistent tone make this narrative one of Gobineau's masterpieces.

---

[7] Voltaire, p. 80.

Chapter VII

CONCLUSION

Even though we may consider Gobineau's short stories to be of unequal merit, we must admit that they are never dull and that, with the exception of his earlier works and parts of "Akrivie Phrangopoulo," they acquire added charm with each reading. According to Gobineau himself, such tangible merits are not to be scorned. He once explained to his sister: "Les oeuvres d'art sont faites pour plaire non seulement à l'esprit et au goût critique, mais avant tout au coeur, au tempérament, à ce que sont les gens qui les lisent, les voient ou les écoutent." [1] Gobineau's stories are definitely entertaining, but they have also proven themselves equal to the rigors of critical examination. Our analyses of the stories now permit us to define his narrative technique.

Gobineau's short stories fall into three periods: the *feuilletons* of 1843-1848, which include "Scaramouche" and "Mademoiselle Irnois," the *Souvenirs de voyage* (1872) and finally the *Nouvelles asiatiques* (1876). "Adélaïde," published posthumously, may be considered as a transition between the latter two works. His unfinished "La Cour d'Amour" furnishes a fleeting glimpse of what might well have become a fourth period. Although certain basic themes cut across these chronological divisions, the narrative technique shows a definite evolution toward objectivity, concision and a more consistent third-person point of view.

---

[1] "Sept Lettres du Comte Arthur de Gobineau à sa soeur," ed. A. B. Duff, *RLC*, XXIII (1949), 549.

CONCLUSION

In "Scaramouche" Gobineau gives the first expression to his concept of womanhood by creating two distinct character types. Doña Paula is the prototype of the forceful heroine, the woman who directs her energy to the domination of both family and environment. In the *Nouvelles asiatiques* most of the minor female characters, such as Zemroud and Bibi-Djânèm, may be considered loud and colorful variations of the dynamic heroine. The ideal feminine type, patterned after the transformed Rosetta, reinforces her gentle devotion and generosity with surprising physical stamina. Lucie Conti, Lucy Barton and Aliénor de Foy are the only female protagonists who exhibit a certain frailty, which, however, the former gradually overcome.

The male characters are generally the weaker. Chalais, Gobineau's first hero, suffers from lack of foresight. The humorously portrayed anti-hero can control neither his will nor his reactions. The positive protagonist becomes so "good" that he is often uninteresting, while the antagonist is delineated as a two-dimensional foil; although Jérome Lânza shows added complexity, he proves to be less astute than his goddaughter. Norton and Kassem attain stature through their inner conflicts, Akbar and Mohsèn through their courage and sense of honor. The most complex and perceptive hero is Aga, whose attitudes and ideas, reminiscent of Candide's, parallel Gobineau's in many respects: irony and detachment serve as shields to protect a deep-set love of Persia.

The basic theme which pervades all Gobineau's works is the identification of aristocracy; the characteristics of this elite, which for Gobineau are those of the pure Aryan, include energy, intelligence, will, and a sense of honor. The protagonists of works by Stendhal and Mérimée, authors whom Gobineau admired, exhibit similar traits. The corollary of such an attitude is a disdain for individuals who lack these qualities. Hence Parisian salon society and its values are subject to severe attack. The Gobinian hero attains his apogee in the experience of love; this passion, which overpowers the desire for knowledge, separates the elite from the rest of humanity.

Gobineau incorporated these themes into his stories in accordance with the belief that man exist only as a member of a given society:

> C'est parce que les hommes sont partout essentiellement différents que leurs passions, leurs vues, leur façon d'envisager eux-mêmes, les autres, les croyances, les intérêts, les problèmes dans lesquels ils sont engagés, c'est pour cela que leur étude présente un intérêt si varié et si vif, et qu'il est important de se livrer à cette étude, pour peu que l'on tienne à se rendre compte du rôle que les hommes, et non pas l'homme, remplissent au milieu de la création. C'est là ce qui donne à l'histoire sa valeur, à la poésie une partie de son mérite, au roman toute sa raison d'être (NA: pp. 6-7). [2]

He explicitly contrasts societies in some stories by introducing the representative of a European culture into a foreign country and recording the points of harmony and conflict. Other narratives present a realistic picture of Mediterranean and Oriental civilizations and allow the European to draw his conclusions as to similarities and differences between peoples. "La Guerre des Turcomans" even places the ironic comments in the autobiography of the Persian protagonist, without the narrator as intermediary.

For Gobineau, however, the short story was not primarily a philosophical enterprise, but an artistic creation. In 1873, he confided to Dom Pedro II of Brazil that his narratives represented "un moyen de peindre les moeurs et les idées de l'ancien monde oriental dans sa norme actuelle." [3] While composing the *Nouvelles asiatiques,* Gobineau also wrote enthusiastically to Prokesch: "Je crois vraiment avoir inventé une forme et un sentiment nouveau" (CP: 361). Evidently, he considered technique to be of at least equal importance to the content. This was an opinion he had expressed approximately three decades earlier in his critical article on Musset.

---

[2] Here Gobineau modifies the position he stated thirty years earlier (May 1845) in a critical article entitled "Une littérature nouvelle est-elle possible?" At that time he believed "...que la beauté suprême, comme la diversité, réside surtout dans l'homme, que toutes les modifications des temps, des moeurs, du culte, n'ajoutent à cette beauté ni n'en retranchent; que, pour l'art, l'homme ne cessera jamais d'être neuf, et que, comme tel, il est éternellement beau." Quoted in Ludwig Schemann, *Quellen und Untersuchungen zum Leben Gobineaus,* vol. 1 (Strasbourg: Trübner, 1914), p. 257.

[3] Raeders [toerffer], Georges, *D. Pedro II e o Conde de Gobineau (Correspondencia inédita),* (San Paulo: Companhia Editora Nacional, 1938), pp. 454-455.

In the short stories particular attention is given to the setting. In 1844, young Gobineau criticized the Romantic emphasis on *couleur locale* which he narrowly defined as bizarre vocabulary and over-burdened descriptions. "Ce fut alors qu'on inventa les choses qui ont du *caractère* et celles qui n'en ont pas. La distinction est facile à établir. Plus la forme d'un objet est éloginée de nos habitudes, et plus cet objet a du caractère. Ainsi une table du temps de Louis XIII a plus de caractère qu'une chaise de paille qui n'en a pas du tout; mais un divan turc en possède bien davantage, et un siège chinois est le *nec plus ultra*" (EC: p. 86). The locale in "Mademoiselle Irnois" reflects the influence of Balzac; the dullness of the apartment becomes an expresion of Monsieur Irnois' character. In the settings for his non-European stories, Gobineau follows Mérimée's lead by blending succinct exterior descriptions with colorful panoramas portraying individuals in their culture. Gobineau transforms the material in his travelogues by abridging the scenic passages and developing the anecdotes; the only narrative which failed to undergo this distillation is the somewhat verbose "Akrivie Phrangopoulo." Apparently with the projected *Nouvelles féodales,* Gobineau intended to return to the historical short story with which he had first experimented in "Le Mariage d'un Prince."

Two types of plots predominate. In the intricate plot, the desires of the protagonist conflict either internally or with those of another member of his family. In other narratives the plot is directional, centering on the character development of the protagonist or on a series of adventures. Generally Gobineau follows a chronological sequence in the presentation of relevant incidents. The later narratives differ from the earlier *feuilletons* primarily in their greater concision and tighter construction.

Gobineau as narrator is always present in his short stories, with the exception of the first-person account, "La Guerre des Turcomans." The narrator usually refers to himself as *je,* but frequently prefaces his remarks with the impersonal *on.* His presence is particularly obvious in the earlier narratives, "Le Mariage d'un Prince," "Scaramouche" and "Mademoiselle Irnois." In the later works, Gobineau often uses an interpretive third-person point of view. The weakness of certain narratives stems precisely from brief diversions in the point of view, diversions which occur when Gobineau the traveller interrupts to give an explanation, or when Gobineau the conversationalist-writer inserts an ironical remark.

The ever-present irony and a direct, almost classical style are the distinctive features of the short stories. In combining the themes of energy and aristocracy with accurate descriptions of countries and their cultures, Gobineau gave fictional reality to the experiences of his travels. Moreover, we may assume that the basic research for *Ottar Jarl* had uncovered a wealth of source material for the *Nouvelles féodales*. At the time of his death, Gobineau was engaged in a similar distillation of his historical studies into a group of narratives.

A SELECTED BIBLIOGRAPHY

ALAIN. "Gobineau romanesque," *NRF*, XLII (1934), 198-209.
BARBEY D'AUREVILLY, J. *Les Oeuvres et les hommes: les historiens.* 2ᵉ sér. Paris: Quantin, 1888.
——. *Voyageurs et romanciers.* Paris: Lemerre, 1908.
BELLIARD, PIERRE. "La France et les Mille et une Nuits," *Table Ronde*, Nos. 127-128 (1958), 104-112.
BÉZIAU, ROGER. "'La Cour d'Amour,' dernière nouvelle de Gobineau," *RHLF*, LXIII (1963), 652-666.
——. "Une Opinion inédite sur les cours d'Amour: 'La Cour d'Amour' de Gobineau," *Revue des Sciences Humaines*, fasc. 113 (1964), 67-78.
BLOCH-MICHEL, JEAN. "Mademoiselle Irnois d'Arthur de Gobineau," *Gazette de Lausanne*, 2-3 septembre 1961, 14.
BONNARD, ABEL. "Gobineau," *NRF*, XLII (1934), 179-184.
BUENZOD, JANINE. "Gobiniana," *RHLF*, LXI (1961), 592-599.
——. "Un Inédit de Gobineau," *Journal de Genève*, 16-17 décembre 1961, 1-2.
CARTELLIERI, ALEXANDER. *Gobineau.* Strasbourg: Trübner, 1917.
COCTEAU, JEAN. "Eloge des Pléiades," *NRF*, XLII (1934), 194-197.
COLIN, PAUL. "L'Ame de Gobineau," *Europe*, III, no. 9 (1ᵉʳ octobre 1923), 27-34.
DEGROS, M., ed. *Correspondance d'Alexis de Tocqueville et d'Arthur de Gobineau.* 2 vols. Paris: Gallimard, 1959.
DREYFUS, ROBERT. "Gobineau, qui est-ce?" *NRF*, XLII (1934), 161-168.
——. *La Vie et les prophéties du comte de Gobineau.* Paris: Cahiers de la Quinzaine, 1905.
DUFF, A. B. "En marge d'une 'Nouvelle asiatique,'" *Mercure de France*, CCCVII (1959), 684-702.
DUFRENOY, MARIE LOUISE. *L'Orient romanesque en France 1704-1789.* Montreal: Beauchemin, 1946.
Etudes Gobiniennes 1966. Paris: Klincksieck, 1966.
Etudes Gobiniennes 1967. Paris: Klincksieck, 1967.
FALK, REINHOLD. *Die weltanschauliche Problematik bei Gobineau.* Berlin: Norm-Druck, 1936.
FAY, BERNARD. "Les Légendes du Comte de Gobineau," *NRF*, XLII (1934), 169-178.
GAULMIER, JEAN. "Au Brésil, il y a un siècle...," *Bulletin de la Faculté des Lettres, Université de Strasbourg*, XLII, 483-498.
——. "Connaissance de Gobineau," *RLC*, XXXIV (1960), 602-609.

GAULMIER, JEAN. *Spectre de Gobineau*. Paris: Pauvert, 1965.
GOBINEAU, ARTHUR DE. *Les Conseils de Rabelais*, ed. A. B. Duff. Paris: Mercure de France, 1962.

———. "La Cour d'Amour," ed. R. Béziau, *Mercure de France*, CCCXI (1963), 260-299.

———. *Les Dépêches diplomatiques du Comte de Gobineau en Perse*, ed. A. Hytier. Geneva: Droz, 1959.

———. *Ecrit de Perse, treize lettres à sa soeur*, ed. A. B. Duff. Paris: Mercure de France, 1957.

———. *Essai sur l'inégalité des races humaines*. 5e éd. 2 vols. Paris: Firmin-Didot, n.d.

———. *Etudes critiques (1844-1848)*. Paris: Kra, 1927.

———. *Histoire des Perses*. 2 vols. Paris: Plon-Nourrit, 1869.

———. *Histoire d'Ottar Jarl, pirate norvégien*. Paris: Didier, 1879.

———. *Lettres à deux Athéniennes*, ed. N. Méla. Athens: Kauffmann, 1936.

———. "Lettres à Marie Dragoumis," *NRF*, XLII (1934), 276-288.

———. "Lettres de Gobineau à la comtesse de La Tour," ed. J. Mistler, *Table Ronde*, no. 28 (avril 1950), 36-46; no. 29 (mai 1950), 39-67.

———. *Lettres persanes*, ed. A. B. Duff. Paris: Mercure de France, 1957.

———. *Mademoiselle Irnois suivi de Adélaïde*, eds. A. B. Duff and F. R. Bastide. Paris: Gallimard, 1961.

———. "Le Mariage d'un Prince," ed. R. Guise, *NRF*, XIV (1966), 357-384.

———. *Le Mouchoir rouge et autres nouvelles*, ed. J. Gaulmier. Paris: Garnier, 1968.

———. *Nouvelles*. 2 vols. Paris: Pauvert, 1956.

———. *Nouvelles*, ed. J. Mistler. Paris: Hachette, 1961.

———. *Nouvelles asiatiques*, ed. J. Gaulmier. Paris: Garnier, 1965.

———. *Nouvelles asiatiques*, ed. Tancrède de Visan. Paris: Perrin, 1913.

———. "Nouvelles lettres athéniennes," ed. J. Mistler, *RdDM*, CXXIV (1954), 406-442.

———. *Les Pléiades*, ed. J. Mistler. Monaco: Editions du Rocher, 1946.

———. *Les Religions et les philosophies dans l'Asie Centrale*. Paris: Perrin, 1865.

———. *La Renaissance*, ed. J. Mistler. Monaco: Editions du Rocher, 1947.

———. "Sept Lettres du Comte Arthur de Gobineau à sa soeur," ed. A. B. Duff, *RLC*, XXIII (1949), 541-561.

———. *Souvenirs de voyage*, ed. J. Mistler. Monaco: Editions du Rocher, 1948.

———. *Stendhal par Gobineau*, ed. C. Simon. Paris: Champion, 1926.

———. *Trois Ans en Asie*. Paris: Hachette, 1859.

———. *Voyage à Terre-Neuve*. Paris: Hachette, 1861.

GOBINEAU, ARTHUR DE, AND MÈRE BÉNÉDICTE DE GOBINEAU. *Correspondance 1872-1882*, ed. A. B. Duff. 2 vols. Paris: Mercure de France, 1958.

"Gobineau et le mouvement gobiniste," *NRF*, XLII (1934), 289-310.

GOURMONT, RÉMY DE. *Promenades littéraires*. 2e sér. 5e éd. Paris: Mercure de France, 1913.

HENRIOT, EMILE. *Romanesques et romantiques*. Paris: Plon, 1930.

HYTIER, JEAN. "Gobineau peintre de l'Orient," *La Revue des Vivants*, VII (1933), 657-670.

HYTIER, JEAN. "Vie et mort de la tragédie religieuse persane," *Cahiers du Sud*, XXII, no. 175 (1935), 127-134.
JOURDA, PIERRE. *L'Exotisme dans la littérature française depuis Chateaubriand*. Vol. 1, Paris: Boivin, 1938; vol. 2, Paris: P.U.F., 1956.
KAUFMANN, JOSEF. *Gobineau und die Kultur des Abendlandes*. Duisburg: Duisburger Verlagsanstalt, 1902.
KRETZER, EUGEN. *Joseph Arthur Graf von Gobineau, sein Leben und sein Werk*. Leipzig: Seemann, 1902.
LACRETELLE, JACQUES DE. "Gobineau romancier: *Les Pléiades*," *Europe*, III, no. 9 (1923), 87-95.
LANGE, MAURICE. *Le Comte Arthur de Gobineau, étude biographique et critique*. Strasbourg: Istra, 1924.
MISTLER, JEAN. "Avec Gobineau, en Grèce," *Nouvelles Littéraires*, 31 août 1961, 6.
MORLAND, JACQUES. "Gobineau romancier (*Les Pléiades*)," *Mercure de France*, LV (mai-juin 1905), 5-21.
RAEDERSTOERFFER, GEORGES. *Le Comte de Gobineau au Brésil*. Paris: Nouvelles Editions Latines, 1934.
―――. *D. Pedro II e o Conde de Gobineau (Correspondencia inedita)*. San Paulo: Companhia Editora Nacional, 1938.
RIFFATERRE, MACHAEL. *Le Style des Pléiades de Gobineau*. New York: Columbia University Press, 1957.
ROWBOTHAM, ARNOLD H. *The Literary Works of Count de Gobineau*. Paris: Champion, 1929.
SABA, GUIDO. "Gobineau, 'Mademoiselle Irnois' e Vigny," *Studi Francesi*, VIII (1964), 229-238.
SCHEMANN, LUDWIG, ed. "Une Correspondance inédite de Mérimée," *RdDM*, LXXII (1902), 721-752, 836-861.
―――. *Gobineau, eine Biographie*. 2 vols. Strasbourg: Trübner, 1913, 1916.
―――. *Gobineau und die deutsche Kultur*. Leipzig: Teubner, 1934.
―――. *Quellen und Untersuchungen zum Leben Gobineaus*. Vol. 1, Strasbourg: Trübner, 1914; vol. 2, Berlin: Gruyter, 1920.
SEILLIERE, ERNEST. *Le Comte de Gobineau et l'aryanisme historique*. Paris: Plon, 1903.
SERPEILLE DE GOBINEAU, CLÉMENT, ed. *Correspondance entre le comte de Gobineau et le comte de Prokesch-Osten*. Paris: Plon, 1933.
SOREL, ALBERT. *Notes et portraits*. Paris: Plon, 1909.
SOUDAY, PAUL. *Le Livre du Temps*. 2ᵉ sér. Paris: Editions Emile-Paul, 1929.
SPRING, GERALD M. *The Vitalism of Count de Gobineau*. New York: Publications of the Institute of French Studies, Inc., 1932.
STREIDL, RUDOLF. *Gobineau in der französischen Kritik*. Würzburg: Mayr, 1935.
TENENBAUM, LOUIS. "Love in the Prose Fiction of Gobineau," *MLQ*, XVIII (1957), 107-112.
THOMAS, LOUIS. *Arthur de Gobineau, inventeur du racisme*. Paris: Mercure de France, 1941.
VILDRAC, CHARLES. "Sur les 'Nouvelles Asiatiques,'" *Europe*, III, no. 9 (1923), 96-98.

www.ingramcontent.com/pod-product-compliance
Lightning Source LLC
Chambersburg PA
CBHW021843220426
43663CB00005B/377